ROMAN
GLOUCESTERSHIRE

On a sudden it struck me that a short account of the Romans in Gloucestershire might serve to while away an hour or so on a dull winter's night, and might present some novelty, at least to those of you who have not had the opportunity of pouring over sundry voluminous works to trace out a tolerably connected local history ... I am fully aware that some of the conjectures and suggestions in it will not be received with the same amount of confidence which I place in them myself ... It will be my plan to give you the facts, such as I gather them, from well known authorities, together with sources from whence I have gained my information, and then draw from them what appears to me a most interesting and plain conclusion, leaving you to accept it or not, as you may feel inclined.

Rev. Samuel Lysons, MA, 1860

For Gavin

ROMAN
GLOUCESTERSHIRE

Best Wishes

TIM COPELAND

Tim

The History Press

For Teddy, Rupert and Rory – the Future

First published 2011

The History Press
The Mill, Brimscombe Port
Stroud, Gloucestershire, GL5 2QG
www.thehistorypress.co.uk

British Library Cataloguing in Publication Data.
A catalogue record for this book is available from the British Library.

ISBN 978 0 7524 5783 3

Typesetting and origination by The History Press
Printed in Great Britain
Manufacturing managed by Jellyfish Print Solutions Ltd

CONTENTS

ACKNOWLEDGEMENTS

The experience of the Reverend Samuel Lysons, writing about the Romans in Gloucestershire to 'while away a dull winter's night', and mine when completing this book in a year could not be so different – he did not seem to have had as many helpers. I am grateful to so many people for their support. Lorna Scott of the University of Gloucestershire Archives and Honorary Librarian for the Bristol and Gloucestershire Archaeological Society has been invaluable, not just in making sources accessible to me, but in reading and commenting on the text. The book would not have been completed on schedule without her help and advice. Louise Clough, also of the Archives Section, cheerfully helped with identifying sources and my continual request for scans. Caro McIntosh, also at the University of Gloucestershire, prepared illustrations for publication using her technological 'magic'. Tom Vivian, my editor at The History Press, gently and kindly gave me many 'hands up' when one or both of mine were out of commission, thereby taking much weight off my shoulders and giving me time to write the book that I wanted.

Information and access to illustrations were readily given by Andrew Young of the Avon Archaeological Unit; Neil Holbrook and Martin Watts of Cotswold Archaeology; Tim Grubb (especially for the LiDAR image of the Cotswold Edge, Ermine Street and Great Witcombe); Tony Roberts and Keith Elliott of Gloucestershire County Council Archaeology; Sarah Lucas and Alex Smith of Oxford Archaeology; and Robin Jackson of the Worcestershire County Archaeological Service. David Mullin of the Museum in the Park at Stroud; Georgina Hiscock and Emma Stuart of Corinium Museum; and David Rice of Gloucester City Museum also made illustrations available to me. Simon James, Tom Moore and Steve Trow allowed me to use material from the Ditches excavation report; Eddie Price kindly gave permission to reproduce illustrations from the Frocester Villa volumes; and Henry Hurst facilitated access to the diagrams from the *colonia* conference proceedings. Philip Moss generously provided the inspiring artwork for the Glevum sections of this book. Peter Guest and Jeff Davies also kindly supplied images of Tar Barrows and the Roman Conquest of Wales respectively. Richard Massey (North Oxfordshire Grim's Ditch) and Peter Salway and Mark George (Chedworth) discussed as yet unpublished material. I am grateful to the Bristol and Gloucester Archaeological Society for permission to use materials from the Transactions. I am thankful to Sharon Laycock and Taz for 'archaeological walks'. Kate Thomson of the University of Gloucestershire gave me a huge amount of professional support through the 15 years that we worked together and I learned much from her that is woven throughout this book.

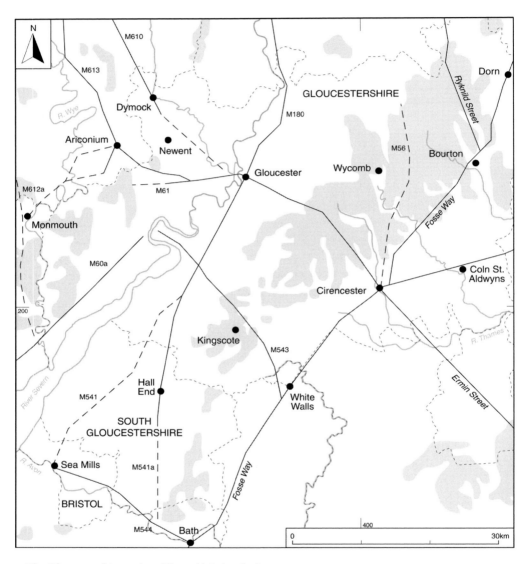

1 The Gloucestershire region. (*Cotswold Archaeology*)

PREFACE

JUSTIFYING THE TEXT

There are always problems with 'county' books as modern boundaries are anachronistic, and Finberg's widely read and highly influential *Gloucestershire Studies* acknowledges that the area now known as Gloucestershire did not exist before AD 1016 at the earliest. Any administrative structure after that time has no relevance and certainly has no relationship to the Roman period. While 'Roman county' books have problems in conveying wider political issues, studies focusing on larger areas do not allow for discussion of the economic or social arenas in which individuals or small groups of people participated. This is especially so with the varied topographies of the Gloucestershire region – the gravels of the Upper Thames Valley, the limestone stream-incised Cotswold Plateau, the alluvial Lower Severn Valley and Inner Severn Estuary, and the raised platform of older rocks of the Forest of Dean – which demonstrate diverse Roman archaeologies and present unique challenges. Roman sites on similar geologies exist in surrounding counties, so while this book is ostensibly about Gloucestershire, it has to be set in the wider Gloucestershire region to give us insights into a more complete landscape.

Two developments have made the writing of this book easier. Television programmes, such as the highly influential *Time Team*, have helped once esoteric terms such as 'geophysics' and 'stratification' become part of the increasingly knowledgeable viewer's vocabulary. Secondly, the internet has supported this increase in public interest with English Heritage producing its 'PastScape' website (http://www.pastscape.org.uk/, accessed 10 January 2010), enabling the interested archaeologist or local historian to search a district or even parish for Roman religion, housing or industry. These individual entries will have references to the *Transactions of the Bristol and Gloucester Archaeological Society* (*TBGAS*), the volumes of which have been digitised (http://www.bgas.org.uk/tbgas/, accessed 10 January 2010), or to Glevensis (http://www.gadarg.org.uk/, accessed 10 January 2010), the *Journal of the Gloucester and District Archaeological Research Group* (*GADARG*), where so many aspiring volunteers have been welcomed and have gained valuable experience. The main source for the understanding of the Forest of Dean during the Roman period is the Dean Archaeological group (http://www.deanarchaeologicalgroup.org.uk/, accessed 10 January 2010).

This has also been a daunting book to write because Gloucestershire has bred or adopted many professional and independent archaeologists who have deservedly become key figures in research, excavation and communication of their particular periods nationally and internationally. Since a book such as this depends largely on using the results from other people's

2 Alan McWhirr –
1937–2010. (*Cotswold
Archaeology*)

work, I am sure that they will readily see their influences, and the bibliography at the end of the book makes this apparent. However, this study remains my personal construction of the Roman past of the Gloucestershire region, and I must take complete responsibility for its approach and contents.

The last *Roman Gloucestershire* was written in 1980 by Alan McWhirr, who died in April 2010 aged 73. I do hope that this book has some of the influence that his *Roman Gloucestershire* had on me, my students and many others.

ONE

LOST AND FOUND: DEFINING ROMAN GLOUCESTERSHIRE

The Romans in Gloucestershire?

There were probably very few 'Romans' (in the sense of Italians) in the Gloucestershire region – as opposed to 'Roman citizens' who might come from any part of the empire, if they qualified for the status. Certainly, the legate and the tribunes of the XXth Legion, which was probably based at Glevum, were from Rome. The legion was raised in Italy by the Emperor Augustus probably in 31 BC and each legionary had to be a Roman citizen. Before coming to Britain over a hundred years later, the XXth was at Neuss in Germany and no doubt recruitment of local men would have taken place if they had Roman citizenship, which was usually acquired by having a legionary as a father. Certainly, the ex-legionaries at the *colonia* at Glevum would have been Roman citizens. Auxiliary troops which would have been part of the legion's command were from other parts of the empire and gained Roman citizenship after 25 years' service and many would have retired locally. So, there is a distinction between being from Rome or Italy and being a Roman citizen, and eventually every 'free' person in the empire was granted citizenship. However, it is highly unlikely that there would have been any 'Romans' at Chedworth Roman Villa in the sense of being from Rome (and certainly no legionary infantry was there despite the 'living history' performances!). So, when we talk about 'Roman Gloucestershire' we are mainly identifying people living in the region in AD 43–410 who had adopted Roman culture and who were unlikely to have been from Rome. Richard Reece suggested that Romanisation never existed: 'Britain (Gloucestershire) became more Gaulish, more Rhinelandish, more Spanish, a little more Italian, a very little more African, and a little more Danubian.' It was not just a one-way process as 'in return Gaul became a little more British and so on'.

Roman 'life-ways'

How do we recognise something as being Roman or called *romanitas*? There are easily recognised, standard, empire-wide aspects of organisation of life between the first and fourth centuries, such as the infrastructure of the army and its equipment, and the predictable planning and design of administrative buildings at the core of towns such as forums and basilicas. There are a range of deities to be found, such as the Capitoline triad of Jupiter the sky god (the Greatest the Best) and symbolic of Rome, Minerva goddess of war, wisdom and crafts, and Juno the goddess of women and femininity. There are well-developed communications – roads, canals, bridges and ports – that form networks to facilitate movement of the army and, later, goods, finances and 'ideas' about what being Roman entailed. This network enables the distribution of a wide range of objects from local, regional and distant localities, most important perhaps being Roman state coinage, but also fast-wheel-thrown, high-fired and often highly decorated pottery that also embody Roman identities.

Roads determine sites of towns after the military presence has largely moved on. Aspects of control can be seen in the evidence for uniform planning, in towns in the form of the street grid, water supply and rubbish disposal. Public buildings are in evidence for community activities and, where the status of the elite can be demonstrated, forum/basilica complexes, baths, amphitheatres, theatres and temples. Important public buildings in towns and private buildings in both urban contexts and in the countryside, such as villas, are built in stone with Roman forms of decoration, such as columns topped with Corinthian capitals. High-status settlements, such as administrative towns, demonstrate the highest aspects of becoming Roman, but small towns also develop alongside roads, facilitating the movement of official travellers and perhaps acting as centres for tax collection.

Although often unsuitable for British weather, the cultural tastes of the centre of the empire are based on a warm Mediterranean climate as seen through wall painting, the detail of mosaic pavements and naturalistic statuary, often having representations of Roman deities, myth and legend. These are especially prevalent in rural villas.

These are the criteria that tell us about 'being Roman', but the implication is that the absence of these characteristics in an area of Gloucestershire means that it did not become Roman to any real extent.

Where can we see 'Roman' Gloucestershire?

Surprisingly, there are not many survivals of the Roman occupation above ground, and most of those are the results of the discovery of the foundations of high-status stone structures that could be reconsolidated for public view. The city of Gloucester suffered from considerable disturbance of Roman layers during medieval and modern times, and has few visible remains. Its Northgate and Southgate streets are on the lines of their Roman predecessors, and the *colonia* walls are most accessible in the basement of the museum. The East Gate and its medieval successor can be viewed from the modern pavement through a sunken, glass-covered basement. A modern statue of a mounted Emperor Nerva, inspired by fragments of a statue and its possible base found in the area, is at the entrance to Southgate Street. A stainless steel time capsule was incorporated within the statue's hollow plinth, filled with items relating to the foundation of Glevum. The Gloucester City Museum has benefited from a successful Heritage Lottery Fund bid and the museum displays the Roman finds from the city and the surrounding area in an exciting and engaging way. Cirencester has a covering of state-protected medieval structures and this has limited exploration of the Roman levels below. Sections of the town wall remain as large banks in several places along the east side, but are best seen in the excavated sections reached from the housing estate of Corinium Gate opposite the end of Beeches Road. Outside the walls the banks of the amphitheatre can be inspected (and the traces of the various back-filled excavation trenches) set in the quarries that provided at least some of the stone for the *civitas* capital of Corinium Dobunnorum. The lack of sites is more than made up for by the Corinium Museum, which has an extensive collection of sculpture and has an emphasis on individuals from the Roman town as well as much material from the surrounding countryside. However, at neither Gloucester nor Cirencester is there any archaeological evidence that they were named Glevum and Corinium.

Major Roman roads traverse the countryside of the region as modern routes or lanes: Fosse Way, Ermine Street and Akeman Street. Disappointingly, that much vaunted and photographed section of the paved road at Blackpool Bridge in the Forest of Dean is not Roman but most likely of post-medieval date. Some parts of the County of Gloucestershire are famed for their Roman villas, but only two can be seen comfortably. Chedworth lies to the north of Cirencester and Great Witcombe lies south-east of Gloucester. Except for their mosaics, both have undergone considerable reconstruction. Chedworth was excavated in the Victorian period, and what was unearthed then is what you see now; although there has been considerable 'tidying up', the cores of the visible walls are likely to be Roman. Great Witcombe suffered unsympathetic re-laying of the foundations after an excavation in the 1950s. The once magnificent Spoonley Wood Villa lies in a copse above Winchcombe. It is accessible only by footpaths, but is worth a visit if only to appreciate the aesthetic tastes of the upper classes in the Roman period through the stunning views across the Severn Valley and Malverns. At Lydney, overlooking the Severn Estuary, is a Roman temple in private parkland, accessible only at certain times of the year.

Recovering Roman Gloucestershire

The name of the Reverend Samuel Lysons (1763–June 1819) will appear a number of times throughout the book as the 'Father of Gloucestershire archaeology', even if his way of excavating sites was more akin to clearing them out to discover Roman mosaics and artefacts rather than 'rude native pottery'. He and other antiquaries opened up some of the most important rural sites that we know about today, especially Great Witcombe and Woodchester villas. Chedworth Villa was discovered in the 1850s and Spoonley Wood Villa was excavated in the 1870s. Each of these explorations was connected with the rural gentry or the clergy with classical educations who had access and, being educated, a 'right' to the archaeology. Accidental finds were made in the towns most frequently during the laying of sewage pipes and water mains as sanitation was improved.

Through much of the twentieth century very competent excavations were carried out by individuals without an archaeological academic background and, unusually for the time, by women, such as Mrs Elsie Clifford at Bagendon, among other sites, and Helen O'Neil, especially in the Cotswolds. A large amount of information was retrieved to be published in the *Transactions of the Bristol and Gloucestershire Archaeological Society*, with particular individuals turning up volume after volume. This tradition of independ-ent archaeology continues in the work of the Gloucester and District Archaeological

Research Group, and especially that of Eddie Price at the Roman villa and surrounding settlement at Frocester.

The 1960s, 1970s and 1980s brought extensive redevelopment to the two large towns of Gloucester and Cirencester and, in advance of the construction 'rescue archaeology' funded by the then Department of the Environment, saw extensive excavations. The results were to give significant insights into both the military and civic aspects of the towns and enabled a much tighter chronology of their development to be established. The genesis of the Gloucestershire archaeological units was at this time. In the late 1970s and early 1980s, large parts of the Upper Thames Valley were being destroyed by gravel extraction and investigated by the Oxford Archaeological Unit through moneys made available for job-creation schemes. Large open-area excavations confirmed the complexity of the landscapes of the late Iron Age and Roman periods that had been discovered by aerial photography. These initiatives have resulted in agreements between archaeologist and the gravel extraction companies that have ensured continued research through excavation and have resulted in the exploration of a whole relict landscape.

The last *Roman Gloucestershire* was written by Alan McWhirr in 1980 and since that time there have been the most profound additions to our understanding of the region. Many of these are the result of the way that archaeological research has been organised. Contract archaeology has ensured that archaeological assessment and excavation has taken place before commercial developments, such as pipeline construction and housing estate building. These have shown us that the Tewkesbury and Bishop's Cleeve areas had an unexpected full Roman landscape used for agriculture and dotted with Roman villas, villages and perhaps a small town. Academic research into the development of agriculture and settlement in the Lower Severn Valley from the Severn Bridge area to Gloucester has provided insights into late Roman land reclamation from the Severn wetlands. Both of these examples demonstrate a change of emphasis from single sites to whole landscapes, and although our knowledge of Roman Gloucester and Roman Cirencester has little changed since 1980, attempts can now be made to link these urban sites with developments in their rural hinterlands. With the full publication of various Thames Valley excavations carried out ahead of gravel quarrying, it is now possible to consider how these sites related to the Cotswold villas and in turn how both were related to Corinium. The period has been especially important for the widespread use of geophysical technology, as well as the development of LiDAR, using radar from aircraft to identify earthworks on the ground.

How did Gloucestershire become Roman (if it did)?

A recent television programme had the title *What the Romans did for us*, which would be an unproblematic approach and readily accepted by the general public now and in the recent past, and it indicates interpretations of the evidence based on the concept of 'the *Roman Empire* in Gloucestershire'. Questions which are not so straightforward are now being asked by archaeologists: 'When did a Roman way of life arrive in Gloucestershire?', 'Who was "us" in Roman Gloucestershire?', 'Did the Romans plan to do anything for us or did we ask for it?', 'Did we make our own versions of what the Romans offered us?', 'What did we do for the Romans?' This is more about '*Gloucestershire* in the Roman Empire' and interrogates the archaeological record for signs of individual or community identities rather than the simplistic general 'Romans and Natives' scenario.

Underlying both approaches are two main interpretations of what happened. The idea of 'Rome in Gloucestershire' characterises the view that the 'natives' of Britain were backwards and that they willingly adopted the superior civilisation of classical Rome and Greece. This perspective maintains the 'native' elites, spontaneously sought to emulate the Romans to distinguish themselves from the rest of society. It was politically pragmatic to use the symbols of Rome to reinforce their social positions in the new reality of living in the Roman Empire. Eventually, the non-elite willingly adopted Roman ways in order to achieve a better life. This view is partly a result of the excavation of villas and towns where a small minority of the population lived. It is also very much that of 'colonisers' and perhaps replicates the British experience with its now faded empire.

A contrasting current interpretation of the archaeology for the Roman period which supports the 'Gloucestershire in Rome' is 'post-colonial', where the idea of being Roman is underscored by accepting that people had to make choices concerning the Roman 'package' and could have selectively adopted Roman goods alongside local culture depending on the situation. Individuals may have juggled between the two but used them to their own ends, and thus these artefacts and buildings came to represent a new Romano-British (or a distinct Romano-Gloucestershire or Romano-Severn Valley) culture. Individuals within a settlement may have had a greater or lesser affinity for a Roman identity and these groups and their meanings would have affected the choices they made. Of course, there would have been a gradient of acceptance from the elite, who were freer to adopt more Roman styles of living in the *civitas* capital of Corinium, but may have reverted to a more late Iron Age package when away from the town. The peasants' lifestyle was little changed throughout the whole Roman period and their choices may well have been limited to materials such as pottery or cheap brooches.

A false impression of the range and depth of the acceptance of Roman culture across all sectors of society is given by pottery, the most ubiquitous material found on Roman sites. At the Roman Conquest there were local potters who might have wanted to make a good living within the new economic system and who moved from making household hand-made items to producing Roman-style wheel-thrown pottery. The potter might well have just been responding to the new Roman 'reality', which was not necessarily intentional or imposed by Rome. In doing so, the potter was accepting, negotiating with and exploiting the new Roman scheme – in other aspects of his life there might be no traces of *romanitas* whatsoever. Richard Reece has suggested there was a 'veneer' of Roman culture over the local traditions and, since the large majority of the population lived in the overwhelmingly agricultural Gloucestershire region, it remained determinedly late Iron Age in character. This implies that rather than being a late Iron Age background to the Roman period, it is very much a late Iron Age foreground throughout the 13 generations of the Roman period, and as such had an impact on the political, social and economic aspects of the whole Roman occupation of Gloucestershire.

TWO

THE LATE IRON AGE
FOREGROUND

Rules of Engagement

Before the material evidence of sites and artefacts is laid out, it is perhaps best to define the rules of the engagement. In terms of the archaeology of the area, Tom Moore has suggested that it is no longer acceptable to refer to a 'middle' and 'late' Iron Age, but instead a 'later' Iron Age reflecting the fluidity of material and settlement change between fourth/third century BC and the first century AD, and a 'late' Iron Age between the first century BC to the mid-first century AD. What does this 'fluidity' mean? Chronologies are closely tied up with the notion of change, usually progressive change. If we consider the use of pottery as a marker of change then later Iron Age pottery is usually accepted as being handmade, whereas late Iron Age pottery is seen as being wheel-thrown. If this is so then we have to explain why, at the Bowsings site at Guiting Power, later Iron Age pottery was in use, but a radiocarbon date indicated an early-mid first-century AD (late Iron Age) occupation of the site. The excavator, Alistair Marshall, commented that it seemed that a local elite were using traditional material goods and were not able to participate in exchange or trade of finer, late Iron Age items and were of a considerably lower social and economic rank compared with the groups at the main 'tribal centres'. There is also evidence that the potteries at Malvern Link were producing both handmade and wheel-thrown items well into the second century AD. We might see a late Iron Age 'package' (known as 'Belgic' in early reports, though the term is now outdated) as the presence of coinage, the adoption of Roman cultural traits, especially concerned with food and feasting evidenced by the use of imported pottery platters from Gaul and further afield acquired and used to display status, and brooches from Colchester. It does not follow that the lack of these artefacts suggests an earlier date for a site, for what the archaeological record may be indicating is that different cultural packages were being used in different localities. While both packages had much to do with the contacts of specific groups of people in terms of their origins, political, social and trade networks, the late Iron Age package indicates wider trade networks, particularly with the south-east of England and the Roman Empire.

The Late Iron Age and the Dobunni

The Dobunni have always loomed large in accounts of pre-Roman Gloucestershire, and is typified by Mrs Clifford's assumption that the Bagendon site was the capital of this late Iron Age people before Cirencester became the Roman Corinium Dobunnorum. The most often quoted historical source for the existence of a pre-Roman political entity called the Dobunni is that of Dio Cassius, writing in the second to third century AD, although he may have been using earlier sources now lost to us. He details the events following the arrival of the Roman army in AD 43 and states that the Roman general Plautius 'secured the surrender on terms of the part of the Bodunni tribe who were subject to the Catuvellauni' (verse Book LX, 20). Accepting the fact that the 'Bodunni' are the Dobunni, the discrepancy being the result of an error in transcription by a medieval copyist, there is the problem of whether Dio was writing about the second-century administrative area, which would have been better known to his contemporary audience, or if he was describing and naming the entity that existed in the AD 40s. So it has been argued that the location of Corinium refers to Bagendon.

There has been much debate recently on the relationship between the literary and archaeological evidence, and even of the very existence of the Dobunni as a late Iron Age regional people or political entity. (The term 'people' will be used here rather than 'tribe', which has unfortunate connotations of a lack of sophistication.)

Coins and the Dobunni

In the decades early BC and early AD, individuals such as Curio, Bodvoc, Anterig, Comux, Eisv and Catti appear on the coins and have been seen as leaders with the distribution of the coins being an indication of their areas of influence, prestige and status. Attempts have been made to construct dynasties from the finds of particular individuals in specific areas. Unfortunately, the relationship of these individuals with the Dobunni is part of a circular argument on the part of numismatists: the coins are examples of the so-called 'Western Series', the area that they are found in corresponds to that of the Dobunni, so any Dobunnic coins are part of the Western Series, and even though we are not sure where Dobunnic territory is, it must correspond to the find spots of these coins. There is a little evidence for the minting of coins within the region. At both Bagendon and Ditches, and possibly also at Wycombe near Andoversford, coin flans have been found that are thought to have been used to produce the pellets that were impressed with the images of these significant individuals. The Ditches used a 'touchstone' for testing the purity of gold but there is still no evidence of an actual mint or whose coins were produced in these areas.

The role of coinage is hotly debated, but here it is taken as a way of encouraging social obligation, a return for certain items or services. It was the face on them that was important, not as a medium of exchange or any sort of monetary function, although some of the issues in non-precious metals might have been used in this way. There is also the possibility that rank was used in gift-giving, with gold, silver and bronze denoting status. To establish some sort of stable identity in an area, and to encourage the idea among elites of some form of attachment to a group, coinage used locally as a gift had the function of drawing individuals of the same status together and yet demonstrating their equality and independence. However, coinage gifts used over geographically long distances can have the effect of shortening social distances and help develop strategic relationships with other elites. If coins were used as political and social entities, find-spots do not necessarily indicate place of manufacture and territory, and so we should look at the distribution of coins not in terms of where they were made, but where they ended up. Clearly find-spots are important, but are more significant if the coins' movements to those places can be explained. At Weston-under-Penyard there are a large number of coins of great variety, not just in terms of the Western Series, but of south-eastern peoples of whose identities we are surer, and a similar geographical distribution is also the case at Bagendon. There is a problem with find-spots, however, which is that nearly all the 'Dobunnic' series of coins identified have been found in early Roman contexts, and Tom Moore suggests that this might be related to deposition in the face of a changing political system. There is also the possible 'curation' of coins as curiosities by members of the Roman army or their use of coins as currency because of the scarcity of Roman denominations.

Trying to establish the borders of an entity called the Dobunni before or after AD 43 is also extremely difficult, no matter how convincing lines are on maps in the books about the period. For example, the supposed border between the Dobunni and Catuvellauni along the River Cherwell in Oxfordshire was based on the distribution of the coins. Finds of the Dobunnic/Western Series appeared to thin out at the river; therefore, logically, that is where the territory of the Dobunni ends. Many of the coins used to make these conclusions were from accidental finds or from sporadic excavations on known sites. Since the 1990s metal detectorists have been examining the areas around the Cherwell with some energy, and the finds of coins they have retrieved has shown that any border between the two postulated entities of the Dobunni and Catuvellauni was much more blurred that had been previously suggested; a permeable 'periphery' rather than a fixed 'boundary', with no clear evidence of discontinuities between peoples. Western Series coins have been found in some abundance at Evenley and Duston, the former being some 9km (5.6 miles) west of the Cherwell and the latter 30km (18.6 miles) west of the river. Although metal detectorists have also been active on the west side of the Cherwell, there has been no increase in the number of Catuvellaunian coins. Clearly, there must be caveats to these results. Many areas are inaccessible for research because of woodland and permanent pasture. There is also a word-of-mouth factor in that metal detectorists can find 'honey-pot' sites and search them rigorously while other less promising sites are left unexplored.

The border between the 'war-like' Silures to the west and the 'peace-loving' Dobunni is usually seen as the River Wye, but the Vale of Gloucester has also been considered. However, both areas lack significant coinage and, again, it is physical, not cultural, features that are used to form a border.

The Cotswolds – *Oppida* and the Late Iron Age

The highest incidence of late Iron Age pottery imports from Gaul and elsewhere in the Roman Empire – Samian Ware bowls, platters, amphorae for the transport of wine and olive oil – are particularly related to the practice of eating and hospitality, and occur at certain sites on the Cotswold uplands, usually related to valleys and enclosed by banks and ditches (also referred to as dykes). The term *oppida* is usually used to identify sites of this type, though their function is hotly debated since the term originated to describe defendable sites in Gaul, and is used very loosely by archaeologists in England. As with the Continental examples of *oppida*, each of the English sites has many functions, such as religious, industrial, agricultural and domestic areas, but these can be spread over a wide area which is often outside that enclosed by the earthwork dykes. In the Gloucestershire region, the sites known as *oppida*, North Oxfordshire Grim's Ditch (NOGD) and Bagendon, are highly individual in the way they are organised geographically, but do share some common structural characteristics, especially the earthworks demarcating large areas of land. The dispersed sites at Weston-under-Penyard in Herefordshire (later known as Ariconium) have many of the characteristics of a late Iron Age *oppidum*, though without evidence as yet of enclosing earthworks. Other candidates on the Cotswolds share some of the characteristics of *oppida* such

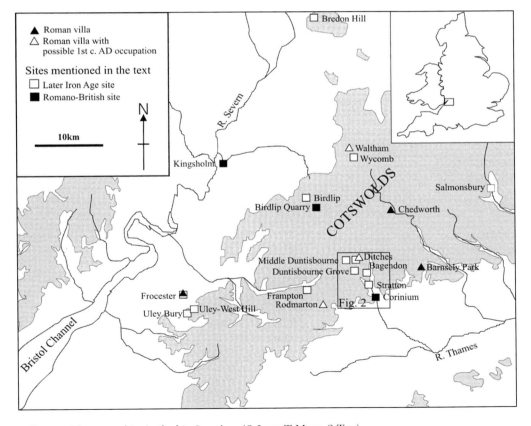

3 Roman Gloucestershire in the late Iron Age. (*S. James, T. Moore, S. Trow*)

as earthworks, but were constructed in the later Iron Age. The 'valley fort' at Salmonsbury, on the River Evenlode, and the possible Cranham/Cooper's Hill/Great Witcombe complex (hereafter referred to as the Cooper's Hill complex) above the Cotswold escarpment have also produced late Iron Age finds. The earthworks above Minchinhampton have been largely discredited as an *oppidum* as the individual components appear to be of dates ranging from the later Iron Age to medieval wood enclosures, though late Iron Age and early Roman metalwork indicates some sort of settlement at Rodborough.

The Bagendon Complex

Bagendon has traditionally been seen as the capital of the late Iron Age region because of its potential relationship with Roman Cirencester just 6km (4.5 miles) to the south-east. The mouth of the valley of the Bagendon Brook, a tributary of the River Churn, is delineated by nine dykes which do not have evidence of a palisade on top or seem to be a coherent whole for defensive purposes. A road, the Welsh Way, climbs obliquely up the steep valley side to the south and has been proposed as the late Iron Age route from the Cotswold Plateau to the highest navigational point on the Thames at Lechlade.

There have been two campaigns of excavation, one in 1954–56 by Mrs Elsie Clifford and a small-scale excavation was carried out by Richard Reece and Steve Trow inside the Bagendon dyke system in the summer of 1981. A section through the inner of the eastern ramparts by Mrs Clifford in 1954–56 showed it to be of typical 'Belgic' construction, with a V-shaped ditch 1.8m (6ft) deep. Finds, including Arretine or similar imported pottery wares, dated the construction to pre-AD 20/25. Excavations at site B revealed ditches with evidence of ironworking dating from mainly Tiberian times (AD 14–37). Above these ditches were several layers with stone platforms, hut sites and iron-smelting furnaces, giving evidence of occupation up to *c.* AD 50/60, when it was presumed that the Bagendon population was transferred to Roman Corinium. Site C appeared to have been occupied from late Tiberian or early Claudian times (*c.* AD 40), and the discovery of many coins there, and clay moulds for casting coin flans, suggests it may have been a mint. Coins from the excavations include 25 un-inscribed and 2 inscribed Dobunnic/Western Series coins, a silver coin of Epaticcu and a bronze coin of the Durotriges peoples of the Wiltshire/Hampshire area.

One of the intentions of the 1981 work undertaken by Steve Trow was to acquire a fairly large and well-stratified body of material from which it would be possible to evaluate the significance of the rather confused material from the Clifford excavations. An area, *c.* 150 sq. metres (179 sq. yards) was stripped by hand immediately to the north of Clifford's site. In the southern part a few scattered patches of rough cobbling appear to represent the edge of the cobbled floors discovered by Clifford. This was reinterpreted as a roadway leading through a gap in the dykes and is flanked by areas devoted to metalworking and rubbish disposal. To the north of this a series of 12 large pits were revealed, filled with domestic and industrial refuse (including large quantities of animal bone). Metalworking activities were represented by iron slag and fragments of coin mould, and the general wealth of the site was attested by imported glassware and pottery, large numbers of brooches and several base silver Dobunnic/Western Series coins. The dating of the imported fine wares suggested that

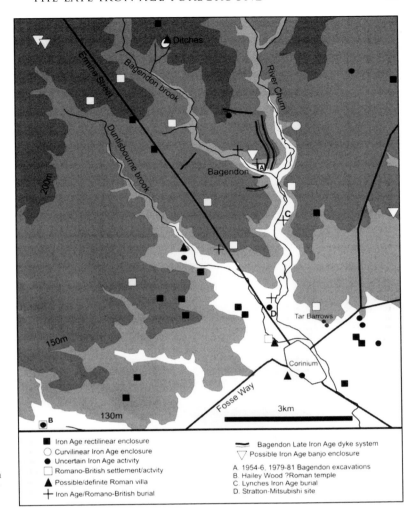

4 Map of Bagendon environs. (*S. James, T. Moore, S. Trow*)

although there is a small quantity of material pre-dating the Roman Conquest present, the filling of the pits took place during the early Roman period. The excavators interpreted the evidence as indicating that the site looked less like a 'Belgic *oppidum*' and more like an early Roman industrial centre. Fieldwalking around the site showed that contemporary occupation spreads over an area in excess of 16ha (40 acres), mainly on the sloping valley sides.

The Ditches site, just west of Woodmancote, hangs on the edge of the northern valley side of the Bagendon Brook above a set of springs, though it cannot be seen from the Bagendon dykes 3.5km (2.17 miles) away due to a valley spur in between them. The chronology of the site begins at a probable late Iron Age date, with evidence of the construction of an outer enclosure ditch and the later addition of an inner one, as well as the digging of storage pits. The double-ditched oval enclosure's southern and eastern sides are slightly flattened and a pair of ditches defining a trackway which led from the entrance at the north-east corner into a dry valley east of the site. To the south-west a curving 'antennae' ditch ran from a second entrance into a second dry valley to the west. Within the enclosure a ditched

5 The Bagendon earthworks in 1913. (Ed. J. Burrow)

trackway, abruptly changing direction twice, joined the north-western and south-western entrances. In a proposed second period between *c*. AD 45 and 50 there appeared to be considerable activity, with the inner enclosure ditch being in-filled and a causeway across the ditch. In the late first century, a Roman-type villa was constructed on the site, but more of that later.

Although only about 2.5 per cent of the site was examined, the excavators, Steve Trow, Simon James and Tom Moore, have suggested that the description of the enclosure as a 'hill-fort' with a rock-cut ditch and an internal dry-stone rampart would seem inappropriate as the size of the site and its features do not indicate a defensive function, nor, with easy access on three sides, does the position. Excavation and aerial photography suggest that there was a large number of storage pits, which when excavated indicated that the site was consuming grain rather than producing it. A specialist report identified that the crops were grown on slightly damper soil than those of the limestone in the immediate vicinity, which might indicate arable activity either in the area around Cirencester or even possibly as far as the Thames or Severn valleys. These pits appear to have been back-filled around the early-mid first century. Although the geophysics indicated a possible structure in the centre of the enclosure, the general lack of evidence might well be because of erosion or because the type of building did not have detectable postholes and sat on the ground surface. It is possible that any settlement was outside the enclosure, the inside being used only for storage. That there was some sort of activity after the filling of the inner ditch is testified by imported pottery of the early first century, and an Augustan gemstone found during fieldwalking. The diet suggested by the bones found appears to be 'cattle-rich', which is more like a Roman diet, rather than the preponderance of sheep or pig which would have been more common in the area.

The most important finds were undoubtedly those indicating the smelting and smith-ing of copper and iron, demonstrated by slag and crucibles, which indicated the possible manufacture of coinage. Baked clay pellet moulds, usually accepted as being used in the manufacture of coins, were also found. The mould sizes corresponded to the production of large gold and smaller silver denominations, and this was reinforced by the recovery from the inner enclosure ditch of gold foil and a touchstone with traces of gold on it. It is tempt-ing to see Ditches as a manufacturer of coins and all the prestige that accompanies this, but strictly speaking it only indicates the production of coin blanks.

The Ditches site appears to dominate the upper parts of the Bagendon Brook Valley and the plateau route to the River Severn and might be seen as proclaiming where the source of political power and wealth lay. The marshy area and springs below the site might have been of potent ritual significance. Similarly, the Bagendon dykes may have been built to display a sense of power by dominating the confluence of the Bagendon Brook with the River Churn. The relationship of the Ditches with Bagendon suggests that the former is of high-status occupancy and at Bagendon, immediately behind the dykes, was an area focused on production and, therefore, it is unlikely that there was any competition between the sites. Richard Reece has suggested that the Bagendon Valley was a private park of an elite based at Ditches with a later settlement behind the dykes.

Other sites associated with the Bagendon complex may well be an extensive settle-ment under the Cirencester golf course, to the east of the Bagendon Brook Valley, and at

6 Bagendon bank and ditch alongside the Welsh Way. (*Oxford Archaeology*)

other locations on the plateau immediately outside Shrubditch. The most significant sites have been identified at Duntisbourne Abbots and Duntisbourne Grove, at the head of the Bagendon Valley, where enclosures have been located and dated to late Iron Age. Pollen indicated that the structures had been built in a wooded area and the presence of pig bones, which were often connected to ritual, could indicate the nature of the sites as part of the whole Bagendon complex.

North Oxfordshire Grim's Ditch

The North Oxfordshire Grim's Ditch complex (NOGD) is a series of banks and ditches enclosing about 80 sq. kilometres (30.9 sq. miles or 8000ha or 19,789 acres) in between the valleys of the Glyme, Evenlode and Windrush, and is just 10km (6.2 miles) outside the present Gloucestershire county boundary and 40km (24 miles) north of Cirencester. It seems to have been constructed between AD 10 and 50 in two distinct phases, the second apparently never finished and possibly connected with the early Roman period. In both phases there was a bank, a ditch and possibly a palisade on the outer lip of the ditch. There was no trace of a wooden or stone barrier on the top of the bank, and so it would appear that the earthworks were to delineate rather than defend the area inside. Phase 1 of the complex, enclosing 13 sq. kilometres (5 sq. miles, 13,000ha 321 acres), seems most appropriate to discuss here as its form is closely related to other examples of *oppida* in southern England.

The dykes of this first phase enclose the spring-fed Ditchley Dell/Devil's Pool stream, although they do not appear to have any relationship to the contours of the valley. A late

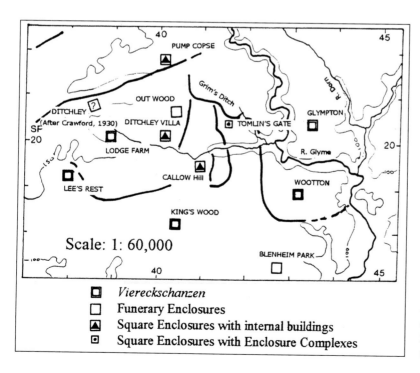

7 North Oxfordshire Grim's Ditch, Phase 1. (*Richard Massey*)

Iron Age site at Ditchley situated near this water source was followed by an early villa, which is a characteristic of many *oppida* sites. Overlooking the valley was another early villa site at Callow Hill, also enclosed by the earthworks and with late Iron Age antecedents. Both the Ditchley and Callow Hill sites had Gallo-Belgic pottery and other imports from the south-east of England and the St Albans area. With the largely empty enclosure of the NOGD, Richard Massey identified evidence for a number of *Viereckschanzen*, late Iron Age ritual or religious enclosures characterised by a generally square or subsquare outline with a single entrance usually facing south or south-east. Most examples cover areas of less than 1ha (2.5 acres). It appears that sites in this class were constructed and used between the later 1st century BC and the 1st century AD. Taken together, the evidence from the area defined by the earthwork circuit suggests a political, social and religious centre with a rather empty interior. Using aerial photography, Richard Massey also located a large and unsuspected high density of late Iron Age and Roman settlement to the east of the River Glyme, with some structures appearing to be of high status and indicating a well-developed hierarchy. It may well be from these settlements that the labour used to construct the enclosing earthworks of the Grim's Ditch originated.

Weston-under-Penyard

This site, 59km (37 miles) from Cirencester has many of the characteristics of an *oppida*-like settlement, but without, as yet, evidence of enclosing dykes. Areas of potential late Iron Age activity have been identified alongside two major Roman roads believed to have Iron Age origins linking the location to the Herefordshire basin, the Severn Estuary by way of the River Wye, the Forest of Dean and the Lower Severn Valley. This would give access to a possible crossing near Gloucester and beyond to the Cotswold scarp and Bagendon. The settlement appears to have had no clear nucleus, rather it comprised of several foci, although some occupation appears to be at the head of two streams, with present-day pools perhaps marking the position of marshy ground in the late Iron Age. A shrine or temple is suspected above the northern stream. Of major importance is the presence of early-mid first-century Gallo-Belgic fine-ware imports comparable to examples from Bagendon and its hinterland, but which are rare elsewhere in the region, especially to the west of the Severn. Brooches made before the end of the first century BC show a similar range of contacts with the south-east and the Continent. That Weston-under-Penyard was a centre of some economic importance is demonstrated by the large number of coin finds, the majority of these being local Dobunnic/Western Series issues and the total only being exceeded by Bagendon. An important element of the assemblage is represented by the five non-Western Series coins, showing contacts to the peoples of the east and south-east: the Corieltauvi, Atrebates and the Trinovantes/Catevellauni. The late Iron Age Weston-under-Penyard locality would appear to be part of a distribution/trading network associated with Bagendon, and its economic status and widespread trading links may have resulted from wealth generated by involvement in an iron production industry based on the Forest of Dean. The site appears not only to have been producing iron, but may have had a more specialist function as a centre providing control over the production

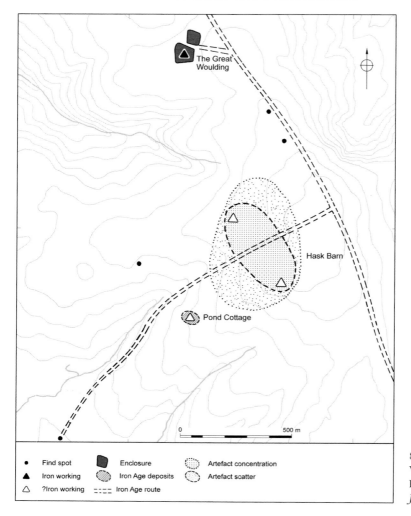

8 Late Iron Age
Weston-under-
Penyard. (*Robin
Jackson*)

and distribution of iron regionally. The lack of defining dykes may indicate a different
relationship with the local population, who would, in other circumstances, have provided
the labour for their construction.

Salmonsbury

This later Iron Age 'valley fort' lies on the eastern margin of the village of Bourton-on-
the-Water, on the east side of the Cotswolds in an angle between the River Windrush and
the River Dikler. The 'Camp' is almost square in plan, with banks enclosing about 22ha (56
acres). The defences consist of two closely set ramparts, each with an external ditch, and
there are two entrances and a gap for the stream, which passes across the interior of the
camp into a marshy area. The stream was not navigable even by flat-bottomed boats, but
must have been used for everyday water needs. An annexe of 6ha (15 acres) lies outside the

main enclosure, and has its east side open. Dunning excavated the site in 1931–34, identifying some evidence of occupation from Neolithic to the early Bronze Age, but the main use of the site appears to be in the early to later Iron Age, followed by the arrival and domination of 'Belgic' culture. The presence of wheel-turned pottery, imported Gallo-Belgic, Terra Nigra and early Roman wares, as well as two Dobunnic/Western Series coins and brooches of iron and bronze, prompted Dunning to date the 'fort' to the early first century, from *c* .AD 30–50. He also suggested that Salmonsbury was connected to the expansion of the influence of the Dobunnic capital at Bagendon, 21km (13 miles) away. This assumption was mainly due to the pottery forms, which were broadly the same as Bagendon, but of a different fabric, possibly related to those being produced in the Thames Valley, and are similar to those from the NOGD complex. There was evidence of connection with more distant places from two Roman Republican coins, a denarius of VIBIUS (49 BC) and M. VOLTEUS (*c.* 78 BC), perhaps arriving through trade. There was later evidence of Roman

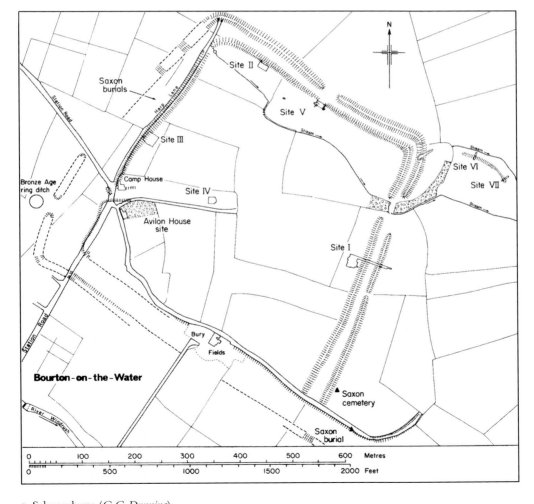

9 Salmonsbury. (*G.C. Dunning*)

occupation, though the main settlement appears to have drifted towards adjacent Bourton-on-the-Water on the Fosse Way, a military road which cut through the area. Geophysics has identified a Roman rectangular structure within the enclosure but no date has been assigned to it as yet.

Cooper's Hill

The inclusion of this site here is highly speculative and depends on the size of the enclosure, its position in relation to Bagendon, 12km to the south-east (7 miles) and the presence of a possible early villa at Great Witcombe below. In her report on the Bagendon excavations, Clifford suggested that even though it had never been described as a whole, the clearing of tree cover at the time enabled the Cooper's Hill complex of ditches to be seen as a 'Class One' enclosure, such as Bagendon. The land enclosed by the dykes was 81ha (200 acres), similar to Bagendon, and more probably a site which was densely inhabited. Witts, in 1881, had also commented that the earthworks were 4.5m (15ft) high in places and must, from its size and appearance, have been an extensive British settlement rather than a camp. The Royal Commission for Historic Monuments could not confirm the height of the bank, but was able to identify some of the damaged earthworks. Below the Cooper's Hill complex are copious springs, some evidence for a late Iron Age settlement and also a very early Roman structure which developed into Great Witcombe Roman Villa. Any route from the crossing of the Severn at Gloucester or from the Vale of Berkeley up on to the Cotswolds through Cooper's Hill would have had a less steep incline than that followed by the later Ermine Street at Crickley Hill, largely because steep valley contours could be negotiated obliquely. There are routes in the modern landscape from Cooper's Hill to the Duntisbournes and the Bagendon complex using modern footpaths and bridleways, which might reflect earlier courses.

Oppida and the Landscape

The archaeology indicates these *oppida* settlements were the centre of economic, social and political activity. What may be significant is that the large complexes at the NOGD, Bagendon and Weston-under-Penyard appear to have been founded in areas where there was no, or little, previous later Iron Age settlement activity. As a result of this, Bagendon and the NOGD have been described by Tom Moore as 'liminal', on the edge of, or between, other groups of longer-established communities, such as those at Salmonsbury or Cooper's Hill.

There does not appear to be any evidence for coercion of local people in the design of the *oppida* and this is probably because no one was displaced by the new arrangements This 'liminality' might be the result of new systems of exchange and the growing volume of commerce with the south-east and the Roman Empire in the period of *c.* AD 10–40. What might be highly significant is that both the NOGD and Bagendon complexes were on tributaries of the River Thames, which in turn connected them with the south-east, Gaul and eventually the Iberian Peninsula, and this could have been an important factor in the choice

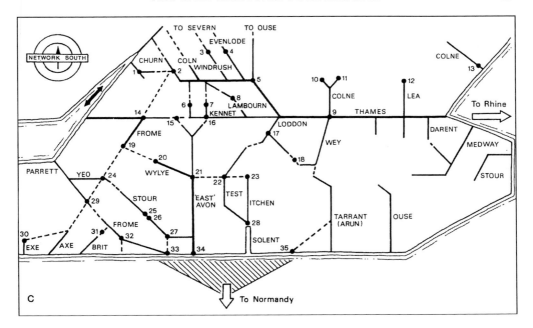

10 Andrew Sherratt's transport network for the late Iron Age. Bagendon = 2, Salmonsbury = 3, North Oxfordshire Grim's Ditch = 4, 11. (*'Verulamium'*, Oxford Journal of Archaeology, *Vol. 15 (2), p. 213*)

of locality. The incomers, with a much more developed understanding of the geography of the longer routes and how they could be used for trading, could act as 'brokers' between trade routes and commodities. The NOGD, Bagendon and Weston–under Penyard might also have been an attraction for the peoples of the wider region because of the opportunity of increased trade, with local produce being moved alongside more precious commodities. In this way the relationship between the wider hinterland landscape and the *oppida* may have resulted in an important economic role, inevitably promoting political and social obligations, including the raising of the earthworks.

This relationship between large incomer settlements, such as Bagendon and the NOGD, and other smaller groups of people not necessarily related to each other might have been the final economic and political situation before the arrival of full Roman power.

So, Who Were the Dobunni?

The name Dobunni could derive from any of these large settlements or just from one of the groups within the area. Lysons suggested that Dobunni was derived from the 'British' term 'Duffen' or 'Dwyn', signifying a vale (the modern Welsh being *Dyffryn*). The Cotswold dip-slope is dissected by many valleys, which are tributaries of the River Thames, and the River Severn is also a major feature in the landscape. Indeed, compared to the counties around it, the Gloucestershire region has many more stream/river/valley features, and although it would be a fanciful speculation, the idea of the Dobunni as the 'valley peoples' is an attractive and satisfying one.

After all of this, we are still left with the problem of Dio's 'part' of the Dobunni. Neil Holbrook has suggested that Dio's comments about the 'subject-ness' to the Catuvellauni might indicate family ties. The political centre of the Catuvellauni was at Verulamion, present-day St Albans, and besides the archaeological evidence for trade there are factors that might support the supposition that the Bagendon area was being referred to by Dio. Verulamion was founded in an area with little later Iron Age settlement, was delineated by dykes and situated in a tributary valley of the Thames. It had a high-status site, Gorhambury, in a similar position to Ditches and also has evidence of coinage production. An important piece of comparative evidence is the burial of an elite member of the Catuvellauni at Folly Lane, above what was to become the Roman city, and which controlled its future layout. Outside of Corinium was a burial site at Tar Barrows, pre-dating the Roman town and controlling its siting and the routes of the main Roman roads around it. The same arguments might be put forward for the NOGD, with Callow Hill representing a Gorhambury-type site, although so far there is no evidence of coin production. A mound at Ditchley House, above the Ditchley Roman Villa, has been described as a tumulus but it has never been explored.

If this part of the Dobunni that surrendered to Plautius was in the Bagendon area, then much might follow – the foundation of a major fort at Kingsholm on the Severn very early after the conquest with little obvious military support needed behind it, the lack of direct supervision by the army during the early years of the conquest, the respect for the burial site by the Romans and the later site of the *civitas* capital being at Cirencester.

Even if this seemingly ongoing process of political, social and economic development in the region was arrested by the Roman Conquest, it is perhaps best to consider it as interrupted for a while until the area was under Roman control. Then the Romans, who preferred to use structures already in place, manipulated the idea of the Dobunni as a major unit of administration and taxation, as well as providing a new arena for the display of individual status of the rich and powerful late Iron Age elites. Of equal importance is that a late Iron Age way of life was to be found on most non-elite sites in the region throughout the Roman period.

THREE

SECURING THE SURRENDER:
FORTS, BOUNDARIES AND
A 'LOST' GARRISON

It is certain that the Roman Empire already had numerous trade and military contacts with Britain, so it is difficult to find an adequate term for the events of AD 43. Usually known as the 'Invasion', this term might not apply to some areas of southern Britain, which had had links with the Romans and would have welcomed them, but this is probably the best name for the event itself. 'Conquest' again might not apply to peoples already 'on-side', but with the presence of five legions it certainly was meant to feel like it, and was a process that took a couple of centuries, if it can be seen as ever being completed. 'Occupation' again lasted for 400 years, 13 generations, and does indicate that the Romans wanted the taxes and resources of Britain and not necessarily to civilise it. The term 'Roman Annexation' might better indicate the way that Rome decided to formalise forcibly relationships with compliant peoples.

The Literary Evidence

As well as informing us about that Aulus Plautius secured the surrender of part of the Dobunni, Dio Cassius then makes the tantalising statement that the governor 'left a garrison there' (Dio Cassius LX, 19–22). The submission has traditionally been seen as happening somewhere in the Kent area through which the major advance route ran, eventually ending up at Camulodunum (Colchester), the capital of the Catuvellauni and Trinovantes, who vehemently opposed the occupation. Eberhard Sauer, among others, has suggested an alternative route for the invasion forces that would have had a greater impact on the Gloucestershire region. There is evidence for pre-conquest and early Roman military bases at Fishbourne, near Chichester on the South Coast, at or even before the invasion. Sauer sees this as a possible starting point for at least one, if not all, of the 'three divisions' reported by Dio. Sauer proposes that the progress of these units making up the division(s) was through friendly Dobunnic territory and then onward to the mouth of the Thames. In this scenario it would have been near or even in Dobunnic territory that the embassy to Aulus Plautius took place. If this was the case there remains the problem of what type of 'garrison' was left, where was 'there' and 'when' did it happen, as the Dio account does not necessarily indicate that this was immediate on the submission of the Dobunni, since Aulus Plautius was governor until AD 47.

Limes, Garrisons and Units

One of the problems of studying the Roman military throughout the period of the occupation is the dating of fortresses and assigning legions or other units to them, particularly as military historians and archaeologists can't abide an unnamed garrison. The challenge has become even more difficult with the recognition, mainly through aerial photography, of the strategic bases, places for the assembly of operational battle groups of mixtures of legionary heavy infantry contingents and swift mounted auxiliary troopers, known as vexillation fortresses. These bases may also have been used as campaign winter quarters. Frustratingly, the Roman army did not consider future enthusiasts by insisting on inscribed stones recording the units occupying the installations.

The archaeology of the military establishments discovered in the Gloucestershire area has produced three main strategic scenarios, each of which may have implications for the identification of Dio's 'garrison' left in Dobunnic territory (if it ever was). The first interpretation of the available evidence involves what is now known as Akeman Street, linking St Albans and Cirencester, and its use as a *limes*, the boundary of conquered territory. The second setting is focused around the use of the Fosse Way as another possible early boundary to a province that was never meant to have included the mountainous parts of Britain in Wales and north of the Midland Plain. The third involves the possibility of the Dobunni being friendly enough for the Romans to leave their lands largely ungarrisoned and to make a break for the River Severn to control, or at least stop, incursions by the war-like,

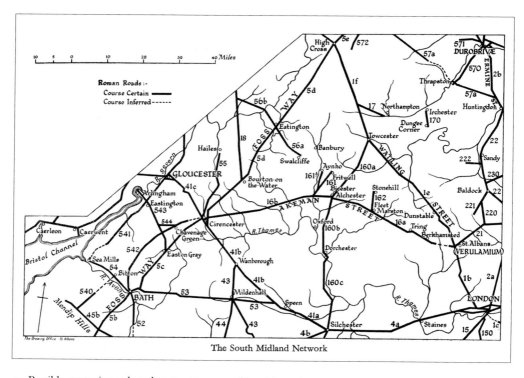

The South Midland Network

11 Possible strategic roads and routes AD 47–49. (*Ivan Margary*)

'swarthy' Silures. Each of these hypotheses will be discussed in some detail as they put the main early military sites in the Gloucestershire region into a strategic perspective and also give an insight into the make-up of the battle groups in the first stages of Britannia becoming a Roman province.

The *limes* proposal is argued from the presence of forts at a day's march apart along Akeman Street and then the Fosse Way to a vexillation fortress at Lake Farm, near Poole in Dorset. With the discovery of a proposed vexillation fortress at Alchester, Oxfordshire, the *limes* schema became more attractive geographically. Alchester is at the northernmost point of the bow-shaped Akeman Street, which appears to be facing outwards, providing a longer perimeter into anti-Roman areas than a straight road. A fortress containing a mix of legionary and auxiliary troops at this location would be in a very good position to control roads crossing from Chichester to the south and the east–west route beginning at the fortress at Colchester. There is a possibility that the battle group was a vexillation of the IInd Augustan Legion, under the leadership of Vespasian, the later emperor. Another part of this legion is thought to have been based at the Lake Farm vexillation fortress at the other end of the proposed *limes* in Dorset.

Without doubt, the discovery of a military base at Alchester is one of the most significant events of the recent Roman military archaeology. Fieldwalking and metal detectorist activity indicated that there had been mid-first century military activity in the area, and this was confirmed by the analysis of aerial photographs followed by further fieldwork and excavation. The aerial photographs showed a marching camp, a parade ground and a Roman fort. The most important aspect of the discovery of this military complex is its gateposts, which have been dated by dendro-chronology (tree-ring dating) to late AD 44 or early AD 45, within a year of the invasion events: a rare 'absolute' date in archaeology which usually relies on broad relative dating of decades. The excavator, Eberhard Sauer, suggested the site was active for just one phase of AD 44–late 50s or early 60s.

The discovery in 2008 of a smaller, and probably earlier, fort in a much better defensive situation for the control of Akeman Street might put the proposed vexillation fortress into a later context. In this scenario, the all-important dated gateposts might have been reused from the fort. The possible early date of this fort certainly makes it a candidate for Dio's 'garrison', especially as its position would enable it to protect the eastern part of Dio's 'Dobunnic' territory from the powerful Catuvellauni to the east. The Alchester area is especially significant strategically in relation to the Boudiccan Revolt of AD 61, which must have caused a great deal of consternation among the occupying forces. It is possible that the Roman version of this event given by Suetonius hides a much wider insurrection and Alchester would be in an important strategic position for a larger and more mobile monitoring force to react to threats following the main uprising.

Unfortunately, this *limes* proposal fails on the 'forts a day's march apart' criterion. There is no current evidence of a fort at St Albans, and although a large collection of Claudian coins was found near the Wilcote settlement west of Alchester, these need not necessarily be related to an army presence. A marching camp of 0.85ha (2 acres) has been identified by aerial photography near Asthall, on the Oxfordshire-Gloucestershire border. The ploughed-out earthwork was located on the south side of Akeman Street and aligned to it, indicating that it must have been later than the road's construction. This undated overnight fortification

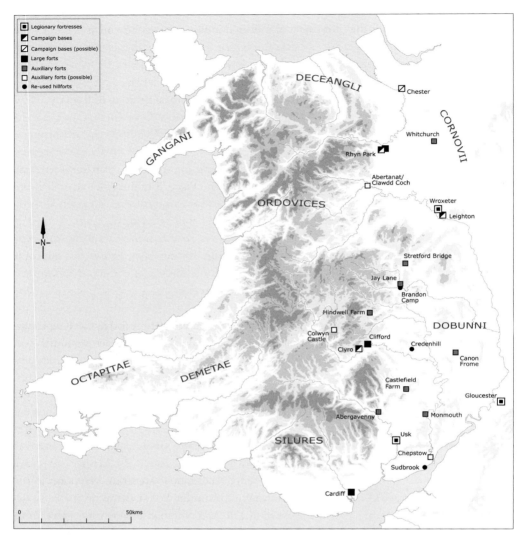

12 The Kingsholm fortress and the Welsh campaigns AD 50–69 (*J.L. Davies*)

for troops on the move is likely to be for units in transit or for making the presence of Rome felt in a peaceful part of the province. The discovery of a long-suspected fort/let under Cirencester at the end of Akeman Street has also been seen as a support for the *limes* strategy and Dio's garrison, but more of that below.

Another proposed *limes* strategy is that based on the Fosse Way, whose construction is usually dated AD 47. This route, running across country from Exeter to Lincoln, has been seen as the 'perfect' Roman road because of its apparent straightness, but in reality it is made of straight alignments (possibly of different dates), producing the illusion of complete linearity. The Fosse Way has also been a subject of a lot of discussion among archaeologists as to whether the route was intended to be a frontier, which might suggest that the Romans only intended to conquer the more agricultural rich lowland part of the province, but were forced into other areas in order to provide security for the fledgling province. At the present time, evidence for early forts at regular intervals has not been demonstrated, with the military bases that have been discovered, such as Cirencester, being later and probably related to supporting westward expansion. The establishment of early forts in front of the Fosse Way, such as the vexillation fortress at Rhyn Park in Shropshire and Kingsholm in Gloucester, hints at an expansionist policy, with the attractions of the mineral resources of the north and west being as important as the well-developed agricultural land to the south. A much more complex and fluid situation has arisen with the identification of other vexillation fortresses, such as that at Longhope in Cambridgeshire behind the Fosse Way line. This may indicate that some people were less willingly to accept Roman rule than others, and needed to be supervised. Although the Fosse Way was certainly a strategic route indicating the general limit of secure control, possibly in the late AD 40s, it is best seen as the spine of a broad, well-garrisoned band of territory, a rearward communication uniting battle groups in front of it as well, ensuring pacification and co-operation behind the line. The fort/let at Leaholme in Cirencester has been suggested as a significant component of the Fosse Way *limes*, but it is actually oriented on Ermine Street.

The third scenario involves the early construction of the vexillation fortress at Kingsholm in Gloucester, partly beneath the rugby stadium in which battles still take place. Ermine Street was certainly surveyed with the site at Kingsholm as its terminus; however, the early fortress is set at an oblique angle to the road and thus it is possible that the military establishment was laid out before the road was built, hence making it a very early feature in the strategic landscape. The military installation at Kingsholm seems not to be supported by other forts close by, therefore implying that the Dobunni were not seen as a threat. Throughout the late Iron Age, the site of the lowest crossing of the Severn at Gloucester was important as a communication route and this was emphasised by a probable settlement of indeterminable size close to the Roman Kingsholm base. It could be that the trade route from Bagendon to the Severn at Kingsholm, and possibly further on to Weston-under-Penyard, was under the influence of the part of the local people mentioned by Dio, and who had already surrendered. The presence of the late Iron Age settlement might explain the siting of the Roman fortress on the river floodplain rather than on the higher ground, at a more natural river crossing point, where the later city centre fortress and *colonia* were to be located.

It has often been presumed that this fortress was garrisoned by the XXth Legion, which had left Colchester in AD 49 in order to contain the war-like Silures. However, the small size of this first phase of the walled site has been estimated at *c.* 9.5ha (23.5 acres), and this is about half the size of a later legionary fortress. The evidence for at least a part cavalry garrison opens up the possibility that Rufus Sita of the mounted detail of cohort of Thracians, whose tombstone was discovered in the area, was associated with this first fort, as well as a legionary helmet cheekpiece. Such a small military installation is more likely to have been the base of a typical vexillation group of combined legionary infantry and mounted auxiliary troopers able to strike quickly.

The fortress' strategic position on the lowest crossing point of the Severn may have more to do with supplies coming up the Severn, than in relation to a route along the northern bank of the river to the Wye and into Wales. The most likely advance route for any Roman

13 Bronze military helmet cheek-piece. (*Gloucester City Museum*)

force would have been through the broad valley of the Leadon, between May Hill and the Malvern Hills to Ross and the middle Wye Valley. Evidence of forward positions in a strategic plan for the conquest of the Silures is still lacking. Dymock and Weston-under-Penyard were considered fort sites until recently, but surveys of old discoveries and recent excavations have found no traces of military occupation. Similarly, Stretton Grandison, in southern Herefordshire, was suggested to have been a permanent fort, but the site is now considered to be a small civilian settlement. Presumably the campaign forts or marching camps were very temporary structures which may have been ploughed out or even hidden in the uplands of the Forest of Dean. The Silures continued to oppose the Roman army and, in the guerrilla warfare of AD 51–52, an attack left a *praefectus castrorum* (a camp prefect and third most senior member of the legion) dead; eight centurions were also killed, as well as an unspecified but certainly significant number of legionary soldiers. Evidence for another military compound or annexe just outside the circuit of the Kingsholm fortress' defences might indicate a supply base or winter quarters for further attachments of troops, or both. It is thought that the XXth Legion may have been moved to the fortress at Usk about AD 57, which as we will see complicates matters even further. The connection between the Usk fortress and the XXth Legion comes down to the evidence of a small bronze roundel, 2cm in diameter, bearing the sign of the charging boar, the familiar insignia of the legion. That certainly is a case of grasping at boars.

Kingsholm

Moving away from the strategic board game of locating Dio's garrison, it is time to look at the archaeology of the individual sites. The first military establishment at Kingsholm was founded in the mid to late 40s, with evidence of timber buildings of post-in trench construction and gravelled roads, ditches and other features typical of an early site. The rampart was faced with turf and clay, had a sand core (possibly over a 'corduroy of timber' for stability) and was 5m (16ft) wide. It was separated by a narrow berm from an eroded V-shaped ditch, 3.7m wide (12ft) and 1.4m (4.5ft) deep. Just outside the ditch was an irregular slot containing angled stake-holes, interpreted by the excavators as the remains of a thorn bush and stake emplacement. Further evidence that the site was of military origin is the recovery of equipment, including an unfinished cheek-piece from a cavalry helmet and three cavalry pendants. Two Claudian copy coins were found in the upper fills of the period one ditch. The ditch began to silt up quickly with sand from the ditch sides and the face of the rampart, which must pose the question about how long the fort was used in this phase. Still on the Kingsholm site, and with the same alignment, another, larger, installation was built

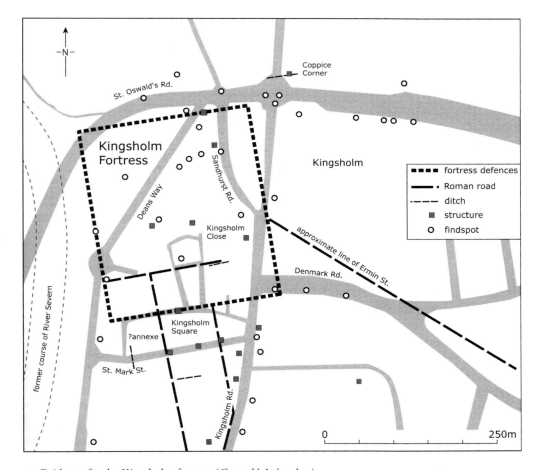

14 Evidence for the Kingsholm fortress. (*Cotswold Archaeology*)

c. AD 60, with the approximate size of 17ha (42 acres), relating more closely to that of a full legionary fortress. In this phase timber sill buildings were constructed. On the Sandhurst Road site the defensive sequence was almost completely rebuilt on a much larger scale, with clay being used much more extensively to add stability to the rampart. A ditch was dug 2.5m (8.2ft) to the north of the earlier feature and it was considered that it was not exposed for long as it was seen to be very sharp in the section of the trench. Malcolm Atkin compared the weather-boarded rampart front of the XXth Legion's previous base at Colchester, and subsequent base at Wroxeter, to the Kingsholm defences, but without any correlation. The destruction pits of this later installation contained coins dated from AD 64–68.

There is evidence of a further area of military occupation to the north of the main Kingsholm site, with evidence of ditches and one possible building. It is clearly extramural to the early site and aligned with Ermine Street, which may indicate a later military founda- tion of some sort considering the objects found, which point towards a date no later than the AD 60s. Whether this occupation represents a later fort, annexe or a supply base is not known at present.

There is also some evidence of a contemporary settlement on the site of the later for- tress and approached by a branch road off Ermine Street. The route of this branching road is on a similar alignment to the Kingsholm military base, which suggests that both settle- ments are contemporary. A series of pits and small ditches indicated a lack of structure and planning, with no overall alignment obvious within the occupied area of some 0.7ha (1.7 acres). The presence of a cemetery south of the Kingsholm site and the active waxing and waning of the military establishment in response to operations in Wales would indicate a need to be at a distance from the fortress, whilst still providing a range of services from provisions to pleasure.

Cirencester

In each of the scenarios examined here, the military base at Cirencester appears to be pivotal; however, there is limited evidence for the exact status of any army establishment at Cirencester in the early Roman years or of the function it may have played. The discovery of the tombstones of two auxiliary troopers from cavalry regiments, Dannicus, a tribesman of the Raurici, and Sextus Valerius Genialis, a trooper of the ala Thracum, are certainly evidence of a military presence somewhere in the area and this has in turn been extended to suggest two periods of occupation for a putative fort. The problem lies in the archaeological evidence for the Leaholme fort's design and garrison as excavations have provided somewhat sparse and ambiguous evidence for such a military base. A pair of parallel and very insubstantial ditches 0.65m (2ft) deep and 1.25m (4ft) formed a very unusual configuration for those of a fort and a geophysical survey provided inconclusive results about the course of the ditches on other sides of the proposed fort. The dimension of the ditches might be explained away by a high water table, making it unnecessary for any deeper features as the shallow ones would form a moat. Analysing this evidence led the excavators to suggest that they represented a *hibernia* (winter quarters) associated with the early years of the invasion and early military contact. This activity has been dated *c*. AD 50/55, but its duration

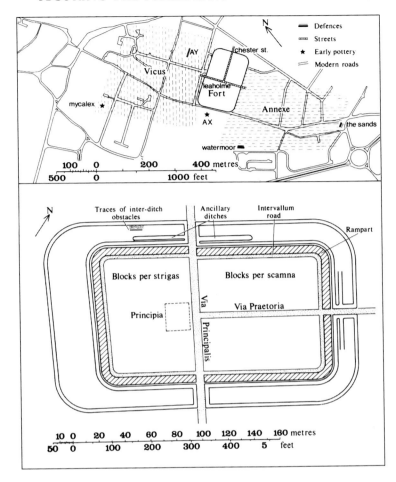

15 The Cirencester
period II 'fort'.
(*Cirencester Excavation
Committee*)

is problematic and Reece suggests on coin evidence that if there was a military presence it
was a passing one of no more than six months. Such a fort might have been sited to act as
a reserve base for the fortress at Kingsholm, and Neil Holbrook has suggested that it was
possibly founded to reassure a Dobunnic hierarchy at Bagendon during the early phase of
the Welsh campaign, which may have produced unsettled conditions in the Cotswold area.
It may also have had the role of supervising them.

The date of the second phase of the defensive circuit of the Leaholme fort has been proposed as *c.* AD 65/70, although it might have been earlier and as a response to the news of
the Boudican rebellion travelling quickly along Akeman Street, causing anxiety among pro-
Roman groups. There is also the possibility that the revolt, or its local sympathisers, reached
as far as Silchester, where the excavator, Mike Fulford, has found considerable evidence of
burning related to this period.

The internal buildings of the proposed fort appear to have been of timber and of both
individual post and post-in-trench construction, and with possibly with three phases, but
sufficient evidence for plans of the buildings to enable understanding their function has
not yet been recovered. What needs to be explained is the type of garrison which might

undertake a substantial role yet fit into a fort of just 1.8ha (4.5 acres). Certainly 500 men in a cavalry regiment and with the need for stables would have had problems with that amount of space. That a military establishment of some type did exist is most probable, but the lack of the expected timber lacing in the rampart of the second fort, none of the small finds recovered from this site having any particular military associations and the unusual configuration of the ditches does make identifying its function difficult. The Leaholme fort (or fortlet) was laid out on the axis of Ermine Street, the primary strategic route through the area, and that there was some connection with the military establishment at Kingsholm is indicated by the pottery retrieved during the excavations on the fort site, having the same fabrics and styles as that from the vexillation fortress. What is clear is that the dating of the site is too late for either of the *limes* strategies or as a candidate for Dio's garrison.

Gloucester: the City-Centre Site

The city centre fortress on the site of the later *colonia* was established in about AD 67, probably the result of rationalisation of legionary deployment, since the XIVth Legion was removed from Britain to fight in Nero's war against the Pathans, always seen as Rome's traditional enemy in the Middle East. With this lessening of military strength, any campaigns were put on hold and if the XXth had been at Usk it would have been moved back to Gloucester at this time to keep an eye on the Silures and the Midlands, with the IInd Legion at Exeter securing the south-west. If the legion had remained at Kingsholm, and there does seem to be an overlap in dates, this might also have been the time to construct another fortress on higher terrain. A part of any overlap in time might have been the result of the Kingsholm site being used as a construction camp for the new fortress. Nero's eastern wars never actually began, since he was overthrown by a series of military rebellions and the Roman world was racked by civil war. Four emperors claimed the throne within a single year before Vespasian emerged as victor and the conquest of Wales was resumed.

The layouts of legionary fortresses always corresponded to the physical features of the site, but certain elements had to be present. The site of the *principia* (headquarters), with its shrine where the legionary standards were kept, was always the first structure to be laid out, if not built, at the centre of the fortress. Once the land for the headquarters had been allocated, the *Via Principia*, the main road through the fortress, was laid out in front of it. The *praetorium*, the commandant's house, could either have been next to the *principia*, as at Usk, or behind it, as at Chester, which was to be the permanent base of the XXth. Along the *Via Principia* were the six tribunes' houses and also that of the *praefectus castrorum*, the camp prefect, who had been promoted up through the ranks of the centurions. The prestigious first cohort made up of double centuries routinely had its barracks near a gate on the main road. Granaries would have to be placed near the gate with easiest access to the river, and the baths were usually close to the *principia* and on a main road to allow easy access for water pipes along it and drains underneath. The whole legion would need 63 barrack blocks and accommodation for at least 150 men and horses of the ala auxiliary regiment that accompanied it. Each barrack block would be located immediately around the defences with access to the rampart and held a 'century' of 80 legionaries. Within the blocks, a *conteburnia* of eight

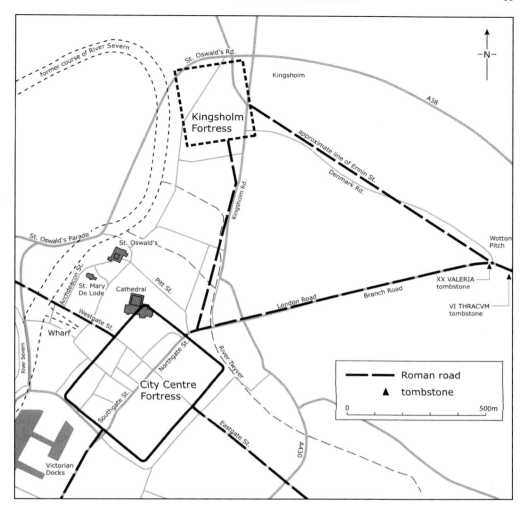

16 The relationship of Kingsholm to the city centre fortress. (*Cotswold Archaeology*)

men had one room for sleeping, probably in bunks, and the other for storage and cooking. A *conteburnia* messed and tented both when in camp and on manoeuvres. The centurion's quarters at the end of the block would contain his accommodation and the administration for the century. Between the rampart and the barrack blocks was the *Via Sagularis* (the road of the cloak), the road where each century lined up for inspection and duties.

At Glevum, the fortress on the city centre site covered *c.* 17ha (43 acres) with a turf-faced rampart, timber interval towers and a single ditch, all of which indicates that it was designed to be only a temporary installation. Only the Eastgate has been thoroughly investigated and two timber posts of this phase were found. Internal buildings were of a post-in-trench construction, except for the back and end walls of the *conteburnia*, which appear to have had base structures for the wall of stone and clay ground sills, probably for timber and clay walls. A small fragment of a building identified at 11–17 Southgate Street as the *principia* had a gravelled courtyard defined by foundations of stone and clay. Parts of the barrack buildings for four centuries were found at 13–17 Berkeley Street, and the barracks for the six double centuries of the prestigious first cohort at 10 Eastgate Street and New Market Hall. The granaries have not been found yet and were probably constructed near the west gate in order to be close to the quays. Since the fortress was probably only garrisoned for eight or nine years as a temporary campaign base, it is unlikely that the full legion was ever in the fortress at any one time and the pressures of maintaining a frontier might have precluded building the stone bath building. The priorities for a campaign base can be clearly seen at the fortress at Inchtuthill on the Tay in Scotland, located in a similar strategic position as that at Gloucester, and which was only garrisoned for three years between AD 83–87. Inchtuthill was timber built and had a *principia,* tribunes' houses and an exercise basilica, as well a hospital, granaries and barracks. The only baths were for officers in a compound outside

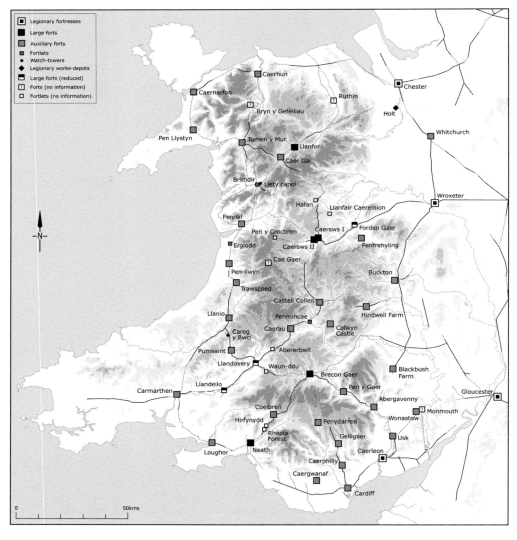

17 The city centre fortress and the Welsh campaigns AD 69–96. (*J.L. Davies*)

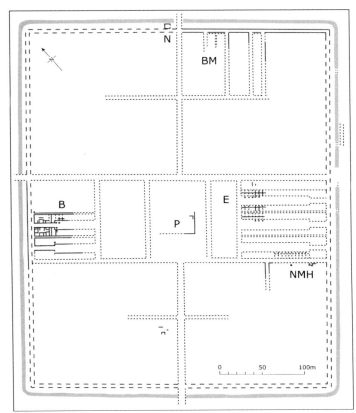

18 Gloucester: plan of
fortress. (*H.R. Hurst*)

N = 45–9 Northgate Street
BM = Bon Marché
B = 13–17 Berkeley Square
P = *Principia* (11–17 Southgate
    Street)
E = 10 Eastgate Street
NMH = New Market Hall

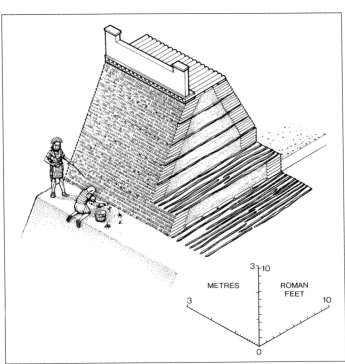

19 Gloucester: the legionary
rampart turf and corduroy of
logs. (*Philip Moss*)

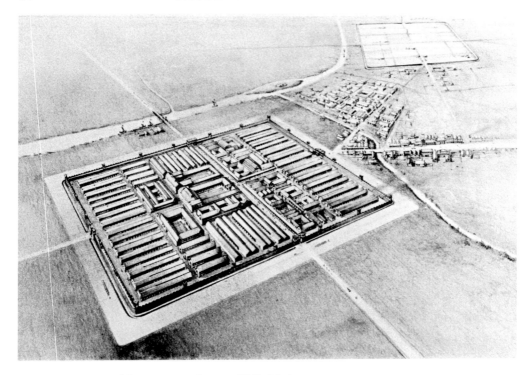

20 Reconstruction of the city centre fortress. (*Philip Moss*)

the fortress. At both Caerleon and Chester, which were destined to be permanent fortresses, the baths were built in stone very quickly (in Caerleon's case, probably at the time of the foundation of the fortress). If the legionary baths had been built at Gloucester they would have been a statement of imperial power with a cathedral-like exercise basilica next to them, and the buildings would most likely have survived into the *colonia* period and throughout it.

Rapid movement and mobility were the basis of Roman military might, and roads would have been laid out as the troops advanced, ensuring a straightjacket of communications in areas already subdued. Just as important, these routes also enabled the movement of the trade, taxes and the mineral resources that the Roman administration had wanted when it decided to make Britannia formally part of the empire.

FOUR

ROMAN ROADS:
A STRAIGHTJACKET FOR
THE REGION

Shrinking Time, Maximising Power

In the late Iron Age routes responded to geographical constraints and were integrated with natural features using river systems, following valleys and connecting large settlements spaced along them. More local routes probably constituted boundaries of social and family networks. In contrast, the Roman road system represents a manmade contribution to the cultural geography of the inhabitants and, by shrinking the 'time-distance' ratio between strategic places, enabled the growth of imperialism and empire. The Romans changed the way that space was organised in Britain by building a network of roads whose compulsive straightness showed clearly that they could travel far, forcibly and fast. The planners of Ermine Street, Akeman Street and Fosse Way were concerned with issues of ideology and power; they wanted to provide symbolic evidence for the coherence and extent of Roman influence in terms of exercising physical dominance over local populations. Roads represented the identity of the Roman state, using the straight, surveyed road measured in Roman miles and imposing a sense of dominated space through the landscape, a determined assertiveness and an authoritative understanding of the land.

The work of the planners and the effects on an individual's sense of place can be experienced by walking Roman roads and especially along long-distance paths such as the 'Roman Way', part of which route follows Akeman Street as it crosses the limestone dip-slope of the Cotswold Hills from Alchester, in Oxfordshire, to Cirencester, in Gloucestershire, and then south-east following Ermine Street across the Upper Thames Valley to the Wiltshire Downs. The walker becomes acutely aware that the route has a hypnotic onwardness as the Roman road ignores everything that went before it, effectively neutering the late Iron Age past.

The Roman Roads of the Gloucestershire Region

All of the main routes of Roman roads in Britain have been identified, usually by researchers with either a military or engineering background, who have been able to second-guess the Roman surveyors. Without doubt, the doyen of the study of British Roman roads and their routes was Ivan D. Margary, who allocated a numbering system for each of the

identified Roman routes that was hierarchical, with its starting point in Dover, the major
Channel port used by the Romans. Single figures were used for main roads, 1 being Watling
Street (the route of the AD 43 invasion), double figures for secondary roads branching off
main routes and three-figure references for local routes (see Fig. 11).

Ermine Street

This route is likely to be the earliest of the roads through the Gloucestershire region as it
runs from around Wanborough, in Wiltshire, and moves through the isolated high point at
Blunsdon Hill. It crosses the Thames Valley, making a deviation, probably to avoid marshy
land, and used a ford or bridge possibly on one of the gravel 'islands', before heading into
the Cirencester region then up the dip-slope of the Cotswolds, descending the escarpment at below Crickley Hill. It then aims for the crossing of the Severn in the region of
Kingsholm, which was the dominant reason for the road and its direction from the Wiltshire
Downs. Ermine Street between Cirencester and Gloucester exemplifies Roman surveying
skills, which were able to minimise the distance and maximise the ease of road construction
between locations in varying physical environments, such as the Cotswold dip-slope and
the Severn Valley floodplain, with a high escarpment in between. It reaches the vexillation
fortress at Kingsholm at an oblique angle rather than at 90 degrees, and it may well be that
the military establishment was founded earlier than the road could have been built, which
must frequently have been the case in the rapid deployment of troops in the early years of
the Conquest.

21 Ermine Street in 1915. (*Ed. J. Burrow*)

Akeman Street

Akeman Street is Margary's 16a and 16b, which ran from St Albans to Alchester, a north–south road crosses it, and then on to Cirencester. Akeman Street seems to have been named some time during the post-Roman period, most likely because it was seen as heading towards Bath, where sick individuals (*aker* in Anglo-Saxon) could get cured of ailments in the hot-water springs and so would travel along 'Acemannesceatre'. In the late Iron Age Akeman Street might have formed an important dynastic connection between the peoples of Verulamion, present-day St Albans, and the Bagendon area. If that was so, the appropriation of the route by the Romans clearly demonstrated their power and it would have been an important military road between Alchester and Gloucester, maximising access to large parts of the Thames Valley and the northern Cotswolds. Assigning a date to Akeman Street is not straightforward as at Wilcote, a settlement in Oxfordshire on the road and possibly an early maintenance depot, the excavator dated the construction of the road to AD 47, but that level of accuracy is rather optimistic. The roadside settlement at Asthall, a few kilometres from Wilcote, has a mid-first century date, but Akeman Street when it approaches Cirencester is seen as being a late addition, *c.* AD 70, to the road system. Neil Holbrook has suggested that Akeman Street was in use in the late 40s but not surfaced until the AD 70s. Since there was no fort at Cirencester at this early stage, this author suggests that the early Akeman Street used the Welsh Way late Iron Age route through the Bagendon Valley, to join Ermine Street near Duntisbourne Grove.

Fosse Way

The Fosse Way, Margary's 5a to 5b Axmouth and Cirencester and 5d to 5f from Cirencester to Lincoln, is the archetypal Roman road, seemingly cutting straight across country with a deceptively unwavering course. The deviation from this straight linear route of the Fosse Way through Cirencester has been the subject of much speculation and suggests that the Roman surveyors needed to take into consideration the presence of an important feature in the landscape, the Tar Barrows. The presence of late Iron Age sites at Bath, Bagendon and Salmonsbury near the Fosse Way, and some indications of changed alignments of the road to these settlements, leaves wide open arguments about whether this was fortuitous or a deliberate policy, though it is difficult to consider that anything would be accidental to the Roman administration.

The Dean Road

In most books about Roman roads, the Dean Road makes an almost obligatory appearance, largely because of the photogenic nature of the paved section at Blackpool Bridge. Walters suggested that the Dean Road was a single entity built in the first century as a route between Lydney and the smelting centre at Weston-under-Penyard. Although a Roman date was accepted by Margary, who catalogued it as route 614, he did have reservations about its age, considering the narrowness of the carriageway. Jon Hoyle, in the Forest of Dean Gloucestershire Archaeological Survey, suggested a number of the arguments against a Roman date and function. A piece of charcoal from a 'sealed context' below a portion of the road gave a radiocarbon date of not earlier than AD 1660. The construction of the road, especially its width of 2.5m (8ft), is similar to that of a pre-turnpike road and not like those around Weston-under-Penyard, which had been excavated and proved to be of a Roman date. Finally, the route of the road respects post-Roman features such as churches and is not used by medieval parish boundaries, both indicating therefore that the road must be post-medieval. Hoyle suggested that the road was built by the government to facilitate transport of timber for naval requirements during the late seventeenth and early eighteenth centuries.

The White Way/Salt Way

The White/Salt Way is one of the most important late Iron Age routes in the Bagendon area as it was probably a pre-Roman ridgeway across the Cotswolds, dropping down the escarpment above Winchcombe and then moving in the direction of Droitwich, the Roman Salinae, a major source of salt. It crosses the River Churn at Cirencester where an earthwork feature and excavated ditch demonstrates its probable original course. It would appear that this road later provided a route to the Leaholme fort and to the Verulamium Gate of the later town. It may then have exited through a postern gate near the amphitheatre and crossed the Thames Valley in a southerly direction as a minor road. The route also became significant in that it connected many of the important villas of the Cotswolds, including Chedworth and Withington, with Cirencester and may have been a contributory factor in their siting.

Subsidiary Routes

Other possible military roads in the Gloucestershire region are route 610 Dymock–Stretton Grandison, although it is now unlikely that forts existed in either locality; route 541 from the port of Seamills (Abonae) to Gloucester, largely following the course of the A38; and route 60a joining Gloucester to South Wales, following the A48 on the north side of the Severn. There are some local roads that would appear to relate to the position of villas and villa estates in the countryside, such as route 542 from Bath to Chavenage Green; route 543 from Eastern Grey to Arlingham; route 544 Cirencester to Kingscote Park, by Coates, Rodmarton and Chavenage Green; and Bitton to Berkeley (no Margary number). There must also have been thousands of tracks in rural areas dating from the late Iron Age and earlier that were used throughout the Roman period, and possibly up to recent times surviving as green lanes or even public rights of way.

Excavating Roman Roads

Perhaps one of the earliest examples of 'rescue excavation' took place in 1939 on the Fosse Way at Culkerton during the emergency war-time expansion of RAF Kemble. As service roads were being laid down, C.E. Stevens observed and recorded 'alternate layers of thin limestone flags and more or less gravelly sand, the whole resting on about 6 inches of decomposed brush over the limestone'. A standpipe hole enabled Stevens to see 'that the lowest layer of flags was laid immediately on this brash'. Excavations on the Fosse Way at about the same time demonstrated similar, if less detailed sequences of construction. Between Stow-on-the-Wold and Moreton in Marsh two sections were dug fairly close to each other – the first found a foundation of pitched stones of varying thickness between 3.8cm and 5cm (1.5in to 2in) and the greatest length being 25.4cm (10in), but in the second trench the road was laid on the solid ground of the natural subsoil. Excavations on Akeman Street in 1952 at Quennington identified a rammed gravel dual carriageway with a shallow gutter in between them and evidence of wheel ruts. Besides responding to local ground conditions, the differences in construction might be due to the local situation of the population maintaining the road surface.

It is not very often that an opportunity arises to excavate sections along an early military Roman road which then survived as an important route through to the fourth century

22 The successive road surfaces seen in section and the efficiency of the roadside ditches in draining its surface. (*Oxford Archaeological Unit*)

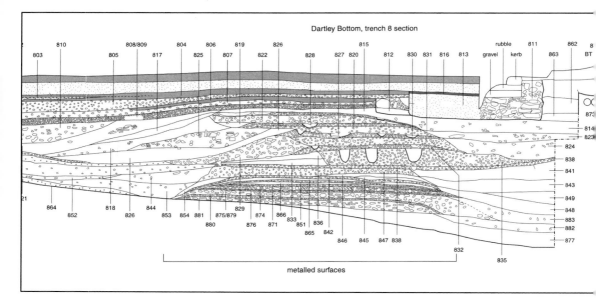

23 Ermine Street: Dartley Bottom (Trench 8). The section shows layer 876 as being the military road surface with the layers below demonstrating the levelling of the road to provide a reasonably horizontal base. (*Oxford Archaeological Unit*)

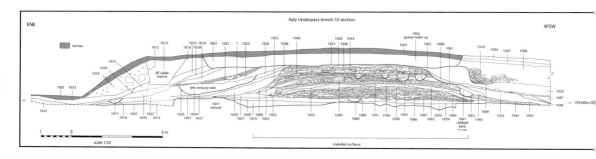

24 Section across Ermine Street at Itlay Underpass. (*Oxford Archaeological Unit*)

and in other guises until the present day. During the A419/417 road improvement scheme in 1996–97, seven sections were excavated across the carriageway and verge of the A419. In each of these sections there was some similarity between the deposits forming the road foundations and surfaces, but it was clear that at each location the engineers, responding to different ground configurations, had used differing techniques to address different challenges. As might be expected there were problems of dating, with little pottery being found, and artefacts such as horseshoes were probably intrusive as they would have most likely have been lost in potholes or ruts in later road surfaces. Post-Roman road construction had also removed earlier surfaces by constant wear or digging down through the Roman deposits to form the foundations of the later route-way. In spite of these constraints, two sections through the road were particularly informative about methods of construction, that at Dartley Bottom (Trench 8) and Itlay Underpass (Trench 10). In both sections the Roman military construction was clearly identified as solid rubble foundations up to 0.4m thick and capped with limestone metalling. Pitched stone sealed with local clay was used in some sections as a foundation or as road edging to stop the spread of the metalling under the weight of traffic. Ermine Street was repaired or reconstructed on a number of occasions, especially in the first and second centuries. At Dartley Bottom at least five constructions were identified, and at Itlay Underpass seven repairs were detected, the sixth likely to have been no later than the second century, and probably all before the third century. There was evidence from along the road that it had been maintained and reconstructed as late as the fourth century. It may be that road repairs were limited to specific locations due to topographical problems, especially where valleys were crossed, and this may also be the case with sections where no roadside ditches were apparent. Even in later periods the road appears to have been constructed either directly by military engineers or by civil engineers using a military method.

The evidence for road construction south-east of Cirencester was limited to only one trench and shows a different form of construction where a slight *agger* was visible with a single eroded surface. Previous work in the Thames Valley area at Cricklade confirms the slightness of the make-up of Ermine Street and this does pose issues of the amount of traffic on the road during the Roman period or post-Roman destruction of the upper layers. The different natural environments either side of Cirencester would have provided different, though equally taxing, challenges for engineers.

25 The rutted surface of Ermine Street outside Cirencester. (*Oxford Archaeological Unit*)

Roads and Officialdom

There are no surviving accounts of travel through the Roman province of Britannia, although there is evidence of specific routes contained in late Roman itineraries. The Antonine Itinerary lists 15 British routes (each identified as an 'Inter'); however, they do not follow the 'military' shortest time/distance ratio, but would appear to illustrate the importance of official 'peregrinations' which, even though they pass through the legion-ary fortresses, represent official routes to civilian sites. Each itinerary seems to be circular and no doubt are demonstrating an economic context or political set of circumstances in a landscape no longer controlled by military strategy. Whereas many of the routes begin at the Channel ports or London, the hub of Calleva at present-day Silchester seems to be the most important in terms of direct influence on both Corinium and Glevum. Inter XIV begins at the legionary fortress of Isca, at Caerleon in South Wales, and runs through Gloucester and Cirencester to Silchester, which was connected with Chichester, Winchester and London by Inter XII, Bath (Inter XIV) and Dorchester and Exeter (Inter XV). Through use of these routes, both Glevum and Corinium would in turn have been connected with the other parts of the empire.

These routes were possibly also part of the networks of the *cursus publicus* on which were posting stations (*mansiones* or *mutations*) for official travellers to change horses and, when necessary, to obtain overnight accommodation. These settlements appear to have been deliberate foundations by the Roman administration and appear to be about 20–35km (12.4–21.7 miles) apart. If no facilities were available, the official traveller had the right to requisition animals and require accommodation or stay in *tabernae*. A post-ing station's lodgings might include higher status accommodation, often with entrance halls and heated rooms, but there would also be separate buildings for the staff of the station as well as stabling and large granaries and food stores. Separate parks may have catered for the wagons and slower moving pedestrians would probably have stayed in the barrack-like standard facilities. It is highly likely that provision of the official facilities, usually recognised as large courtyard houses with separate bath house as befitting some-one travelling on administrative business, would be found in Corinium and/or Glevum. Considering the importance of Cirencester as a node for at least three main routes, one would expect to find an early *mansio* there, perhaps in or near the possible Leaholme fort/let. Using the 20–35km (12.4–21.7 miles) apart rule and the importance of Cirencester as the administrative hub at the crossing of three major roads, candidates for *mansiones* on the south Fosse Way might be the Roman site at Easton Grey, to the north of Corinium the walled town of Dorn and Chesterton-on-Fosse in Warwickshire (also with defences). On Akeman Street, Asthall (just in Oxfordshire) is the required distance and on Ermine Street, to the east of Corinium, so is Wanborough. A settlement alongside Ermine Street to the west of Corinium at Birdlip is unlikely to be deliberately founded as it looks like a purely agricultural community and is very close to Gloucester and its suburbs. Gloucester would certainly have been another hub and on the road north to Wroxeter are a number of equally spaced settlements at Dymock and Stretton Grandison in Herefordshire that are candidates for accommodation on the *cursus publicus*. Along the road from Gloucester to Caerwent, first-century Roman buildings at Blakeney might be considered a suitable location. However, the use of waterborne transport must be kept in mind as there was a ferry across the Bristol Channel between Caerwent and Sea Mills near the mouth of the Avon, and Caerleon was also on the navigable Usk. As will be seen later, the Lower Severn might not have had as many navigational hazards in the Roman period as at present and this has implications for travel from the mouth of the Severn to Gloucester, and also ferries across the river above the site of the first Severn Bridge.

Roman Roads, Mobility and Identity

Margary accepted that his books were 'surface descriptions' of Roman roads and admitted that he was not interested in who used the roads, just those who surveyed and built them. While this approach is still of high value and an important achievement, it means that he also represented Roman roads as having an impersonal, timeless, function *inscribed* in the present landscape and therefore disembodied from it and the travellers and settlers alongside the routes. This may well have been the case in the early years of the invasion, when 'inscription' was exactly what was desired to achieve military objectives and demonstrate dominance. However, the roads in the Gloucestershire region were used by travellers for many purposes after the military phase and it is important to try to get a sense of their experiences by seeing the Roman roads as *embodied* in the landscape.

Richard Reece has examined Ermine Street between Cirencester and Gloucester and the possible influence of the road not only on politics, but also the traveller, trade and settlement. He notes that while the two settlements are 22.5km (14 miles) apart, the journey between them is a pull of 8 miles to climb the 182m (600ft) of the gentle dip-slope, with sharp little valleys to cross every so often, then the drop of 243km (800ft) in 1.6km (1 mile) down the steep scarp slope, before a level journey of 8km (5 miles). The return journey was worse, with the need to climb the 243m (800ft) with hardly a level stretch. He states that this would produce a distance between Gloucester and Cirencester of at least 35.4km (22 miles) in direct effort or 'mental miles'. Perhaps with the discipline of the Roman army these 'mental miles' were 'shorter' or even 'less', but in civilian periods the distance would have had a significance in terms of personal, political and economic factors. Reece considers that this steep slope of the Cotswold escarpment might form the natural boundary of the influence of Glevum and that of Corinium, and perhaps the edge of the Severn Valley pottery trade and therefore its distribution. The position of the rather curious military installation at Corinium in the AD 60s may have something to do with these 'landscape miles'. Usually, the fort/let has been considered in terms of journeys through to Glevum or the monitoring of Bagendon. If the direction of travel was seen to be the opposite way then a base at Cirencester would be the natural place to change horses or rest tired officials. During the construction of the A419, a settlement originating in the later second century was discovered at Birdlip Quarry adjacent to Ermine Street. While it might have had some sort of role in servicing traffic along the main road, the settlement was predominantly of roundhouses of the late Iron Age tradition, indicating that the effect of Ermine Street was minimal in influencing the identities of groups of people of low status, even though Roman-style pottery was found there.

Akeman Street bisects the North Oxfordshire Grim's Ditch *oppida* complex, in which by the third century were a number of very wealthy, indeed palatial, villas, comparable to any other similar sites anywhere in southern Britain. With such affluence, and the nearest settlement of any sophistication and power being Cirencester, there can be little doubt that the occupants of the villas had townhouses and travelled between their rural homes and the *civitas* capital frequently. The distance between the villas at Stonesfield and North Leigh to Cirencester is just 37km (22miles), a five-hour day by horse along Akeman Street, as opposed to the 15–20km (9.3–12.4 miles) distance per day on foot with a beast of burden, resulting in two days' travel. The advice of the Younger Pliny (AD 61–*c*. AD 112) in the first book of his *Epistulae* was that easy access to Rome from your villa by good communications was necessary, so that he could travel the 27.3km (17 miles) from the capital without having cut short or hurried the day's work. Such a relationship between the villas and a major settlement such as Corinium could not have happened without shrinking the time-distance ratio. While Reece suggests that these settlements are a 'forbidding distance away' from Cirencester, the pull of the *civitas* capital in terms of economic, cultural or political power must have been considerable and we need not always think about daily travel, but also seasonal.

The increase in mobility and movement had more profound effects on the Gloucestershire area than just minimising the time a journey might take when compared to the routes of the later Iron Age using meandering river valleys. More mobility opened up more possibilities and opportunities to travel to more places and to experience a wider range of actions and events, as well as to experience new ideas. Each of these factors could reinforce or widen a sense of cultural identity through active participation with travellers and in travelling. On the one hand, it could be argued that this increased mobility might have forced a change of identity as the Roman army or representatives of the provincial government could be responsible for 'telling' settlers how to become Roman. New opportunities could also have led to active participation in identity change as merchants and the administration 'sold' ideas to individuals and communities, or elites sought out new goods and personae which, in turn, resulted in modification of identities gradually and through self-determined choices. It was along the roads that the ideas of becoming Roman flowed, the notions of towns and country villas as well as new diets and a new official language.

FIVE

DISPLAYING COMPLIANCE: AD 43–100

While the Roman literary accounts extol the Conquest and would like to indicate a sharp break in AD 43, the archaeology points to a more subtle relationship between the new arrivals and the late Iron Age communities. The Roman approach in the early years appears to be one of forming pragmatic, opportunist and flexible relationships with different areas of the country, and these policies were likely to have been in place before the landings on the South Coast. The Roman attitude was to make or encourage these diplomatic efforts to isolate enemies from potential allies so that military units might be released to fight on another front. The lack of forts along Akeman Street and the continued development of pre-invasion social groups indicates that key individuals had already made pacts with Rome and had for some time been in some type of political and economic relationship with the empire. It is likely that these elites had a special status, 'client kingdoms', and therefore would not have put up any resistance to the conquering army.

The conquest of Britain and its long-term occupation was not an act of benevolence, as the exploitation of land and resources was fundamental to the success of the Roman Empire. Whatever the status of the Dobunni, which we can now call the *civitas* administrative area, the strategic position of the Gloucestershire region must have been marked out as significant before the conquest. Similarly, through long-term trading with the empire, especially Gaul, the people must have been aware of the Roman military machine and its methods, which were brutal, cruel and indiscriminate in the damage they caused, and would not have wanted that repeated on their own lands. Late Iron Age elites, particularly significant individuals, would have probably realised from their Continental contacts that if they did not conform to Rome's wishes they could be replaced with more compliant leaders. Even if the Dobunni was a client kingdom, there is no reason to think that this status continued after the military had moved on to further conquests, or that the peoples were not subjected to paying tribute and that taxes were not imposed. Similarly, forced labour or animals for transport could have been requisitioned and young men may have been recruited forcibly into the army. However, favoured individuals and groups may have had nominal independence, even if their lands remained garrisoned by the army, and this may well be the case with Dio's 'part of the Dobunni'.

Even though the Gloucestershire area, at least that part east of the Cotswold escarpment, might have been part of a compliant kingdom, there was a heavy garrison which was a springboard for attacking the Silures as well as protecting the Severn waterway, which would have been of major significance. There must have been confiscation of lands for the *territorium*, which the fortress at Glevum would need for supplies of food, and it is unlikely that lands were totally returned or supervision was lessened until the years immediately before the founding of the *civitas*, the administrative centre of the Dobunni at Corinium. There was always the possibility that confiscated lands would be held on to as part of an imperial estate or reward for services to the empire for someone living outside Britain. The unusual combination in the same region of an *oppidum*-type settlement, a *civitas* capital of Corinium Dobunnorum and a *colonia* for retired soldiers, replacing the fortress at Gloucester, poses many questions about change and continuity of civilian life alongside the military activity.

Tar Barrows

As we have seen, Fosse Way and Akeman Street follow rather eccentric courses when approaching Cirencester. Richard Reece has argued that the Tar Barrows, two features of ritual importance, may have been responsible not only for these rather unexpected alignments but also for the unsuitable location of the *civitas* capital of Corinium Dobunnorum, where the high water table caused problems of flooding (see Fig. 4). In the most perfect of Roman worlds, Corinium would have been sited near Tar Barrows and both Ermine Street and Fosse Way, on straight alignments, would have formed a crossroads at its centre. The approximate date of the construction of Fosse Way near the town is *c.* AD 47 and that its course respects the barrows indicates that they must have been constructed, or that the land was sacred, before that time. This indicates either a very early Roman or, more likely, a late Iron Age date for the Tar Barrows. Geophysical prospecting and fieldwalking suggests that the eastern barrow was set in its own enclosure and there were at least four other ditched features arranged around the barrow which have been interpreted as *mausolea*, set within funerary enclosures. Pits holding possible cremation burials were also set in ditched enclosures that ran along Fosse Way. This activity seems to have been the focus of a settlement covering an area of approximately 350m (383yds) by at least 200m (218yds), and the northeast to south-west alignment indicates that it post-dates both the Fosse Way and the original settlement at Cirencester. The possible pre-Roman or at least pre-*civitas* date of the barrows and *civitas* date for the settlement may point to a continuity of ritual, power and memory between Bagendon and Corinium.

Akeman Street linked Corinium and Verulamium and this connection between the two Roman towns highlights a striking concordance between Tar Barrows and a similar enclosure outside the built-up area of Roman St Albans. The Folly Lane Burial, dated to *c.* AD 55 and excavated between 1991 and 1993, was a rectangular enclosure and consisted of a high-status cremation burial and a shaft with a sunken, timber-lined funerary chamber in which were the remains of the funeral pyre. The chamber also contained burnt grave goods, including the remains of an ivory mounted couch, 2.5kg (5.5lb) of silver and a complete tunic of iron chain mail, bronze and enamel horse gear. The site was interpreted as a royal grave and implied that the cremation was of an individual who had served in an auxiliary regiment at some time in his life. The position of the feature on the skyline, overlooking the area of what was to become the Roman town centre, seems expressly designed to ensure that the person buried there continued to dominate the local community in death, as he had done in life. This may suggest that for the first few years after the conquest this site was based under the client rule of a trusted chieftain, as the Romans preferred to deal with individuals rather than groups of elites. If the Tar Barrows are pre-AD 47, it implies that the features may have been the burial place of the local leaders, though there is no reason to discount their later use for a similar function or that an important personage who lived after AD 47 is also buried there. The resemblance of the position of the barrows in the Bagendon areas and St Albans further supports Holbrook's suggestion that there may have been family ties between the two late Iron Age communities.

Ditches

Ditches is an important site because of it earliness as a Roman villa of about AD 70. Continuity from the late Iron Age may well be seen in the tantalising 2006 geophysics results, where what may be a late Iron Age roundhouse was detected in the middle of the enclosure. Since the early Roman structure respects the possible roundhouse site by being

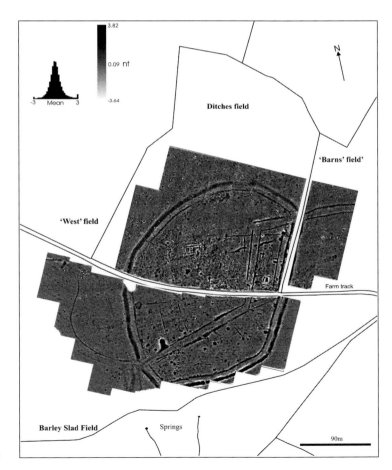

26 Ditches: the geophysical survey. (S. James, T. Moore, S. Trow)

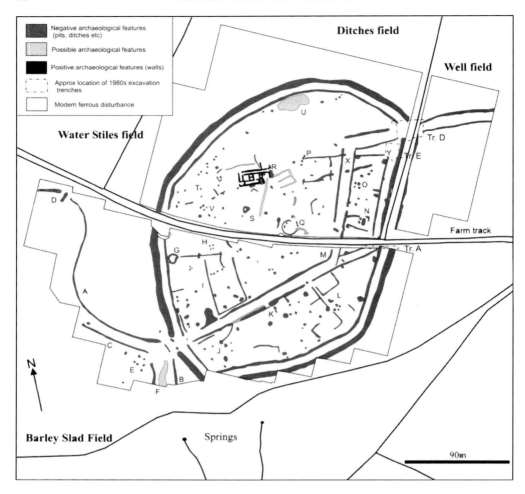

27 Interpretation of the geophysical survey showing the possible roundhouse and early villa. (*S. James, T. Moore, S. Trow*)

built to the north-west, it could be that the early feature was still standing, and perhaps being lived in, when the villa was constructed. Early villas have been described as 'square roundhouses' as the way of life in both types of structure may well have be similar.

The Ditches Villa appears to have been built during the third quarter of the first century AD and there seems to have been at least one ancillary structure, possibly for accommodation or storage. The early date at once separates the edifice from the other known villas in Gloucestershire, which are usually of the second to fourth centuries. The structure was a 'row-type' house, in that it consisted of six rooms, and possibly in the early second century a timber-framed corridor or veranda was added to the front of the row, if not on all sides of the block. The timber veranda was replaced by a stone-built corridor running around this main block (and obliterating evidence of the timber phase). The villa structure seems to have been refurbished some time before the early second century, with a cellar being built at the east end. After the construction of the masonry-built corridors and at some time in the early–mid second century, the southern arm of the corridor was modified to provide a shallow wing at each end of the main block.

The layout of the Ditches Villa has correspondence of design with some similar types of structures around Verulamium, and also the Ditchley and North Leigh villas within in the NOGD. The first phase of the Ditches structure also has parallels in northern Gaul and this may indicate a Continental influence in this design – an 'indigenous' Gaulish adaptation of Roman design. While there was little evidence for interior decoration of the villa or for a tiled roof, the stone construction, including a cellar and well-built walls, suggest an imported technology, possibly the result of the owners commissioning Gallic masons. The previous position and importance of the late Iron Age high-status site will have been part of the everyday experience of those in the valley. This new opulent, foreign-designed, symmetrical structure built of mortared stone and at least 3m (10ft) tall with possible pillared colonnade would have astonished local people and travellers. The building would have confirmed not only political power, but economic and social dominance. If individuals or groups had high enough status to be allowed inside the villa, the window glazing and the plastered and painted walls would have given a very direct message about the aspirations of the owners. In the late Iron Age the enclosure's entrance antennae faced in the direction of the valley, and it would appear that it was designed to be seen from the Welsh Way, the postulated route from the Thames to the Cotswold escarpment and therefore the direction of travellers of higher status. The change of orientation of the villa to face south-east, thereby

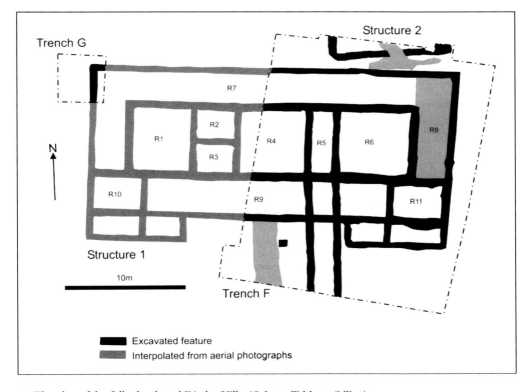

28 The plan of the fully developed Ditches Villa. (*S. James, T. Moore, S. Trow*)

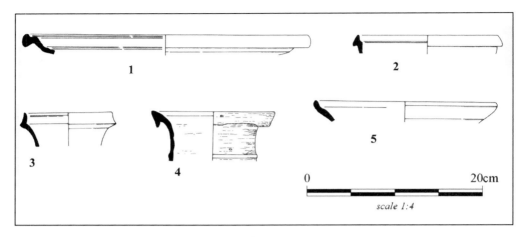

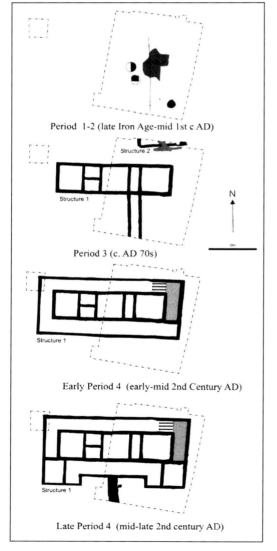

29 Imported pottery from Ditches: the Samian Ware bowl (No 2) can be dated AD 40–55. (S. James, T. Moore, S. Trow)

30 The chronology of Ditches Villa. (S. James, T. Moore, S. Trow)

giving a commanding view of Ermine Street, probably compensated for the continued occupation of such a weather-exposed site. This new arrangement not only suggests a display of status, but advertises to the traveller along Ermine Street that the owners of Ditches were focusing on the future. The building of the Ditches Villa is indicative of the aspirations of an individual or family group, a private act with different motivations from the display of material culture in a communal context that was to take place later with the construction of the *civitas* capital like Corinium. Just because a group of people want to adopt a Roman lifestyle doesn't mean that they supported the Roman Empire or its army. Adapting this very personal display of Roman cultural lifestyles might have come to rapidly signify good taste and social eminence rather than being associated with alien conquerors. The complexity of this process is reflected in the title of the excavation report for Ditches: 'Becoming Roman, Being Gallic, Staying British'.

There are similar early Roman villas in prominent positions at St Albans (Gorhambury) and the North Oxfordshire Grim's Ditch (Callow Hill) with commanding views into what seems to be a largely empty space in a valley. In both localities there were ritual structures present and these may have emphasised the continuity of ancestors and present power structures. An early villa at Withington appears to be on the edge of a late Iron Age enclosure and is just 2km (1.2 miles) from the contemporary shrine at Wycombe. Although such a feature is not known yet in the Bagendon Valley, such an empty space with a ritual aspect would have made the villa overhanging the source of the brook even more visually and symbolically impressive. If the roundhouse had remained in the enclosure, at least in the preliminary phases of the villa construction, the memory and continuities of power would have been even greater.

Around AD 150–75 part of the eastern wall of the cellar collapsed into the chamber and was filled with rubble and rubbish. At the same time the roof was stripped deliberately. This may have caused the abandonment of the villa. Around the early third century AD the eastern end wall of the main villa block collapsed or was deliberately toppled. The excavators have suggested a scenario in which the villa was destroyed in an accidental fire, although whether this destruction was because the family had lost power and wealth or it had grown wealthier and no longer needed to demonstrate status in such an exposed location cannot be known. If a new site was needed to demonstrate prosperity, rank and standing then a move further around the headwaters of the stream now occupied by a grand house called Cotswold Park would have given a gentle valley slope to expand down, a spring nearby for water and ritual and also have retained a view from Ermine Street, but in a much more sheltered position. Unfortunately, much of this site has been landscaped, with possible damage to the archaeology.

Bagendon

While the Ditches site appears to have been continually occupied at this period, it is probable that activity at Bagendon ceased about the AD 60s, after having a short period of intense activity. As suggested above, the settlement behind the dykes looks less like a 'Belgic' *oppidum* and more like an early Roman industrial centre and it was this production role that was different from the high-status consumer settlement at Ditches. The settlement occupied a very small area and it does not seem to be of great intensity or complexity, with very little evidence of people living there in any numbers at all. Any immediate post-invasion role might have been to be part of existing exchange processes between the early Roman province to the south-east and the areas to the north-west, such as the Midlands or the Welsh borderlands. Even though the Roman army would have been campaigning far west from the Bagendon area, trade routes would have probably survived as it was in the interest of the province that these should continue and develop. With the increasing civilian use of the Fosse Way, Ermine Street and Akeman Street, it was probably inevitable that the focus of trade would move to the crossroads at what was to become Corinium. So, there is no reason to think that any of the trading connections of the area would have ceased, but the new road configuration would have made travelling easier.

There is no evidence from either of the excavations undertaken at Bagendon to suggest a town or proto-town behind the dykes, so it is unlikely that the growth of Corinium was at the expense of Bagendon or that there was a wholesale movement of people to the new location. If Bagendon was abandoned in the AD 60s, Corinium, as a replacement *civitas* capital, was unlikely to have been in place until *c.* AD 80–100. Aerial photographic evidence suggests that settlement on the western slope of the Churn Valley between Bagendon and Corinium did survive the founding of the *civitas* capital. At Verulamium in the AD 40s and early AD 50s one of the most pronounced features was a shift in the pattern of settlement away from the plateau edge to the lower slopes, where it was centred on the site that was to become the later forum/basilica complex of the Roman town. There is some evidence that this might have occurred at Corinium.

Gloucester: Colonia Nervia Glevensis

The date of the foundation of the *colonia* on the city centre fortress site at Glevum has been a matter of some debate and demonstrates the problems of using epigraphic and archaeological evidence together. At a conference in Gloucester in 1999, an 'historical archaeologist, Mark Hassall, and Henry Hurst, 'a dirt archaeologist', undertook such a debate and the evidence for, and conclusions of, can be read in the conference publication listed in the bibliography. Hassall suggested that the *colonia* was actually founded in the reign of Domitian (AD 81–96), but since he was disgraced and his name removed from all inscriptions after his death, *damnatio memoriae*, this would support the argument that the fortress on the *colonia* site had indeed been abandoned after AD 75, with the foundation of a fortress occupied by the IInd Augustan Legion at the Caerleon on the River Usk. This would give a chronology of the XXth Legion as being at Colchester from AD 43–49, Kingsholm AD 49–*c.* 55, possibly from AD 55–67 at Usk, then AD 67 on the city centre site until *c.* AD 75, when it moved to Wroxeter, eventually ending up at its permanent base at Chester in AD 87. Hassall also suggests epigraphic evidence of inscriptions of the XXth after the removal of the legion indicates that centuries or cohorts were helping to build the *colonia* wall in stone. This chronology tends to ignore the evidence of the Kingsholm base surviving until *c.* AD 64.

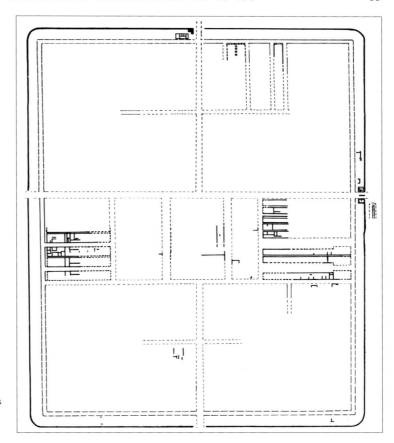

31 Plan of Glevum *colonia* in the late first century with excavations sites as fig. 18. (*H.R. Hurst*)

Hurst maintains that there was a second fortress built in one episode to replace the timber buildings in AD 86/87, but the *colonia* is most likely to have been founded in AD 96-98. Hurst admits that units of the XXth Legion might have been helping the colonists build a walled circuit. Perhaps the different approaches demonstrate that an archaeologist like Hurst would have to accept broad dating, in this case between AD 80 and 100, as being a 'tiny' difference, but an archaeologist using written evidence, especially epigraphic which is inscribed on stone, would demand much more precise dating!

Here it is accepted that the fortress on the city centre site was abandoned *c.* AD 75 with the foundation of Isca Silurum at Caerleon, and that the new part stone-built structures were those of the *colonia*. Which leaves the issue of what happened at Glevum in between *c.* AD 75 and *c.* 86/87 and in what state were the buildings at the time of the foundation of the *colonia*? For a brief period in the late AD 70s and 80s there were more fortresses than were needed by the four remaining legions in Britannia due to movements of troops up to new theatres of war to carry out Vespasian's expansionist policies. We can only guess at why the Roman army kept hold of these defunct sites. They may have been unwilling to demolish them until it was absolutely certain that strategies would not change again, forcing a legion back to its previous location. Another significant reason, perhaps more so, is that until the provincial government had an alternative use for the fortresses, they were of less value to it than the land around them – their *territoria*. With the removal of the XXth Legion, it is unlikely that the army would have felt any responsibility for the substantial community of people outside the defences and those who had serviced the fortress with food etc. The legionaries' 'unofficial families' (they were not allowed to marry) would have moved with them, as would the traders. It was the *territorium* containing a significant amount of farmland still under control of the army that was important.

The function of the *territorium* was to provide at least part of the raw materials and supplies needed by a legion, and since the IInd Augustan's fortress at Isca was on a green-field site, it may have been a priority to use Gloucester's *territorium* as a resource until the new fortress was completed. The navigability of the River Severn, its estuary and the Usk up to the Caerleon fortress site was clearly an essential factor in this process. Wroxeter, the new base of the XXth Legion, was on the site of a previous fortress and the legionary demands might have been less. Once the *territorium* of the new fortresses were fully developed, productive and self-sufficient, the old ones would become increasingly irrelevant and their redevelopment for public use could be considered. In Gloucester's case, this was as a *colonia,* in Wroxeter's as *civitas* capital of the Cornovii. Any 'caretaker' garrison left at Gloucester might have been preparing the site for the arrival of the colonists and have left inscriptions to prove it.

Michael Fulford has estimated that each year, assuming legionary units were maintained at full strength, between about 400 and 800 legionaries, and an equivalent number of auxiliaries, would reach retirement age. So, between the invasion of AD 43 and the foundation of the *colonia* of Glevum, with the almost continuous service of the four legions in Britannia, the number of retired soldiers may have been 20,000 men or more. Even if only half of these men and their dependent families, let's say of three people, were to stay in Britain, that would give a total of some 6000 over a decade. Many military men may have decided to return to the town of their birth or settle elsewhere in the province. At the close of the first century, most of the veterans who joined the legions in the AD 70s were probably from outside Britain; however, after 25 years of service most soldiers would have lost contact with their homeland and, in the case of the now redundant fortress of Glevum, many men of the XXth Legion might have decided to return to their last posting. In the second century, local recruitment would have been the norm and legionaries may have retired back to families living close to the fortress in the extensive settlements around it.

The idea encouraged by Romanists in the past has been to see the *coloniae* – Colchester (Colonia Claudia Victricensis), Lincoln (Colonia Domitiana Lindensium), as well as Gloucester – as reported by Tacitus, 'to protect the country against revolt and familiarize the provincials with law-abiding government'. Evidence at Gloucester suggests that the ex-soldiers were not valued highly by the provincial government and were moved into accommodation worse than the barrack blocks they had left at active fortresses. If Glevum had remained under a caretaker garrison for up to 15 years or more, it is likely that most of the buildings were in a poor state of repair. At Berkeley Street it appears that accommodation for the ex-soldiers were the part-stone structures built on the 'footprints' of the original timber barracks. It would only have been the stone fortress baths, if they had been built, that would have survived more or less intact, with the huge structure giving the message 'We are here to stay!'

Cirencester: Corinium Dobunnorum

The fort at Cirencester has been considered to have had a *vicus*, a small settlement outside its walls which was developed by traders or camp-followers, including soldiers' unofficial families. Although a *vicus* has been seen as the precursor to the *civitas* capital, the evidence for it is scanty and it may be that the Leaholme fort was never substantial enough or its garrisons permanent enough to establish one. At Cirencester the fort/let had been abandoned by *c.* AD 65–70, but the *civitas* capital is unlikely to have been formalised until perhaps the late first century or the early second. Recent discoveries demonstrate the existence of some form of the street layout at an angle to the later one, within the southern part of Cirencester around the Watermoor area. Short lengths of metalled street and fragmentary traces of timber buildings pre-dating the town's street grid have been found at a number of locations; notably a street associated with pottery dated before AD 69 has been seen beneath the courtyard of the forum. In two other cases in the Watermoor district, streets at different angles to each other were covered by dumps of materials containing pottery of the period AD 69–96 and were buried beneath the rampart of the second-century defences, therefore being outside the subsequent walled area.

The earliness of these developments can be compared with progress at the neighbouring *civitas* capitals at Calleva (Silchester) and Ratae (Leicester), and which may demonstrate the role of roads in 'shortening' distances and transporting ideas. At Calleva, just 77km (48 miles) south-east along Ermine Street, the recent *Insula IX* excavations, by Reading University's Department of Archaeology, discovered a rectangular structure on a different alignment to the street grid, hinting at an earlier layout. This was also seen in the junctions of several main roads at the centre, which were diagonal to the subsequently imposed street grid and resulted in anomalies in the later planned town. Calleva boasted buildings with tiled roofing by the AD 60s and amphitheatre in 60s–70s, a revised street grid some time in the 70s or 80s and a timber forum complex *c.* 85. This comparison with Corinium begs the question of the lateness of its development. At Ratae, 119km (74 miles) along Fosse Way, traces of Iron Age roundhouses of the conquest phase later gave way to rectangular buildings on a variety of alignments, but at an angle to the later street grid which appears to date to *c.* AD 100. Are we seeing at Corinium signs of the local elites not challenging each other to develop personal identities, but developing a community identity by competing with the next large later Iron Age settlement down the road, in this case at Calleva, which was to become the *civitas* capital of the Atrebates?

The *Civitas* Capital of the Dobunni

The idea of wholesale movement from Bagendon to Cirencester was a commonly held belief in the recent past; however, as we have seen, Bagendon seems not to have been heavily populated and the site appears to have been abandoned well before the beginning of the building of the *civitas* capital. There were signs of late Iron Age elites emulating the Romans in terms of fine dining, importing wine and table ware, as well as producing coinage that might be seen as ways of establishing and affirming their positions, but it was not necessary to move to a new site to continue this process. As the power of elites was based on the funds got from long-distance trade, there probably were markets operating in a variety of places, and new ones did need to be constructed at Corinium to replace them. Why then should the population, especially the elites, abandon ancestral sites, found a capital from scratch, gather their dependents from their residences, spend immense sums of money on foreign architects using some building materials that could not be locally sourced and indeed came from considerable distances? In many ways the Roman policy was to let the local hierarchies be responsible for city development, as elites would have wanted to use the new social and political arena for display of their status. It was also that this was probably the most effective ways of ensuring compliance since the privileged would have the most to lose. Such huge undertakings were unlikely to have been funded by the central government so no doubt loans from the rich in other parts of the empire were needed. The grander housing in Corinium seems to have been of a later date, perhaps because it took many generations to pay off the debt and funds were not available for domestic structures. It is possible that the local hierarchies were they still on their ancestral lands, but came to Corinium when necessary for communal duties in the Dobunnic capital.

The public buildings, such as the forum and basilica, were no doubt constructed to impress subordinates, especially local inhabitants in the countryside, who made up the majority of the population, and this display of wealth replaced pre-Roman ways of demonstrating power. This would have been more so if the creation of these substantial structures provided employment for others of low status through the redistribution of resources. One of the major results of the public building programme might have been the consolidation of a community that the Romans had already determined was to be called the Dobunni. Similarly, participation in the wider Roman Empire gave opportunities to the elites of the provinces to consolidate their power on a more extensive stage. A key part of this process would be in impressing the provincial administration, specifically the governor who would have gone on peregrinations to sit in judgement and to hold audiences with local powerful individuals and their families. These visits by the governor would put the community in its place in the structure of the empire and inspire it to reach higher. The *romanitas* of the town and its builders would be seen through the layout of the street and the vistas along them, as well as the major buildings, statues and possibly inscriptions in stone. Citizenship may not have been available to the populace of Corinium in its early years, but participation in the building of civic structures demonstrated wealth and power and reaffirmed the position of the privileged individuals before the conquest.

SIX

ROMANS AND COUNTRYMEN: GLEVUM AND CORINIUM

One factor that makes the Gloucestershire region unique is the proximity of two important large urban settlements, Glevum and Corinium. Some fortresses became *civitas* capitals, for example Wroxeter (Viriconium) or Exeter (Isca Dumnoniorum), but a fortress becoming a *colonia* so close to a *civitas* capital was unusual and their economic, social and political identities need exploring. Both were founded at about the same time and presumably because of the selection of Corinium as the 'tribal capital' (which may have been decided on much earlier, perhaps in the first decades after the conquest) and Glevum was the result of unforeseen military conditions because of large numbers of troops retiring in the area due to interrupted military progress. Even after conquest had been achieved and the peoples had submitted, the legions were kept on the edge of province in order to keep their military power and influence as far away from Rome as possible, so the *colonia* may have been placed for the same reasons.

Glevum: Colonia Nervia Glevensis

Due to the use of Gloucester as an administrative and important commercial centre throughout the medieval period and continuing development into the present, the opportunity for open-area excavation has been limited. This has resulted in little being known about some aspects of Roman Glevum, and what is known is patchy due to the small areas available for excavation and medieval features cutting into the Roman layers, thereby destroying evidence of earlier structure.

The development of the wooden-built early *colonia* into being stone-built gives insights into the aspirations of the soldier population. At about AD 100 or even earlier, the ditch of the fortress was filled and its turf rampart had a stone wall inserted into its front, with limestone rubble filling the gap between the two. The wall was constructed of squared local oolitic limestone blocks with a 'rusticated' surface and it was between 4m and 5.5m (13ft by 18ft) high. It is likely that the gates were also rebuilt at the same time as similar blocks of stone built in a dry-stone fashion were also apparent. The impression of this new design was probably meant to indicate that the fortress had turned from a temporary military establishment into a permanent town. The design of the wall circuit was to change at least three times during the life of the *colonia*. In the late second century an earth bank was added to the existing one and stone interval towers were built inside the wall. Some

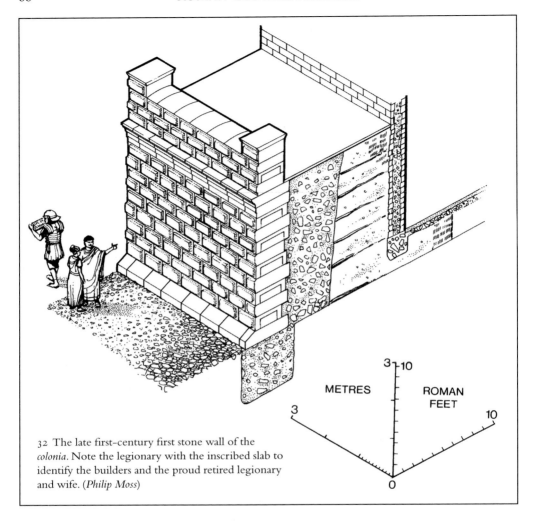

METRES   ROMAN FEET

32 The late first-century first stone wall of the *colonia*. Note the legionary with the inscribed slab to identify the builders and the proud retired legionary and wife. (*Philip Moss*)

time in the third century the walls were rebuilt, except for 30m stretches either side of the gates, and the interval towers were retained. In the late third or early fourth century, probably in response to threats from attacks by opportunist brigands coming up the Severn, the walls either side of the gates were rebuilt and projecting towers were added. As always with such linear constructions, it is likely that each of these phases are of long periods as resources became available and repair to the walls was probably a continuous process. There were four gates of which the construction of only two are known from excavations directed by Carolyn Heighway in 1974. The north gate of the *colonia* appears to have had two arched carriageways flanked by symmetrical guard chambers. The east gate appears to have been very different, with solid towers and just a single opening. Henry Hurst pointed out that the *Porta Praetoria*, the main gate of the fortress, served traffic coming from both the east and north, and therefore it might have been of a triumphal arch design. Why this should be in a *colonia* is unknown, but features such as this normally commemorate victorious campaigns.

33 The *colonia* mid-second century: W = Westgate, F = Forum. (*H.R. Hurst*)

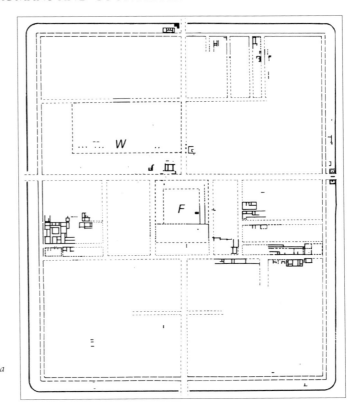

34 A reconstruction of the *colonia* in the mid-second century. (*Philip Moss*)

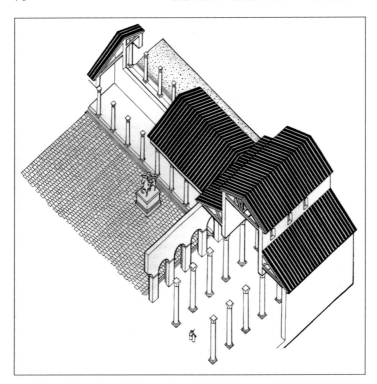

35 A reconstruction of *colonia* forum. (*Philip Moss*)

A forum/basilica on the site of the fortress *principia* became the administration centre of the *colonia* and measured 95m by 65m (311ft by 213ft). Little is known of this forum/basilica complex, but the excavator suggested that there were three successive buildings on the site: the first, the fortress *principia*; the second structure also had a gravelled area, walls of Lias limestone, including one at the front of the supposed basilica, and can be seen as the first *colonia* forum. The forum's third building episode was a substantial structure which made copious use of oolitic limestone and was constructed about AD 120. There was a certain amount of colour in the complex, with a courtyard paved with greenish stone flags from the Forest of Dean and, at ground level, a gutter of old red sandstone, also from the forest. The colonnade facing the courtyard had columns 0.6m (2ft) in diameter. Three steps in oolitic limestone then led up to the partly open basilica and here the nave and two aisles had columns of 1m diameter at shaft level. In civilian towns the forum was a public space used as a small market with the basilica used for the meeting of the *ordo*, the council managing the town's affairs. There is no reason why this should not be the case in the *colonia*. However, the presence of a statue base in the courtyard, *c.* 4m by 3m (13ft by 10ft), at some time carrying a bronze equestrian statue whose cut-up pieces have been found, indicates a high-status formal space which may have been less public.

There are a number of features that would be found in a Roman town close to the forum, but the most important would have been a temple. The location of this structure has still not been located with absolute confidence, but a row of oolitic limestone columns about a hundred metres long and known as the Westgate Colonnade has been found piecemeal over an extended period from the nineteenth century and has been the subject of much

speculation. Since the shaft bases of the columns are 1m in diameter, they clearly form a
building of some substance, which would be taller than the forum/basilica and therefore
would be unlikely to have been a bath building. When the Upper Quay Street/Westgate
Street Sewer Renewal Scheme was the subject of a watching brief in 1991, archaeologists
retrieved evidence for a building, with a possible veranda fronting on to the east side of
the street, behind the west defences of the *colonia*. In this structure's final phase, the east
wall was rebuilt and set on a very substantial oolite plinth. To the east of this wall there
was no evidence of any other buildings for a distance of 129m (423ft). So, an open space
would appear to have been defined by the Westgate Colonnade on its south side, a range
of buildings to the east side, with the proximity of a large mosaic as well as the structure
with the plinth defining the west side. The possible isolated masonry plinth opposite 30/40
Westgate Street may have been the base of a monument within this open space. This
evidence suggests a single major building, which appears to have fronted the forum and was
possibly a temple, lying between St John's Lane and the defences.

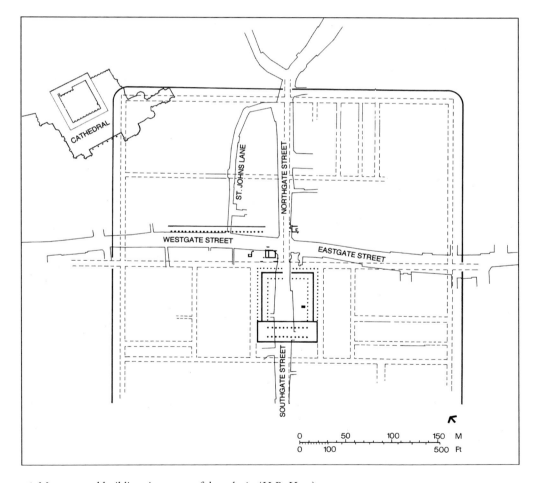

36 Monumental buildings in centre of the *colonia*. (*H.R. Hurst*)

There is very limited evidence of the domestic buildings of the *colonia*. A stone house structure developed over the barracks at Berkeley Street that has links to a military form. It was square with sides of *c.* 28m (92ft) and had a central paved courtyard which led to ranges on all four sides. What appeared to be the base of a stone cistern was found and this appeared to be connected with a monumental stone feature. Except for a black and white mosaic in the centre of the east range, all the floors were of mortar. The plan of this structure is very similar to the standard tribunes' house in fortresses. A tribune was an equestrian (a 'knight') who would have had a three-year posting with a legion to gain experience and undertook military duties. At the end of this period the officer would have certainly returned to Italy. However, the excavated building of the *colonia* period did not front on to the *Via Principalis*, as a tribune's house would have done, and so perhaps the plan of this was being copied later to ape the status of the rank by a person who had private means.

At Eastgate Street, on the site of the prestigious first cohort's barracks, and indeed almost in the same position and orientation, a substantial townhouse was erected of at least 70m by 22m (229ft by 72ft), with a paved courtyard towards the east end and ranges of rooms surrounding it and another central room or courtyard to the west end. There were at least 12 to 14 mosaic floors in the building complex and at least one room with a hypocaust heating system. There was at least one mosaic of the 'Corinium School' design, dating the building to fourth century.

Corinium Dobunnorum

As at Gloucester, there have been no large-scale excavations in Corinium since the 1980s. Since then research opportunities have been limited to watching briefs and keyhole excavation before the foundations of new build structures have been started. Much of the work of these archaeologists concerns designing ways of protecting, not excavating, the archaeological resource. At the Angel Cinema site, which itself had destroyed archaeological strata, only small test pits could be used to locate the position of the forum walls. That much is still remaining from the Roman town can be ascertained from observations during the construction of the Cotswold Mill complex in 1998–99, where Roman walls standing 16 courses high were visible, but not excavated.

The Development of the *Civitas* Capital

It is clear that at least in the first 50 years of the town's existence the street grid, the public buildings of the forum/basilica and perhaps the main temple were the main construction projects. Most typical private buildings in the AD 100–150 period were strip houses with street-front shops and workshops in the area around the forum/basilica. From about AD 175 the housing stock rose sharply and large, stone-built and elaborately decorated with mosaics significantly had probably come to dominate the landscape by the end of the third century. As early as AD 150, and possibly before, a circuit of the defensive earthworks was

37 Excavations at Admiral's Walk, Cirencester, in the 1970s. (*Cotswold Archaeology*)

38 An evaluation test pit for the Corinium Development. (*Cotswold Archaeology*)

constructed, enclosing an ambitious area of 96ha (273 acres) making it, next to London, the largest defined area in the province. By AD 250 the defences were being reconstructed. Each of these projects diverted finance from the construction of private housing.

The Street System

Since the site of the town was in a marshy area due to a more appropriate site being impeded because of the existence of Tar Barrows, important works had to be undertaken to divert the River Churn from the braided channels that ran through the future town site. Whether the date of these works was related to a new course outside the defences, the setting up of the defences or even an earlier bank that has been detected around the town that perhaps acted as some form of flood defence is not yet known. The large size of the area within the walls of Corinium was not built over completely and one wonders why it should be so substantial. There may be competition with Calleva as a factor, but it may have been the mimicking of the shape and area of the Bagendon-centred settlement further up the Churn Valley.

   The relationship of the setting out of the street grid to the development of the town can be seen in two ways: it may have been from the beginning of the settlement and have determined the positions of the public structures in the centre; or the public structures may have determined its alignment. In both cases, sturdy road foundations would have been needed to take the weight of construction traffic in an area with a high water table. The town was built on two main axes planned from the very beginning to create syn-chronised 'public space' from gate to gate. The *Cardo Maximus* was the main thoroughfare – the High Street – and followed the route of Ermine Street from the Silchester Gate to the north-east and the Gloucester Gate on the opposite side of the town. The chosen line gives an indication of the importance of these two settlements in the organisation of the province. It is also at angles to the prevailing wind from the south-west, thereby ensuring that most of the time the street was not a wind funnel. The *Decumanus Maximus* joined the Verulamium Gate to the Bath Gate. The Fosse Way and Akeman Street were on the same alignment and left through the Verulamium Gate. The pattern of the street grid on either side of these main routes is not regular, as small excavations during recent urban devel-opment have emphasised, and was probably laid out as the town expanded. The *insulae* south-east of the *Decumanus Maximus* would appear to have been laid out at the same time and date, whereas many of the blocks to the north-west of the street are offset. It is possible that extensions to the grid were added as the town expanded, yet all within the walled circuit, so perhaps much of the area near the defences was empty and used as gardens for growing food. Where the road has been located it would appear to have been resurfaced every 15 years or so, but there must have been much localised patching and repairs. The increasing level of the internal streets because of these refurbishments meant that the floors in shops and other structures also had to be heightened to avoid the spread of debris caused by traffic outside. Another effect of the building up of sediment on the road may well have been a shifting of its line laterally where there were no houses.

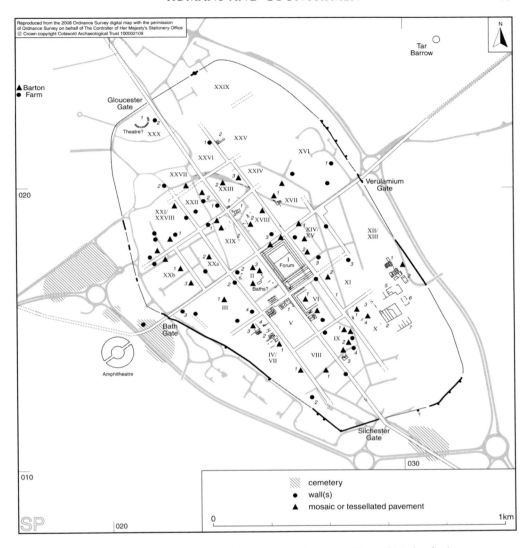

39 The Corinium street system, buildings and the location of mosaics. (*Cotswold Archaeology*)

The Early *Insulae* – the Public Buildings

Navigating around Cirencester is difficult, with little match between the Roman plan and that of the present day, and it is important that the size of the monumental buildings is appreciated. From the forum car park (not on the site of the forum!) turn into South Way and follow it until the junction with Lewis Lane, which follows the line of the *Decumanus Maximus* from the Bath Gate to the Verulamium Gate. Cross over this road and you will find yourself in Tower Street. The crossroads that you have just negotiated is at the north-western corner of the forum. Walk a little way down Tower Street and look back and you will see the line of the *Cardo Maximus* and Ermine Street. As you continue down Tower Street, the long axis of the forum in *Insula I* is on your right and *Insula II* on your left. Cross The Avenue,

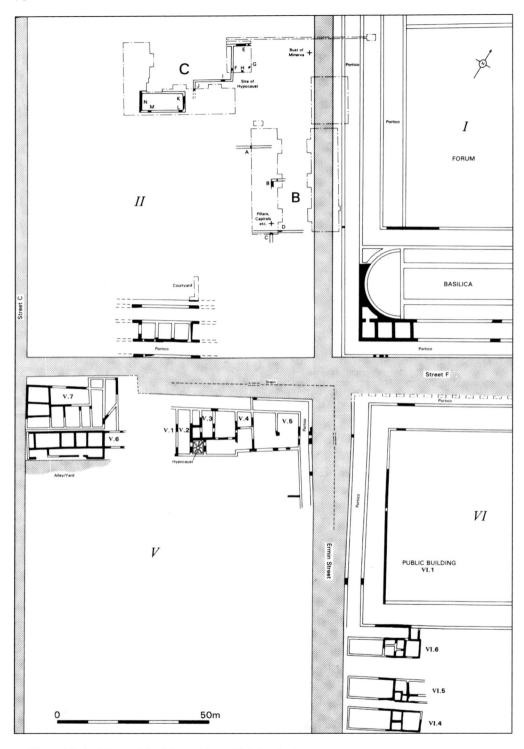

40 The public buildings of Corinium. (*Cotswold Archaeology*)

which marks the line between the forum and basilica, and you will find yourself in a cul de sac, which is also on the line of Ermine Street. Here the line of the apse of the basilica is laid out on the modern street surface in lighter stone. Stand in the round apse and face the road. You are looking at the site of the *macellum*, the meat market at the end of *Insula II*. Look back to Lewis Lane and you will see the whole length of the forum/basilica complex and, to the right, the forum in *Insula I*. Turn to the left towards the end of the road and this is on the line of Ermine Street. The lines alongside the apse represent the colonnade that fronted a road. Across that road was *Insula VI*, with a public building based around a courtyard of which we do not know the use, but a baths has been put forward. Across Ermine Street and to your left is *Insula V*, with its shops fronted by a colonnade. Evidence suggests that both sides of Ermine Street, at least along *Insulae I, II, V, VI*, were colonnaded, giving an impressive vista up the main street for the traveller from Silchester to Gloucester, and showing them how sophisticated the *civitas* capital was. To get an impression of the size of the forum, return to The Avenue and turn right, cross the road and turn left up Bingham Close and then left into Lewis Lane returning to the junction with Tower Lane and you will have walked around the four sides of this huge construction. It was likely to be at least as high as the parish church if Continental examples are a guide.

The Forum/Basilica Complex

The basilica and forum occupied the whole of *Insula* I and were 168m and 140m (551ft and 135ft) wide. The basilica was at the administrative heart of the town, and possibly of the Dobunni. It comprised an aisled hall 100m (337ft) long and 24.4m (79ft) wide with flanking aisles, each 5.5m (18ft) wide, and to the south-west the nave terminated in an apse. On the south-east side of the great cathedral-like hall were offices for official purposes. The importance of the structure is seen in the use of imported marble as a veneer to decorate the walls and Purbeck marble for mouldings. From what we know from inscriptions elsewhere in the province, there would seem to be an adoption of the Roman model of town councils, paired magistrates and perhaps two junior financial officers. The council, *ordo*, would have met in the basilica and were expected to procure funds for public building projects and temples, and organise festivities and games. Often there was a shrine in the basilica to the emperor and gods which might have represented the community. Since for the Roman state the prime function of local government was to provide the resources that it needed and towns were where they were extracted from, the basilica was a key location. Although the opulence of the structure was in some ways to celebrate the wealth of the elites whose money constructed it, in so many other ways it celebrated the power of the Roman state.

If the basilica was the administrative heart of the town, then the forum was the commercial and social focus of the settlement. It had a piazza estimated at 107m (351ft) long and 68m (223ft) wide north-west of the basilica and may have had two storeys. The length of the forum in comparison to its width is unusual and where this does occur a temple is often present. There is no evidence of this, so the temple must be sought elsewhere, but somewhere close by. As designed, the forum was probably floored with flagstones as these were used in its final phase. It was surrounded on at least two sides by ranges of rooms,

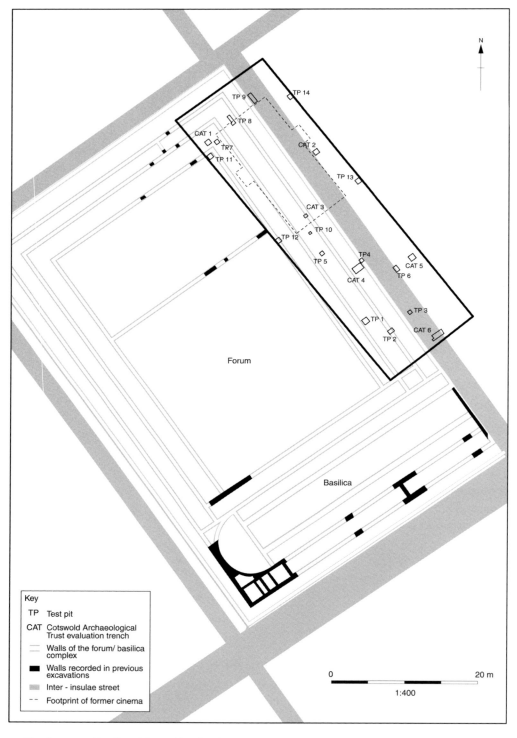

41 The forum and basilica. (*Cotswold Archaeology*)

with internal and external verandas, and compared to other towns it is most likely to have been all four. The main access was probably through the north-east and west sides. The external verandas would have been a welcome provider of shelter for traders or travellers along Ermine Street, as would those inside the forum, which probably held shops with wooden shutters.

The forum was not meant to be as richly decorated as the basilica and in many ways the contrast between the public and state can be seen in the way that the forum was accessible to all, but entrance to the basilica was likely to have been restricted. Any approach to the basilica usually meant climbing stairs from the forum, thereby giving it a position of dominance. This, in turn, made the forum almost a political 'courtyard' to where the main administrative business was done.

The Temple

The site of the main temple is not known for certain, but in many towns it lay close to the forum and at Corinium may have been in *Insula II*. The richness of architectural features, such as columns, is also an indictor of grand buildings outside of the central *insulae* and these may be parts of temples. Temples to Mercury and Minerva are also represented by sculptural finds. No doubt individual households would have had their own shrines, and there may have been others throughout the town on the streets; this might account for the high incidence of Celtic reliefs which would not appear in the classical temples that would be dedicated to Roman deities.

Macellum

A marketplace was situated in *Insula II*, next to the forum, and in its earlier stages was an open space. The forum piazza was used for selling many types of products but it is unlikely that meat, with the odorous and messy butchering process that accompanies it, would have been acceptable in such a prestigious place. The building had an external colonnade facing on to Ermine Street, but this was less to do with the building's function and more to do with the overall vista down the *Cardo Maximus*.

The Baths

It has been suggested that the baths may well have shared *Insula II* with the *macellum*. However, just as it was stated above, the choice of the alignment of the *Cardo Maximus* was used to stop the street channelling the prevailing south-west wind, so the site of a baths, burning huge amounts of wood or coal and producing much smoke is hardly likely to have been to the south-west of the forum, where the fumes would have been blown. At Leicester and Wroxeter the baths are next to the forum but on the up-wind side. At Silchester the baths are to the south-east of the forum an *insula* away and close to the town walls; at

St Albans again the baths are up-wind and near the walls. Evidence of wooden pipes and iron collars was found near the Verulamium Gate and these could have taken water to a baths in *Insula II*, and then disposed of it through a sewer under the *Cardo Maximus* and then through the Silchester Gate into the Churn. At the Firs in *Insula IX*, rich architectural fragments of columns and mosaic pavements have been found alongside Ermine Street. The site might be more appropriate in terms of the direction of the prevailing wind and there would have been no difference in the suggested course of water inflow or disposal except that it would have been used further along the system.

Cirencester may have had a population of between 5000 and 12,000. If each inhabitant went to the baths once a week, then at the minimum this would be 700 a day and possibly a least 100 an hour. Even if these figures are high estimates, considering that slaves probably were not allowed in the facility, a high-use area such as the baths would have meant that being outside of the central *insulae* would have made the management of large numbers of people easier. Also, the echoing noise in the large domed spaces would have been more tolerable to the population of the town as a whole.

The Theatre

The remains of a possible theatre is suggested by a concentric pair of curving walls which have been located in the north-west part of the town. This interpretation is partly on negative evidence as there is no other structure found in Romano-British towns that fits the shape of the building and it compares well in size to other examples. If it is a theatre then the concentric walls define a passage around the outside of the seating area, with radial walls that spring from the inner curve, marking walkways which led to the inner area.

The Defences

The defensive circuit appears to have survived almost intact until the early nineteenth century, having been gradually robbed of its stone since then. Indications of a late first- or early second-century construction of earth defences have been found during excavations of the town. At some date a decision was taken to construct stone gates, possibly before the rampart that forms the core of the defences in all periods was completed. The architecture of gateways probably reflected the impression that the city council wanted the traveller to experience as he or she entered the town. The Verulamium Gate was on the line of Akeman Street and the Fosse Way as they entered the town and they became the *Decumanus Maximus*. It appears the gate was 30m (98ft) wide and had two D-shaped drum towers. The pattern of ruts visible in the street surface suggests that there was a pair of carriageways on both sides of a central *spina*, four openings in all. The gate would appear to have had a monumental appearance as befitting a connection with Verulamium, which had a long history possibly related to Corinium's own, and the entrance's structure and decoration would have echoed this. The Bath Gate was at the other end of the street and became the Fosse Way outside of it. It also had drum towers, but was only 22m (72ft) wide, indicating fewer carriageways, but

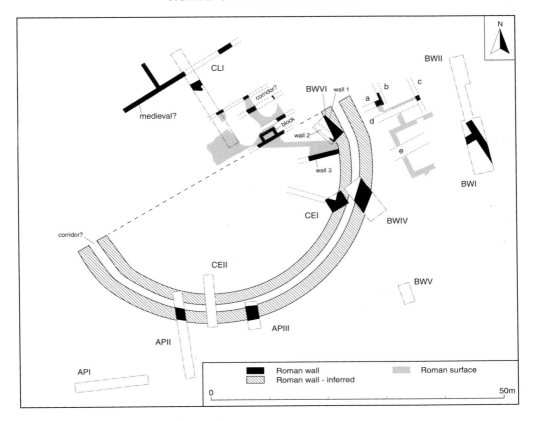

42 The possible theatre. (*Cotswold Archaeology*)

it too had finely carved decorations. It may be that the quality of these was more related to the presence of the amphitheatre than the route to what was the small town of Bath, even though it had a high religious significance. Unfortunately, neither the Gloucester Gate nor the Silchester Gate is well known, but, considering their position on Ermine Street and the *Cardo Maximus*, it would be expected that they were very grand. It is possible that timber gateways preceded the stone structures.

Stone interval towers also appear to have been constructed and embedded in the earthen rampart phase of the defences. The height of the rampart has been suggested as at least 3m (10ft) high. At some stage the face of the rampart was cut back and was heightened as a stone wall was added. This may have taken place after AD 220. At a later date the wall was thickened, but not necessarily around the whole circuit, and external towers (bastions) were added, possibly only at certain parts.

There are two reasons usually put forward for the construction of town walls, that of prestige projects and otherwise defence. The walls would have taken a considerable period to build, possibly in stretches as and when they could be afforded. A consideration of the weak defensive strategies, connected with such a large circuit, makes a prestige role most likely. The town walls would have been magnificent for the approaching traveller, especially with the forum towering over them. However, with the addition of external bastions, there is no reason why the function of the defences might not have changed, especially with the many periods of political instability in the province.

The Amphitheatre

The amphitheatre lay outside the Bath Gate to the south-west of the town and is the most substantial remnant of the Roman presence to be seen in Cirencester. A broadly second-century date seems likely for its construction and in its final form it comprised of an arena measuring *c.* 49m (160ft) on the long axis and 41m (135ft) along the short one, with surrounding earthen banks an average 30m wide. Investigations at the north-east entrance determined that in its original form the dense mass of the soil banks was retained by timber posts and dry-stone walls. Later repairs included the construction of the entrance in dressed stone where supports for vaulting indicates the supply of more seating over it for a growing population. At a later date the dressed stone was replaced by timber posts and two small chambers were built either side of the entrance, with double-doors communicating directly with the arena suggesting animal pens. Although amphitheatres are often thought of as being places of often cruel entertainment, they could also be used for the official gathering of the town's population for civil ceremonies or relating important news. That the amphitheatre is large and is closer in size to a fortress *ludus*, built to hold 5000 men, than a typical *civitas* capital in the south of England and gives an idea of the minimum size of the population of Corinium, may indicate a large population.

Shops

A restricted amount of evidence has been retrieved about the commercial aspect of the *civitas* capital, especially the products of any industry or the items that shops were selling. Shops have been discovered in the central *insulae* of the town, particularly along Ermine Street. The pattern of development from timber to stone structures emphasises the importance of shops in supplying goods in the early development of the town. Evidence demonstrates that continued prosperity resulted in the accommodation behind shops being provided with hypocausts and mosaics.

Houses

The evidence for the population that supported and used the town's public facilities is patchy, largely because it is not always possible to recognise domestic housing or the extent of the structures without area excavation. Usually it is the presence of mosaics and walls that indicate the probable presence of domestic structures. At the police station site in *Insula XVIII* the earliest structures were built from plaster-faced clay and a new house on the site in the early second century comprised a simple row of five or six or more rooms with a corridor on the west side. This pattern is typical of houses of the same date in other towns.

43 The Cirencester amphitheatre in 1913 with traces of the seating. (*Ed. J. Burrow*)

44 A reconstruction of Roman Cirencester. (*Cotswold Archaeology*)

Other houses in the town have been identified as courtyard layouts, which are often seen as a later development from the simple row house. Finds of different styles of house indicates the extent and a date of the growth of the town. An opulent house built no later than the third century, with a courtyard and columns supporting verandas, indicates a Mediterranean plan and must have been owned by someone of some wealth and standing.

The most complete housing complex in Cirencester was excavated in 1971–73 in Beeches Road. The plan of either one complex structure or two more simple houses with associated outbuildings was recovered. One house began life as a simple rectangular edifice, although additions were made to all four sides and included a bath suite. A rectangular outbuilding, a possible barn, lay immediately north-west of the house. South-east of this building was the site of another house of winged corridor plan, which also had a complicated structure, and three associated outbuildings. It seems from the finds that both these structures were built on virgin sites in the middle of the fourth century and from the agricultural nature of the finds it has been suggested that these were working farm units within the walls. The plans of the structures do suggest working villas. What is equally important is that the date of these buildings near the town walls indicates the margins of the town were only built up in a late period of the town's development. The distance between them and other indications of further structures invites the conclusion that this area of the town was sparsely populated.

Contrast between Cirencester and Gloucester

Henry Hurst has argued that the size of the settlements was not vastly different, in that only 75 per cent, about 70ha (179 acres), of the area within the walls of Corinium was developed, as compared with 50–70ha (123–179 acres) at Glevum, which comprised not only of the buildings within the walls but also the extensively urbanised areas to the north and north-east of the town, a possible public market and areas for industry, as well as a river crossing and potential river port. This was partly because of the restrictions placed on the use of space by Glevum retaining the shape of a fortress and the *colonia* growing out of it, whereas Corinium was conceived on a virtually green-field site and was laid out with a new grid formation with the 'fort' outline ignored, if it was still visible. Because of its new beginnings, Corinium was more easily laid as a town with vistas of its grand buildings, a forum and basilica that (deliberately?) dwarfed Glevum's, an amphitheatre and also a possible theatre. The *colonia's* poorly developed city plan has often been seen as a less energetic form of urban creation, a lack of interest being shown by retired legionaries who were more interested in farming the countryside. However, there were grand buildings, possibly a huge temple or other grand courtyard building, and it would be unusual for a *colonia* not to have an amphitheatre. Legally, the judicial power of the magistrates of the *colonia* would have been the greater, and the *civitas* capital would have had less extensive regional responsibilities, though it is likely that it would have supervised some of the small towns and *pagi*, the rural districts in its hinterland. It is likely the lands within the *teritorrium*, or even the wider hinterland of the *colonia*, would have been administered from Glevum. Hurst argues that the difference between the two settlements can be explained by accepting that the two communities were expressing their identities and aspirations reflected in different ways and it is worth exploring this idea further.

The daily life in the *colonia* would have been a continuation of a legionary's experiences and might be seen as being a very conservative and predictable form of *romanitas*. In the early days of the town, retired members of a legion were Roman citizens and shared their identities with others who had common standards of pay, service and conditions. They were used to military discipline and being a part of a hierarchy of command and responsibility. The veterans were probably literate or partly so, spoke Latin, which was the polyglot means of communication within the army, even if it was a colloquial 'camp' version, and had rights and privileges that put them above the ordinary provincial. As part of a settlement of retired soldiers there would have been a comradeship through mutually shared experiences and support (exactly the same aim as the present-day British Legion) and each man would have still felt intense loyalty to his legion. Each rank would have been fixed on retirement, and he would no doubt have pride in the battle awards earned while in action, often in the form of medals, collars or armlets. The veterans would have celebrated the birthday of their legion and, as soldiers, would still have maintained a devout belief in the deified imperial cult. On arrival before or after its rebuilding as a *colonia*, a veteran would have known exactly how to move around the town, as the street system and buildings used the same military space as fortresses throughout the empire. However, the idea of a *colonia* was that the retired soldier was given land, or money which could purchase it, and would mean that the centre of economic activity was as much in the *territorium* and beyond as within the town. It is from the surroundings of Glevum that its success should be judged not just from the structures inside it.

John Creighton has attempted to compare life in Pompeii with what might have happened in British towns such as Corinium. The privileged elite might have wanted to emulate the client system which was one of the very foundations of Roman society. Clients acted as a kind of 'clan' to the patron, who created a kind of welfare network in a state which largely hadn't the means to support the poor and deprived. Patrons were seen as protectors of their group and some noble families could indeed count on the support of very many people, in the cities as well as in the countryside and its small towns. The client system created stability, and the unwavering loyalty of clients could keep families in power for centuries. Status was enforced and reinforced by lifestyles lived day to day in the *domus*, the townhouse, in the theatre, in the forum and elsewhere. At sunrise (*salutatio*) the clients of the great and the good would arrive at their patron's *domus* to pay their respects standing in line, with their positions marking social status and length of the queue measuring the status of the benefactor. Higher-status houses were not tucked away in separate residential quarters but surrounded by smaller houses and shops and, as the procession of the patron who had been holding court that morning wound its way to the forum, it would pass a whole variety of town life. As the parade passed in front of other residents, comparisons could be made of the relative importance of other individuals by the length of the pageant. The forum would have seen an unfolding pattern of power relationships at play in meetings where public business was done between groups of clients and their various patrons. After several hours in the forum in the early afternoon, the patron might pass on to the baths, and clients would follow him. Because of the crucial nature of this social reinforcing of rank through movement through the city, the patron's place of residence needed to be a short distance from the forum, baths and temple to create the possibility of people going about their daily lives seeing the passage of the select few through the city. Had all the public buildings been located together and all the best residences been built close to the centre of the town, then there would have been no opportunity for processions, so residences were dispersed in choice positions throughout the town, and public monuments were often similarly set out. At the theatre or amphitheatre, social status was revealed on the banked seats by the segregation of people according to rank. These patterns of behaviour might not have been very different from those that were practised in the late Iron Age social system, with elites developing 'clans' through trade, social and then political power, and then maintaining these relationships by ensuring that people remained prosperous.

It is too easy to suggest that Corinium was a 'peace and plenty town', with entrepreneurial progress resulting in a higher incidence of fine, well-executed mosaics and sculpture, and totally the opposite to the 'practical', ultra-conservative and introverted nature of Glevum. This view of the *colonia* as a place where retired soldiers saw out their days and the *civitas* capital being vibrant as local leaders sought to display their wealth, may not reflect the realities. Glevum's population had undergone huge changes in their ways of life from soldiers to civilians and this resulted in an explosion of economic activity, producing a high level of social and economic integration that would have a community based on mutual agreement and respect. The possibility of a temple building of considerable size might indicate an important provincial status. The discovery of a monumental arcaded structure outside the north gate may indicate that other substantial structures await discovery. Corinium demonstrated the basic continuity of the hierarchy of the ruling elite which was reinforced by consuming Roman-style goods and, it could be argued, had the more conservative outlook.

SEVEN

CONTRASTING LANDSCAPES, CONTRASTING ARCHAEOLOGIES

Population

The greater part of the population of the *civitas* of the Dobunni was rural, and of those who lived in the countryside the vast majority did not dwell in either the small towns or villas. It is difficult to know the total rural population and how it grew or shrank during the Roman period. Mattingly has suggested that there may have been 1.6 million country dwellers in Britannia (at least 80 per cent of the total inhabitants) with those in urban settings being not more than 200,000 and a similar proportion in the military. He has also suggested the existence of a possible 2000 villas, but this number would comprise only about 2 per cent of the known late Iron Age and Roman rural sites. This suggests that the most typical rural site was not the villa, but small farms and villages. At Frocester, using a combination of field-walking, the Domesday survey of 1086 and tithe records, as well as Victorian agricultural surveys, Eddie Price suggested a population of 130 to 140 adults and working children – 40 to 50 families – in the villa and the two settlements around it. This gives some indication of the density of population in the countryside. To paraphrase Mattingly, if 'Roman Gloucestershire' was the region of the villa, 'Gloucestershire in the Roman Empire' was characterised overall by the roundhouse. These non-villa dwellers are largely invisible in the landscape, due to the difficulty of finding evidence for wooden and thatched structures, whereas villas with structural material such as mosaic tesserae, heavy clay roof tiles and stone walling are easier to locate through fieldwalking.

Landowning

All the land within the Dobunnic *civitas* would have been surveyed by the Roman administration, and, as Reece suggests, not in terms of spatial dimensions, but in terms of the type of land and its productive qualities – an exercise similar to that of the Domesday survey in 1086. Even if it is taken for granted that as a possible 'client kingdom' at least part of the elite of the Gloucestershire region would have been allowed to retain their own lands, some would have been taken for the Glevum fortress' *territorium* and probably more added with the development of the *colonia*, so that the veterans might have their own agricultural holdings. Some of the land would have been retained by the state and leased out to provide revenue for local administration and Corinium was probably given lands to provide an income to support the local administration – parts of the Thames Valley, for example, which show such a move to intensive farming at about the same time that the *civitas* capital was being developed. No doubt, as in other parts of the empire, Rome would have made personal gifts of land to form private estates, in some cases to individuals in other parts of the empire. We might have to consider ownership of land in the lowlands of Roman Britain as being like a mosaic of different areas of the landscape owned by very different interests, none of which can be identified archaeologically.

The relationship between the *territorium* of the fortress and the land owned by the retired legionaries of the *colonia* is impossible to gauge. For legionaries, the area needed for cattle (for food, tents and armour), sheep (food and clothes) and horses, along with further areas for pig-farming, vegetable and fruit cultivation, would require a maximum territory of 90 sq. kilometres (35 sq. miles). In other words, a north–south stretch of about 10km (6 miles) on the east side of the Severn Valley, if not less, and 8km (5 miles) wide near Gloucester. The army is also likely to have land in the Forest of Dean for ironworking and in the Cotswolds for stone-quarrying. What happened to the *territorium* is difficult to know as retired soldiers in the second century onwards were being given grants of land or a large sum of money, and whether it was sold off or the ex-soldiers settled in a wider area, there must have been a significant impact on the ownership and economy, especially agriculture, of the region.

The Thames Valley

In the Thames Valley, the river terraces have been ploughed, and have truncated archaeological features, but what has survived is accessible from the air in the right conditions. On the terraces the soil marks and crop marks of buried ditches and other features cut into the subsoil can be identified through the tall growth and slower ripening of a crop over the moist, deep and fertile soil of buried features such as pits and ditches. This contrasts with the lower growth and faster ripening of the crop where it is growing on the thin soil over dry gravel. Conversely, the alluvium on the valley floor has obscured sites, but in turn they have been protected from damage by agricultural processes and thus are more fruitful when excavated.

Both the Upper and Middle Thames are flanked by extensive terraces in places more than 3km wide, which are the result of hard rock from the Cotswolds being deposited as gravel on to the Oxford clay of the river valley. A period of high discharge of water in the far distant past caused the river to form a braided system of many minor wandering channels. Any late Iron Age settlement sites would have been situated on islands of gravel, and have often moved as the channels of the river migrated. At Thornhill Farm, Lechlade, situated on the floodplain, it was established that in later prehistory the landscape comprised of 'fossilised' water courses and marshy areas which dissected the first terrace, but islands and tongues of gravel provided well-drained sites that were dry enough for settlement. The local environment would have been one of heavily grazed grassland with ill-drained, tussocky, marshy hollows covering several square kilometres of the valley bottom. During the late Iron Age and early Roman period there was a substantial increase in the alluvium from seasonal flooding on the Thames floodplain which could have been the result of clearance and increased cultivation on the Cotswolds, where the soils are relatively thin but dry and light.

45 Excavating at Claydon Pike showing the round temple on the gravel island, which is now being mined. (*Oxford Archaeology*)

Wider cultivation in the hills on either side of the Upper Thames Valley would have two consequences: firstly, pressure would have been put on sheep pasture which was traditionally important in the uplands; and secondly, the need for more traction animals to pull ploughs. These factors could have changed the nature of the settlement in the lowlands of the valley.

Very few late Iron Age sites are known on the floodplain or lower gravel terraces of the Upper Thames Valley, largely due to the alluvium making aerial photography unproductive. Most of the known sites show some kind of continuity from the later Iron Age into the early Roman period, some retaining the dispersed pattern of settlement, with others indicating considerable change in the nature and form of the occupation. These widespread changes are seen in sites being newly established, abandoned or shifting in location, such as that at Roughground Farm. At Claydon Pike, Fairford, the settlement disruption is seen during the mid to late Iron Age/Roman transition (*c.* first century BC/AD), when the settlement shifted to another gravel island to the south and changed from an unfocused mixed farmstead into a specialist pastoral community with an associated series of stock enclosures and droveways used for the management of livestock. Although in reality the settlement was turned into a 'cattle ranch', there was also an emphasis on horses, sheep not being significant in the area. It is difficult to explain these changes in terms of one enveloping factor as they probably took place over many generations, but they may have been a consequence of a growing population in and around the valley due to economic, political and social developments in the Bagendon area to the north. While such settlement disruption is clear at Claydon Pike, at other sites, such as Horcott, Cotswold Community, Ashton Keynes and Thornhill Farm, there is more evidence of continuity, although the intensity, density and functions of the settlement do appear to change over the course of the Iron Age over many generations.

What is clear is that the occupation of the Thames Valley in the late Iron Age was quite dense with an organised agricultural landscape, the higher terraces being used for arable and the floodplain and part of the first terrace, being primarily open and unbroken grassland, used for pasture. Neither Roughground Farm nor Claydon Pike could have been self-sufficient, and arable activity most likely took place on the higher terraces of the river, such as those to the east where arable agriculture is a feature of sites in West Oxfordshire. Unfortunately, the evidence for individual domestic structures is lacking, possibly because houses were built using 'mass-wall' construction techniques that do not require foundation trenches and are therefore difficult to locate archaeologically, and which seem to be traditional feature of the Gloucestershire region.

There does not appear to be any change in the agricultural landscape at the time of the Roman Conquest as new political structures are unlikely to have affected local affairs and the late Iron Age settlement patterns survived. However, there is evidence for another major period of settlement disruption in the late first and early second centuries, which took place over a very short period of time. At Claydon Pike and Somerford Keynes the low-lying first terrace settlements were replaced by large barns and rectangular field systems, joined by trackways on the gravels. These changes are considered to have been initiated as officially fostered centres, perhaps under the control of Corinium, or as an imperial estate. They certainly have the flavour of reorganisation of territory and ownership, and may be reflected in the changes of the second century on the Cotswolds with the foundation of simple villas. Certainly the introduction of a regular supply of money and the development of a market economy would also have been significant factors in development, although the growth of these specialisations might also have been a response to the introduction of a tax regime. Overall the agricultural regime of the late Iron Age continued into the Roman period, with the floodplain being used for the raising of domestic stock, although there was the introduction of hay meadows and the higher terraces having settlements operating mixed farming economies. There is increasing evidence for hedged boundaries defining paddocks and areas of cultivated land for local use. In the middle of the second century Roughground Farm had been transformed from a farmstead into a farming settlement with two masonry structures, one an aisled building for storage and the other a 'proto-villa'. The farm may well have had lands on the first and second terraces together with the floodplains of the Leech and Thames. Regularly organised paddocks are in evidence around buildings as are trackways connecting various field systems. The timber-aisled building, possibly a cattle shed and hay barn, was located at the junction of these droveways A series of enclosures in front of the timber structure opened on to a cleared space, which has been interpreted as a 'green', used for the corralling of animals. A circular raised mound in the centre of the green may have been an elevated platform from which to see stock collection or may have even performed a role in a market.

Some longer tracks/roads also ran long distances along the valley bottom and may have connected estate centres represented by some of villas north of the Thames on the clays at the base of the Cotswold dip-slope and to the south at the foot of the Wiltshire Downs. Overall, it was a well-organised landscape, with some areas of woodland with numerous farmsteads and a small number of villas which operated a variety of agricultural economies and were connected with a comprehensive system of minor roads and local trackways. The lack of small towns, even on the Cotswold dip-slope, supports the notion that local marketing and exchange mechanisms were unnecessary as the produce of the land was already committed to some authority either locally, such as Corinium, or provincially. The evidence of writing and some military equipment at Claydon Pike may indicate some sort of official presence.

The Cotswolds

The identification of Roman sites in the Cotswold area is beset by a number of other problems. The geology of largely oolitic limestone and the presence of the rock just below the ground makes the recognition of stone-built structures very difficult. Flattened earthwork features seen in ploughed land may easily be prehistoric or medieval or also be geological in origin, such as rectilinear cracks in the limestone or the presence of ice wedges or tree pits. The dense and deep ploughing of the land in the last 50 years has destroyed many earthworks of the field systems, trackways and insubstantial non-villa sites, whilst it has made the high-status villa structures more visible. The better preserved landscapes are sited in uncultivated parkland such as that at Barrington and Barnsley. Many of the Cotswold sites were excavated during the Victorian period and the first half of the twentieth century, and there has been a lack of opportunities for contract archaeology in such a rural area. We probably know more about the non-villa settlement and environment in the Thames and Severn valleys than the Roman Cotswolds away from its villas.

Sites of agricultural settlements of the late Iron Age are known mainly from crop marks and show simple forms of settlement rather than the complex ones in the Upper Thames Valley. These settlements were liberally scattered over the landscape, but no site has been excavated in its entirety and comparatively little is known of their character. Truncation by deep-plough erosion is a major problem in interpretations so little evidence of domestic structures has been found. What are known as 'Celtic Fields' (which are usually categorised as late Iron Age) may be Roman or even medieval in origin. Economies of these sites are not well understood, although the evidence so far indicates that a mixed arable/pasture farming regime was generally practised. Cereal production has been detected by the use of pits and stone querns, millstones for hand-grinding corn and the evidence for animal husbandry points to sheep and cattle.

While the main centres of population are known around the three *oppida*, it is the space in between them that is less accessible in terms of aerial photography. Recent research has identified a few later Iron Age and, less frequently, late Iron Age sites, but no farmstead-type settlement has yet produced conclusive evidence for an uninterrupted sequence of later Iron Age, late Iron Age and early Roman occupation. This pattern seems to conform to Moore's proposals that the areas of Bagendon and Salmonsbury were largely under-populated in the late Iron Age. There is evidence of population movements or abandonment of sites due to the reorganisation of land at the beginning of the first century AD, which echo the situation in the Upper Thames Valley.

46 The late second-century roundhouse (structure 1463) under excavation at Birdlip Quarry. (*Oxford Archaeology*)

At Birdlip occupation ceased during the later Iron Age and resumed in mid-first century BC and possibly spanned the late Iron age/Roman transition. The evidence for a mid-first century AD occupation reflects a small rural farmstead even though the pottery assemblage was paralleled at Bagendon, 1km (0.6 miles) away. A gold 'Dobunnic' coin of late first century BC was also found, indicating high status, perhaps related to the prestigious Birdlip Iron Age cemetery close by, which was in use in AD 20–40, though there is no certainty that the agricultural settlement was occupied at that time. Interestingly, in later Iron Age the fills of grain storage pits were full of evidence for the processing of crops rather than of the products themselves, which might indicate exchange of some sort in an area that has already been seen as being on a possible trade route.

During the construction of the A419 a settlement originating in the later second century was discovered at Birdlip Quarry, adjacent to Ermine Street. While it might have had some sort of role in servicing traffic along the main road, the settlement was predominantly of roundhouses of the late Iron Age tradition, indicating that the effect of Ermine Street was minimal in influencing the identities of groups of people of low status, even though Roman-style pottery was found there.

The Guiting Power area of the Cotswolds has probably been explored more fully than elsewhere, although the limited number of sites makes comparison across the late Iron Age Cotswold settlements difficult. At Huntsman's Quarry in Naunton there was another rectilinear, ditched settlement enclosure of middle Iron Age, contracted of during the later Iron Age/early Roman period.

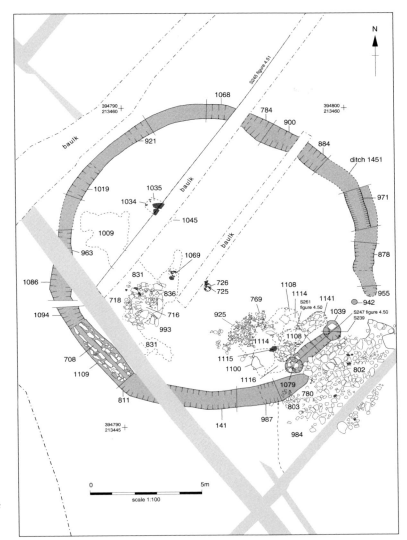

47 Plan of the roundhouse structure 1463. (*Oxford Archaeology*)

In the present administrative area of Stroud, 19 parishes have evidence of villas/possible villas, whereas 70 parishes to the north of Ermine Street have traces of these high-status structures. The settlement pattern around Stroud may well have been influenced by the presence of what might be a major estate/administrative centre at Kingscote, which has only one villa within a 6km (3.7-mile) radius of the settlement. The importance of this possible imperial estate may also be the explanation for a lack of small towns in the area. As would be expected, there appears to be a high density of villa structures around Cirencester, largely to the north and east. The most opulent houses tend to be related to the entrenched valleys whose watercourses drain the hills into the Thames, with far less evidence for wealthy structures on the high plateau or valleys to the west. The further away from Cirencester, the closer to fast roads these villas tend to be, for example at Turkdean near Fosse Way. Within the north Cotswold area are a group of small towns: Bourton-on-the-Water, Wycombe,

Dorn and possibly Coln St Aldwyns. They will be discussed in a section below, but recent surveying suggests more villa structures than was previously thought are within a 19km (12-mile) radius of each of these settlements.

Since many of the 'monumental' Cotswold sites were excavated before there was interest in the environment around them, there is only a small sample of plant pollen, seeds and animal bones to support the finding of agricultural equipment in the large and small settlements, but it does appear that there was a mixed economy, with a growing acreage given over to the cultivation of crops. This development of ploughing on thin soils in what might have been a traditional sheep-raising area could be responsible for the increase in alluvium in the Thames Valley during the late Iron Age and early Roman period discussed above.

Below the Cotswold escarpment two highly palatial villas at Woodchester, near Stroud, and at Spoonley Wood, above Winchcombe, are in rather incongruous situations. Woodchester seems to be more closely related to Glevum rather than the *civitas* capital at Corinium. Similarly, although Spoonley Wood is sited in a combe just below the Salt/White Way and has at least one, if not two, satellite villas with mosaic pavements, it does face the Severn Valley, and again it may be more related to the *colonia*.

Middle Severn Valley

Both the surface and underlying geologies of the Middle Severn Valley largely determines the settlement archaeology in north-west Gloucestershire and south Worcestershire. Fan gravels and sands were created from the deposition of large amounts of fractured Jurassic limestone from the Cotswolds during the last glaciations. They probably formed a continuous sheet across the Severn Valley, but have been dissected and diminished by the Severn's braided watercourses. Settlement not only appears to have favoured the fan gravel islands, but it is on their better drained soils that the more high-status sites existed. It is round the Carrant Brook and Bredon in Worcestershire areas that sites are more easily detected through aerial photography and the organisation of the landscape is seen. The Lias clays, which form extensive areas of the valley floor, produce heavy clay soils and are prone to wetness and flooding, especially when topped with the alluvium of the floodplain. Archaeological sites are difficult to find on these soils because of the lack of the formation of crop marks and even intensive fieldwalking does not pick up substantial settlements. Therefore, the ones that are known of are the results of contract archaeology, where the soil has been stripped for purposes such as road building or the burial of pipeline. The Wormington to Tirley pipeline demonstrated the 'double-edged sword' of contract archaeology. A thin, snaking slice of only between 4m and 6m (13–19.5ft) was available for excavation, though when sites were discovered the area available was extended. However, this arbitrary line through a highly populated landscape did give insights into the density of settlements and different methods of locating sites were trialled.

That some of the fan gravel spreads in the Severn Valley were intensively used for settlement is seen at sites such as those at Bishop's Cleeve, which have been extensively explored due to the rapid development of the town. There is considerable evidence of a late Iron Age agricultural settlement focused on the production of food, as implied by storage pits

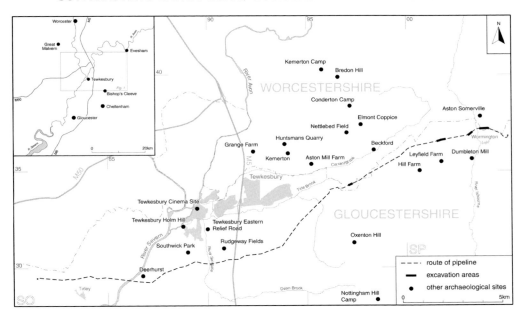

48 The route of the Wormington to Tirley pipeline. (*Cotswold Archaeology*)

and querns, which suggest the growing and processing of grain and other cereals. Evidence for small-scale craft industries, such bone-working and iron-smithing also has been found. Boundary ditches interpreted as being used for livestock management, dominated by cattle, sheep and goats, suggests overall a mixed economy. The other important insight from the Bishop's Cleeve sites was the long-distance trade patterns, with salt being brought in ceramic containers known as 'briquetage' from Droitwich, pottery from the Malverns and quern stones from May Hill. The centre of the late Iron settlement has not yet been identified.

Continuity of settlement into the Roman period is indicated by Iron Age ditches being recut, but the evidence also demonstrates that the community moved westward in the late first century, which is perhaps more evidence of settlement dislocation. Materials found on some of the sites from this period indicate that a villa or small agricultural settlement lies close by, but the Roman masonry structures remain elusive. A possible hypocaust, the presence of *opus signinum* floor tile, tesserae, and wall plaster indicate a well-appointed structure, possibly a villa dated to the third and fourth centuries. The botanical evidence suggests that in the Roman period oats, wheat and barley were grown. Evidence from boundary ditches also indicates that livestock management was dominated by cattle and sheep, the carcasses being butchered and processed for consumption and the use of some by-products. An extensive system of agricultural enclosures indicates discrete zones for horticulture, small-scale industrial activity to meet the needs of the settlement and leather tanning or flax retting. It has been estimated that this settlement may have covered about 3.8ha (9.5 acres) and survived in some form until the fourth century.

These archaeological investigations suggest a well-populated landscape of small, dispersed agricultural settlements on the edge of the Cotswold scarp and valley floor. The spring lines under the Cotswold Edge in the Cheltenham and Bishop's Cleeve areas might be the

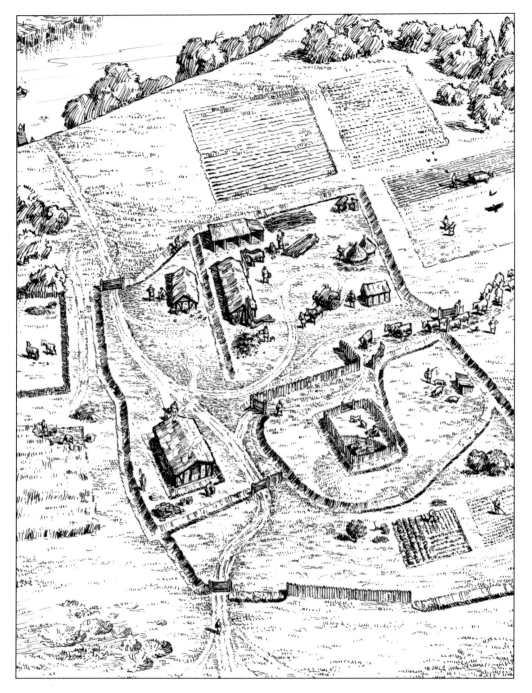

49 A reconstruction of the farmstead at Saxons Lode Farm, Ryall Worcestershire. (*Cotswold Archaeology*)

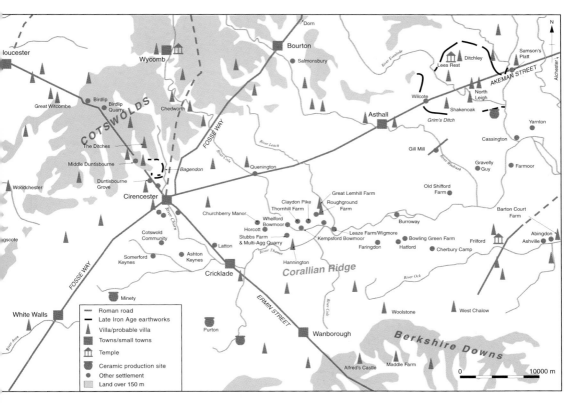

1 Map of late Iron Age and Roman settlements on the Cotswolds and the Upper Thames Valley. (*Oxford Archaeology*)

2 Gold stater of Bodvoc from Badgendon. (*Corinium Museum*)

3 The tombstone of Rufus Sita found at Wotton in Gloucester in 1824 alongside Ermine Street may be associated with the Kingsholm fortress. (*Gloucester City Museum*)

RVFVS·SITA·EQVES·CHO/VI
TRACVM·ANN·XL·STIP·XXII
HEREDES·EXS·TEST·F·CVR

4 The surface of Ermine Street at Itlay Underpass. (*Oxford Archaeology*)

5 Geophysical survey at Tar Barrows with Cirencester parish church in the distance. (*Peter Guest*)

6 The excavation of Ditches Villa, 1984–5.
(*T. Moore, S. James, S. Trow*)

7 Tombstone of Lucius Octavius Martialis, soldier of the
XXth Legion. (*Oxford Archaeology*)

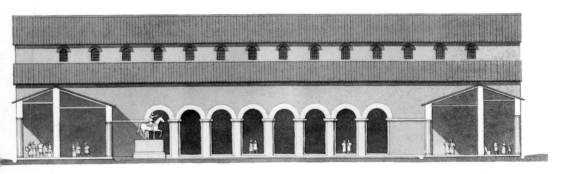

8 Reconstruction of the *colonia* basilica at Glevum. (*Philip Moss*)

9 The forum and basilica at Corinium. (*Corinium Museum*)

10 The Beeches Road townhouses, Corinium. (*Corinium Museum*)

11 The Verulamium Gate at Corinium. (*Corinium Museum*)

12 The Roman defences at Corinium Gate, Cirencester. (*Tom Vivian*)

13 The amphitheatre at Cirencester. (*Tom Vivian*)

14 The Claydon Pike Villa. (*Oxford Archaeology*)

15 LiDAR image of the relationship between Ermine Street and Great Witcombe Roman Villa. (*Tim Grubb, Gloucestershire County Council*)

16 Witcombe Villa and Cotswold escarpment. (*Cotswold Archaeology*)

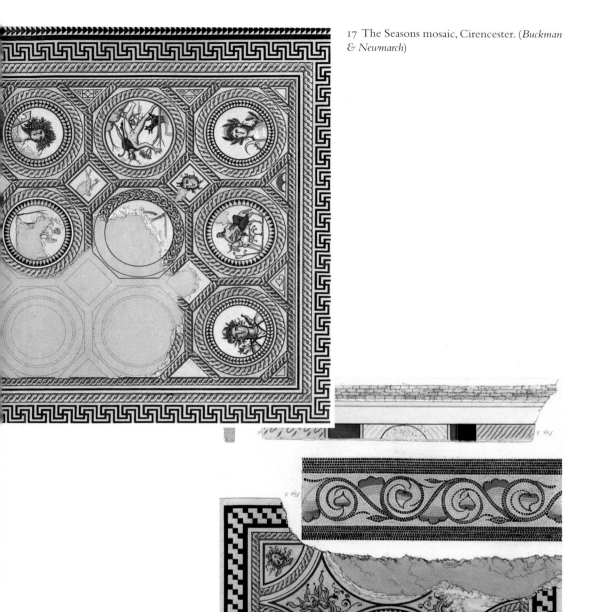

The Hunting Dogs mosaic, Cirencester. (*...ckman & Newmarch*)

19 The Barton Orpheus mosaic, Cirencester. (*Buckman & Newmarch*)

20 Relief of Mercury from Cirencester. (*Corinium Museum*)

21 A water nymph from Cirencester. (*Corinium Museum*)

22 The Lydney fishes mosaic. (*William Hiley Bathurst*)

23 The continuity of sacred space: the Neolithic long barrow of Hetty Pegler's Tump, a possible Bronze Age round barrow, the Roman temple to Mercury and the Uleybury Iron Age hillfort. (*Steve Smith, Stroud District Museum*)

24 Claydon Pike Temple reconstruction. (*Oxford Archaeology*)

25 The tombstone of Martialis, the slave of Corius, Gloucester. (*Oxford Archaeology*)

26 The tombstone of Valerius Sextus Genialis, Cirencester. (*Corinium Museum*)

27 The tombstone of Dannicus, Cirencester. (*Corinium Museum*)

28 An inscription from the base of the Jupiter column restored the governor of Britannia Prim (*Corinium Museum*)

sites of further Roman settlements, especially under present-day communities, such as is hinted at in Southam and at Vineyard Farm, Charlton Kings. There is certainly evidence of field enclosure of the late first to fourth centuries at the West Drive and the Waitrose sites in Cheltenham, both also on sand and above the floodplain of the Severn. This pattern of settlement on the fan gravels can also be seen at villa sites such as those at Whitminster or Eastington, further down the valley, as well as Frocester.

The Frocester Villa settlement was a farmstead until AD 275 and with roundhouses of some form until AD 100. In the Roman period a chain of similar sites were situated astride the 100m contour of the Cotswold escarpment. Clay soils which underlay a large area of the villa's lands had to be drained or they would have turned into the sort of rush waste found in the Thames Valley. There was some evidence for strips or narrow closes on the steeper ground, but these have been largely ploughed out or are under the medieval ridge and furrow systems. As now, the steep Cotswold scarp was probably woodland used for farming purposes and this may well have been the case above Bishop's Cleeve until the onset of quarrying, which made the escarpment a litter of stone spoil.

On the Lias clays, south-east of Tewkesbury on the other side of the valley, two humble farmsteads have been excavated that were sited on poorly drained clay. One was subject to flooding in winter and the other, sited just above the floodplain, would have been highly productive and ecologically diverse as long as the alluvial clays were well drained. The floodplain would have provided excellent summer salt marsh grazing and evidence from bone suggests that sheep or goats and cattle were in plentiful supply. The discovery of grain pits might also indicate a mixed economy. The most revealing sites, largely because extensive geophysical survey could be carried out before the excavations, were at Rudgeway Lane, Walton Cardiff, near Tewkesbury, in 2004–05. No late Iron Age features were found, but a first-century AD unenclosed settlement comprising a number of roundhouses surrounded by individual drainage ditches was revealed. In the second century AD these were replaced by a rectilinear ditched enclosure c. 105m (334ft) long and 50m (164ft) wide, with a track-way on its southern side. The enclosure was sub-divided internally to create areas which may have been used for breeding and folding of stock, the storage and processing of crops, was demonstrated by the presence of a drying oven. The layout of the rectangular settlement with its roundhouse appears typical for these low-lying valley floodplains and the most complete plan was recovered from Ripple in south Worcestershire, which although on gravel has many similarities to the structures on the clay.

The excavations have discovered humble farmsteads with a similar development sequence. Corral ditches and trackways have survived to demonstrate the possibilities of an intricate and extensive, reasonably developed agricultural landscape similar to that of the Upper Thames. The domestic structures themselves have been largely undetectable, probably because of the lack of postholes used in their construction which is more likely to have been mass-built with cob, wattle and daub walls and thatched roofs. At many of the sites structural evidence, such as tile and brick, has indicated the proximity of a larger, possibly villa building in the immediate proximity, which might indicate that the farmsteads were family-owned or tenanted. This was the case at Wormington Farm, where aerial photographic evidence indicated the presence of a courtyard-type villa of the third and fourth centuries close to a modest farm site. There seems to have been a major episode of settlement discontinuity

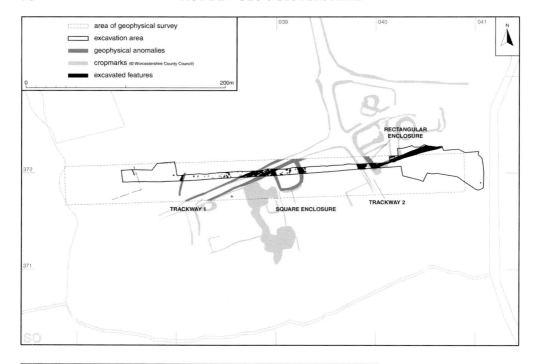

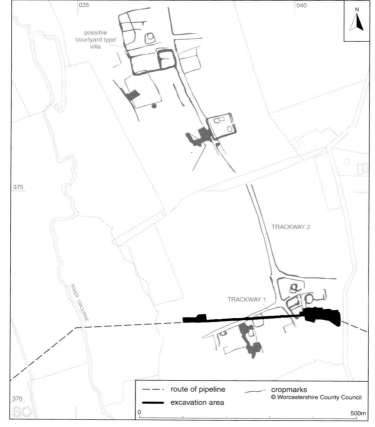

50 Wormington Farm, Aston Somerville, Worcestershire: geophysical, crop mark and excavation plot. (*Cotswold Archaeology*)

51 Wormington Farm, cropmark plot indicating the presence of a possible villa. (*Cotswold Archaeology*)

around the end of the first century or the start of the second century, with earlier enclosures being abandoned and new ones established at Elm Farm and Bank Farm, while at College Farm and Wormington Farm a greatly increased level of activity was apparent. This pattern was also observed at Rudgeway Lane, Walton Cardiff, and Site 1 on the Eastern Relief Road and also at Brockworth, east of Gloucester.

A possible small town in the Oldbury area of Tewkesbury was situated on the higher ground close to these valley settlements and was likely to be a roadside settlement on the route from Gloucester to another small town at Worcester. Possible villas of some pretention have also be detected on the low gravel-topped hills at Tewkesbury Park and Southwick Park, where there have been finds of ceramic roofing materials, tesserae and a wide range of imported samian and amphorae. There are also indications of a villa at Deerhurst and the closeness of these sites to the River Severn indicates a potential for waterborne transport of produce downstream to Gloucester. If this is so, the less pretentious inhabitants of the communities along the lip of the floodplain may well be tenants of these suspected villas. At Stoke Orchard excavations during the construction of the M5 motorway identified a settlement of up to 9ha (22 acres) whose economy may have been based on sheep grazing and weaving.

A similar pattern of sites and structures would appear to have existed in the Roman period around the *colonia* of Glevum, but they have not been explored in any detail to ascertain whether or not there was late Iron Age settlement below them. The evidence suggests that there was a high density of Roman settlement to the east of Glevum. Villas have been detected at Sandhurst Lane, Wells Bridge and on the Eastern Radial Road just beyond the walls of the *colonia*, and that at Hucclecote is well known from excavation. Villas near Abbeymead (Upton Lane) and Quedgeley (Olympus Park), as well as another probably connected with the bath house discovered separately at Hucclecote, demonstrate a zone of higher-status (but not particularly luxurious) buildings further out. Great Witcombe Villa might be included in this list but it is altogether of a different complexity and wealth, indicating a different function and still higher rank.

Recent excavations at Brockworth explored a non-villa site that probably originated in the first decades after the foundation of Kingsholm. The earliest period at Brockworth conforms to similar sites at Walton Cardiff, as well as the Hucclecote settlement, Abbeyfields and Abbeydale Saintbridge, but the indigenous tradition of mass-walled roundhouses made them difficult to detect. In the first and second centuries the older roundhouses were replaced by Roman fields and new roundhouses in rectangular enclosures. Allocating a function to parts of these enclosures has not been possible, but evidence appears to favour mixed farming in the vicinity of Hucclecote settlement. Often there seems to be evidence of, as yet undiscovered, structures of villa type close by, characterised by small quantities of tile and sometimes box tile related to hypocaust systems being found. At Hucclecote Villa the excavator, Mrs Elsie Clifford, suspected a timber structure which was replaced by stone in the middle of the second century. Considering the similarities between Hucclecote and Brockworth, it is possible that they both developed as similar types of farmstead, with only the former developing further into a villa in the third and fourth centuries.

What excavations at Hucclecote and Brockworth have demonstrated is that around the villa there are more humble buildings of an indigenous architectural tradition set in an

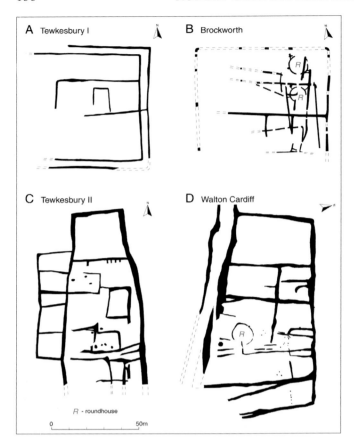

52 Farmstead enclosures in the Severn Valley. A: Tewkesbury 1 after Walker et al.; B: Brockworth after Rawes 1981; C: Tewksbury I, sub-phase 3c after Walker et al.; D: Walton Cardiff. (*Cotswold Archaeology and* BGAS)

extensive system of enclosures connected by a series of trackways, all forming a complex agricultural landscape. This intensive use of the land must surely be related to military supply in some way, either officially imposed or opportunistic. There is no reason why local peoples should not have lived and produced under Roman supervision with a *territorium*. Efforts to find evidence of *centuriation*, the division of the *territorium* landscape in rectangular blocks for settlement of retired legionaries, have so far proved unsuccessful.

The Vale of Berkeley and the Southern Bank of the Lower Severn

As a result of rising sea levels in south-west Britain since glacial times, salt marshes have developed consisting of sediment brought by the tides along the Severn from Gloucester to Awre. In the late Iron Age and early Roman period these areas might have remained wetland and been managed for wild-fowling or seasonal use for cattle grazing. However, reclamations accompanied by the drainage of land by both cutting ditches, as well as con-trolling, widening or diverting existing natural streams, may have begun in the late Iron Age and continued through the medieval, early modern and modern periods. The relative dating of these subsequent reclamations depended on the rising sea level producing higher surfaces on the seaward side of successive seawalls, so the lower the land surface, the earlier it was reclaimed. Fieldwork has identified a considerable body of evidence to indicate the building of massive sea defences like the 'Great Wall', which is still detectable in the land-scape in Elmore parish, in the late Roman period. Research has also demonstrated that at least a half of the 28 sq. kilometres of reclaimed wetlands in the upper estuary were of this late Roman date.

Settlement on the new alluvial farmland on the south bank of the Severn has been located through fieldwalking and the discovery of large scatters of building materials indicating single substantial farmsteads, probably of extended families, rather than in villages. No site has produced evidence of mosaics or hypocausts and the lack of tile would suggest that roofs were thatched. It is difficult to see the manpower and motivation required to build the seawalls and dig the ditches coming from small landowners even if working co-opera-tively, especially as this type and distribution of settlement indicates tenant and dependent farmers. It is possible that finance might have partly come from ironworking at Arlingham, Longley and Awre, which may have been of industrial proportions, but this would have been nowhere near the resources required for such ambitious projects. At this late date it is unlikely that the army was involved, and the lack of evidence for reclaimed land along the

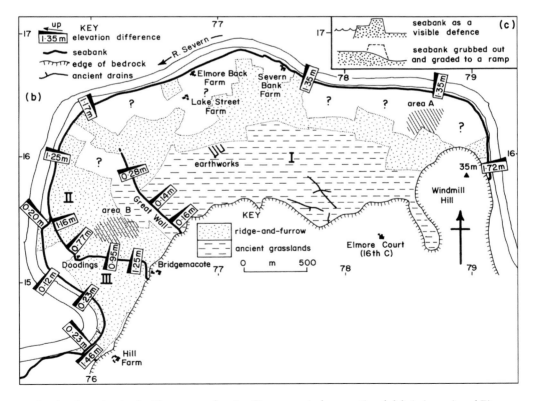

53 Land reclamation in the Elmore area showing Roman period occupational debris (areas A and B). Reclamations I and II are at least as old as the late Roman period and Reclamation III occurred in 1960–61 when a sea defence was raised on an area of marsh apparently never previously embanked. (TBGAS, Vol. 108, p. 18)

54 The 'Great Wall' at Elmore. (*Cotswold Archaeology*)

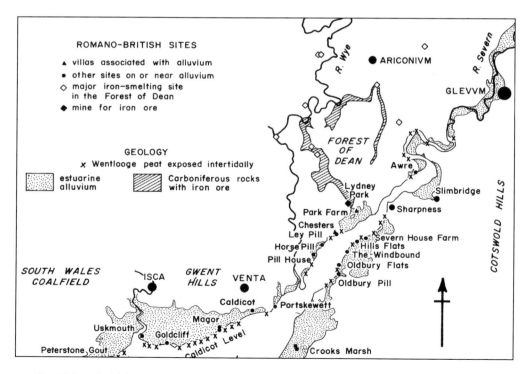

55 Alluvial deposits in the Severn Estuary, after J.R.L. Allen and S.J. Rippon. (Antiquaries Journal, *Vol. 77*, *p. 329*)

river at Gloucester indicates that there was no desire on behalf of the city council or a sub-stantial group of rich individuals to undertake such activity. It is likely that the reclamation activity was in some way related to the pressures of population growth and presence of villa estates on the gravels of the river terraces, such as at Frocester and on the Cotswold escarp-ment. Even these may have been too small to fund extensive works on the wetlands below and perhaps we should be looking for larger villas in the area or consider the role played by the extensive, possibly official, settlement at Kingscote. In the fourth century abandonment of the settlements in Lower Severn may be related to villa centralisation as demand for pro-duce did not wane, as is evidenced in the continuing process of land reclamation.

Romano-British settlement is also being detected further downstream from the Arlingham 'bends'. Wetland landscapes with rich natural resources, such as the grazing of livestock on the marshes and fishing, have been discovered, as has the probable production of salt through boiling sea water. Research at Hills Flats and Oldbury, where there may have been a villa or at least warehousing, has identified pottery, querns, bones, teeth and snails, which point to drainage and settlement as well as suggesting late Iron Age activity. Evidence points to a disruption of agricultural activity seen at the end of the first century and the start of the second century, which is seen elsewhere in the surrounding area. The recent discov-ery of a 'small town' at Wickwar indicates a market for wider and denser rural settlement.

Forest of Dean

The Forest of Dean has almost 110 sq. kilometres (42.5 sq. miles) covered by mixed wood-land, and it is the area where least is known about the late Iron Age and Roman archaeology. Clearly, accidental finds might result from earthmoving to lay forestry roads or in the process of planning new areas of trees, but other forms of fieldwork, especially aerial photography and geophysics, are problematic as trees and tree rooting can be a take up a large part of any area. Burning of timber in the past would also distort the findings of geophysics and would be difficult to undertake in terms of meaningful retrieval of valid evidence. Light Detection and Ranging (LiDAR) has been used very successfully in the Forest of Dean to locate sites, but as yet no confidently accepted Roman ones have been found. However, it is a pos-sibility that this sparseness of inhabitation is an indication of the lack of occupation of the landscape. There are four known Iron Age hillforts, all in strong positions and all highly vis-ible in the landscape – Symonds Yat promontory fort, Lancaut promontory fort, Camp Hill near Lydney and the only recognisable multi-vallate hillfort with three banks and ditches is Welshbury Hillfort. Only Lydney has been excavated and had pottery assigned to the immediate pre-Roman period, but the styles have now been recognised as having continu-ity into the early Roman period. The Symonds Yat site has provided evidence of late Iron Age activity perhaps associated with iron smelting. Whether these hillforts were occupied in the late Iron Age is unknown, even though it is likely in some cases since hillforts on the Cotswold escarpment might also have been inhabited at this time. The possible burial of a late Iron Age warrior from High Nash, Coleford, does not seem to be connected securely with a known site, although a Roman temple may be in the area. There is a similar lack of evidence for any late Iron Age settlements in both Monmouthshire and Herefordshire as little modern excavation has taken place. So, unfortunately, there is no secure evidence for the nature of any transition from the late Iron Age to Romano-British society.

The Forest of Dean also suffers from a lack of known sites in the Roman period and it is easy to come to the conclusion that the area was wooded and only mineral working for coal and iron ore took place. While this might be the case, the present heavy tree cover might be responsible for such a skewed picture. Perhaps the best evidence for other settlements has been provided by villas and also sites in the area around Dean Hall in the form of tiles, tesserae, pottery and iron clinker. There was apparently evidence within the structure of the hall itself to suggest that it might be built over a Roman building. A hoard of over 90 coins ranging in date from the first to the fourth century is said to have been found in 1986 in the make-up of the building.

The majority of Roman reclamations of farming land from wetlands were on the south bank of the river, but there is no geological reason why this the northern bank should not have been extended through the use of seawalls and banks, although it may be the result of a desire to protect the woodlands of the Forest of Dean. Similarly, there are no settlements on the higher ground overlooking the river on the north side, which might reflect the need for land for farming.

What this survey of the rural areas of the Gloucestershire region has demonstrated is that in the Thames and Severn valleys, and to a lesser extent on the Cotswolds, there is a considerable indication that the landscape was drastically reorganised at the end of the first century and beginning of the second century. The growth of Corinium as the *civitas* capital and Glevum as a *colonia* at this time must surely be the instigator of such a large measure of change. While the populating of Corinium might, to a large extent, have been a redistribution of groups from the countryside around, the establishment of the *colonia* would have produced an influx of new individuals and new money. At the time of the Glevum city centre fortress, the *territorium* would have had to support a legion comprised of single men, but the ex-soldiers of the *colonia* would have had dependants, resulting in larger areas of land needing to feed an increasing population. On the evidence that we have, this must have been in the Severn Valley and it is frustrating that this coincides with an area that is not amenable to producing crop marks. However, except for the prestigious architecture of the Cotswold villas, there may have been little difference in the agricultural resources of the areas around both Corinium and Glevum.

Although it is difficult to recover the plans of the lower-ranking houses, the survival of the indigenous roundhouse style of architecture is seen throughout the Roman period, even if embedded in a different complexity of enclosure representing a change in agricultural practice. While this does not appear to be a feature of the Cotswolds, this is probably more to do with the availability of evidence than reality of the situation. There also appears to be a difference in the number of villas and the quality of life enjoyed between the Severn Valley and the Cotswold region, but research has indicated that villa settlements did not just exist on the hills, but throughout the region, even if there are differences in status expressed through architectural pretensions.

EIGHT

SMALL TOWNS: UNIQUE, COMPLEX AND VERY UN-ROMAN

Small towns

If Corinium and Glevum had a charter to establish their separate functions, there were other types of communities which have been defined as 'small towns', or 'minor towns', 'large villages' or 'local centres' by archaeologists. Whatever term we wish to use, these settlements might help us see the degree to which Roman ways of life, as defined in the Introduction, permeated the countryside. The evidence from them could reveal the acceptance, rejection and modification of the cultural influence of Rome by indigenous people. It might also signify whether the provincial authorities chose to interfere in the growth of these types of settlements. In turn, this might give some idea of the Roman attitude to non-urban and non-villa settlements in the countryside. What must be acknowledged is that, taken together, a substantial portion of the population must have lived in these communities either permanently or seasonally.

In the Gloucestershire region it is the Cotswolds small towns at Wycomb and Bourton-on-the-Water that are best known, but this type of settlement has also been recognised at Asthall in Oxfordshire on Akeman Street, Dymock, possibly Weston-under-Penyard, and most recently at Wickwar in South Gloucestershire. At Tewkesbury and Worcester limited evidence points to a role as small-town settlements as they are on a main Roman road and have known agricultural hinterlands. There is also a site at Stoke Orchard in the Severn Valley that was discovered during the construction of the M5 motorway and whose suggested area has been given as between 3.6 and 8ha (9–20acres). Other settlements, such as at Horcote of 2.4ha (6 acres), at Shipton of 'three modern fields', at Swell of 3.2ha (8 acres) and at Poulton of 1.2ha (3 acres), are most likely to have been villages attached to villas, but there is no reason why these should not have had specialist functions such as local markets or a religious foci, which caused the site to be chosen for a villa location. On the whole, these settlements have been explored in a piecemeal fashion, often by earlier antiquaries, and therefore the quality of information can be poor. There do not appear to have been any permanent small towns in the Upper Thames Valley and this further strengthens the case for the area being an estate administered for Corinium. However, as in the recent case of the discovery of the settlement at Wickwar, it is likely that other population centres await discovery in the landscape. The following material is constructed around these settlements' histories, layouts and functions.

Wycomb

The settlement of 11–12ha (27–30 acres) lies in a sheltered valley at the headwaters of the River Coln to the north of Andoversford and is cut by a now disused railway line and the A40 Andoversford bypass. There is considerable evidence of a late Iron Age presence in the community (if not earlier), suggested by a horse bit of a typical design of the period, brooches, 'Dobunnic' coins and imported pottery identified as Claudio-Neronian Samian Ware, and Gallo-Belgic wares, as well as an amphora for wine or olive oil. Perhaps of importance is the possible coin mould found, similar to those from Bagendon and Ditches. The presence of a temple at Wycomb, unfortunately buried by the construction of an embankment for the Cheltenham to Bourton-on-the-Water railway branch line in 1860s, may also have late Iron Age origins as the presence of the spring close by is likely to have attracted ritual attention. Wycomb's position close to the White/Salt Way from Droitwich to Cirencester via Hailes at the foot of the Cotswold scarp may have been of importance, as was the settlement's

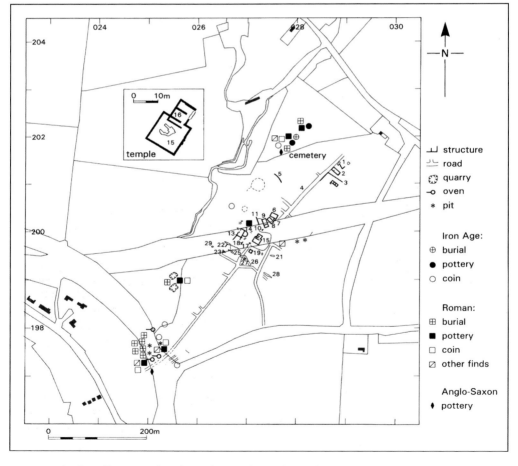

56 Wycomb: plot of known archaeology. The temple is indicated by 15 and 16 and the possible theatre/shrine 5. (*Cotswold Archaeological Trust*)

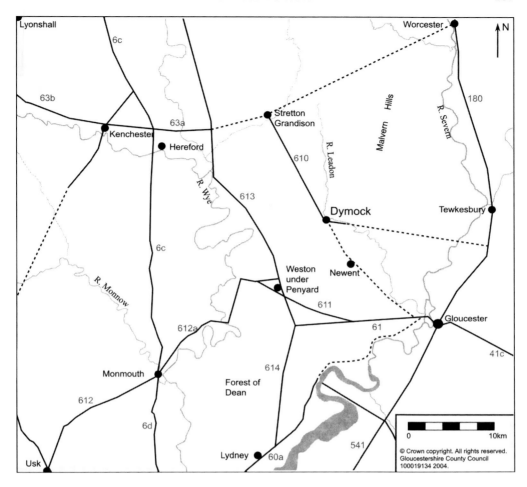

57 The location of small towns west of the River Severn. (TBGAS, *Vol. 125, p. 132*)

proximity to the other 'Salt Way' routes towards Lechlade and the Thames. The proximity of the substantial late Iron Age enclosure at Withington, just 2km (1.3 miles) east from
Wycomb, raises questions about links between elite power and ritual. The settlement
had a single main street running in a north-east to south-west direction, paralleling the
course of the Coln, though not leading to a spring. Evidence of timber structures from the
Andoversford bypass indicate a date of at least the AD 70s or perhaps earlier. Just north of
the temple the street divided, one branch to the south-east and the river and the other to
the south. On either side of the two main roads were minor roads or alleyways between
properties. The presence of the temple structure was obviously important to the existence
of the settlement, if not its origin, and will be discussed in detail below. Indeed, the whole
plan of the settlement looks like a large village surrounding a temple and it is clear that
the specialist function was religious. Parallels can be found at Uley, where structures such
as a priest's house and possible accommodation for pilgrims were postulated. A possible
high-status structure to the east side of the temple enclosure, from which Samian Ware

was retrieved, was also accompanied by evidence for a hypocaust. To the north another complex of buildings with a surrounding wall indicates the possibility of a villa-type site. The original excavator, Lawrence, also suggested the presence of an amphitheatre or theatre within the settlement which would be not out of place in a religious complex. However, it might also indicate a separate shrine. As well as the religious functions of the site, ovens and hearths have been found but it is difficult to identify them as industrial or domestic. There is also little evidence of agricultural practice. Animal bones, such as sheep and goat, might be related to temple offerings, as might boar tusks, horn cores and cow horns. There were querns and ovens found, but the report of the early excavations are very vague about this.

One of the incongruous aspects of the Wycomb settlement is the types of pottery being received in the later Roman period. Nearly all the main industries are present: Oxfordshire, Dorset Black Burnished Ware, New Forest and Nene Valley colour-coated wares, as well as fabrics from the Midlands. While this might be due to the positioning of the settlement at the node of several roads, the assemblage is very rich and varied for a small agricultural community. The explanation that the temple site flourished in the second century to decline by the early fourth and continued as a simple rural community involved in metalworking activities seems not to be borne out by the evidence.

Dymock

Roman Dymock appears to have been a settlement of 14–16ha (35–40 acres) and encompassed an area from north-west of the present village eastwards to the cricket ground, with a focus on the relatively sheltered position on a ridge above the floodplain of the River Leadon, where the church stands. There is little indication of late Iron Age activity in the area, but a limited number of 'Dobunnic' coins have been found. Samian pottery from an excavation at the local sewage works suggests a starting date of c. AD 70 or even earlier. The settlement at Dymock shows signs of a deliberate foundation at the beginning of the Roman period, and may have been sited on a road from Gloucester to the possible fort at Stretton Grandison in Herefordshire. That the roads in the settlement pre-date any form of ironworking that was to occur later is demonstrated by the lack of slag in their make-up. There is no evidence of a military occupation in terms of finds of armour or weapons, but the presence of pottery of Kingsholm-type fabric and the sample of coins found on the site of the first century could be evidence of an administrative role.

In recent excavations at Dymock early Roman timber structures were identified inside a ditched and gated enclosure and consisted of wattle and daub walls, possibly with timber cladding and a thatched or timber roof. The excavator pointed out the problems of the layout of the structures being seen as part of a Roman military establishment. That there were buildings of some pretension on the site is indicated by the discovery of door keys and the recovery of iron nails also indicates a very unusual level of sophistication so early in the Roman period. The excavator was tempted to see the locations as a site for the *cursus publicus*, being 15km (9 miles) from Gloucester and 14km (8.6 miles) south of Stretton Grandison. Although it might be expected that these were short distances for horses carrying official mail, there are other types of official stop-points for various forms of transport.

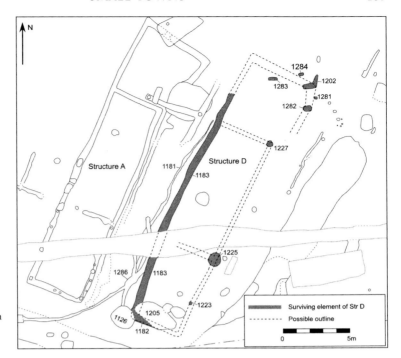

58 Dymock Sewage
works: possible layout
of Structure D based on
Structure A. (TBGAS,
Vol. 125, p. 145)

Mansiones did have different layouts and the enclosure, with a gateway and no rampart, has
been paralleled elsewhere as has the barrack-like buildings at right angles to each other
which might have been a stable and for storage possibly forming a courtyard. However, due
to the presence of the river constricting the area, it is unlikely that the characteristic facilities
of bath houses, granaries and accommodation for horses and men could fit into the available
space. As the excavator remarks, there is no single plan for these establishments and some of
these features might be sited close to those excavated. However, it might also be argued that
because of successful agriculture and metalworking, the unusual high-status items, such as
fine glassware, plated spoon handles, as well as the 'Roman' construction techniques of the
house, might just indicate prosperity and success for local elites. However, the demolition of
the wooded structures and the filling of the ditch in one episode, possibly around AD 100,
are difficult to explain if the structures were of domestic use.

In the second century it seems that part of the settlement was divided into rectilinear
plots with individual dwellings positioned along the road. The evidence for one of these
postulated dwellings excavated at the rectory site indicated that it was built from timber or
wattle and daub with a thatched or shingle roof, and was associated with outhouses, pits and
features connected very much with agriculture. Environmental evidence from the Roman
period layers suggests a mixed farming regime with wheat, barley, grassland and meadow
alongside mixed woodland.

Extensive iron smelting and the casting of copper objects are known to have been important at Dymock and traces of the industry have been found in the form of slag across the
settlement area, but this aspect of the economy seems to have ceased in the mid-second
century. Much of the evidence for the chronology of the Dymock settlement appears to

show that it had shrunk, moved or become defunct by the late second or early third century. Much more evidence is needed from the surrounding area to detect the presence of villa structures and other agricultural settlements before any further functions or chronologies can be suggested.

Weston-under-Penyard

The Iron Age and early Roman core of Ariconium was situated on the south and west facing slopes of the hill and formed a focus for domestic occupation from about AD 100 to 250. A number of other stone-founded buildings probably had timber-framed super-structures, while from crop-mark evidence several enclosures are known which probably represent plots of land beside or behind the main roads entering the settlement. These are likely to have contained domestic properties, ancillary buildings, yards and workshops. There is no evidence for any element of organised planning of the internal street network and an irregular network of tracks, back lanes and access routes linked the domestic and industrial areas, as well as gardens and small fields, within and around the margins of the settlement. Beyond this domestic area, two distinct ironworking zones developed. To the north, extensive spreads of iron slag and a group of shaft furnaces provide evidence of an ironworking area, during the first half of the second century and extending in use through to the early-mid third century. To the south-west, around two road junctions, a second area with extensive evidence for ironworking developed, either at the end of the second century or early in the third. There are also indications of copper alloy working and a watermill, and possibly an associated storage and processing building can be seen as an important component in marketing, processing and redistribution of local agricultural surplus.

Ariconium appears to have fallen in status during the second century, although there are some indications of more wealthy inhabitants evidenced by ivory items and an escutcheon from a copper alloy vessel, an expensive object of some elegance. A stone building excavated in the 1920s was associated with a possible hypocaust system, window glass, painted wall plaster and a tessellated floor. This was clearly a townhouse of some pretension and this building may have had an imperial function as a *mansio*. However, besides some evidence for a temple or shrine, there are no other known public buildings, indeed only a couple of other structures demonstrate any signs of higher status and which may have been the urban residences of local elites. Otherwise, the majority of buildings are most likely to have been simple, rectilinear timber structures, sometimes with stone foundations.

Evidence for occupation in the second half of the third century and the fourth century remains relatively extensive and although the northern industrial area had been abandoned and was used for rubbish dumping, the south-western area of the 'small town' continued to thrive. Ariconium maintained a healthy economy and considerable size until at least the end of the third century. The possible *mansio* appears to have remained in use until the mid-fourth century, while other stone-founded buildings survived at least until the end of the third century. Ceramic evidence certainly suggests that the 'small town' fell into a marked decline in the fourth century and that it may have largely been abandoned by about AD 350.

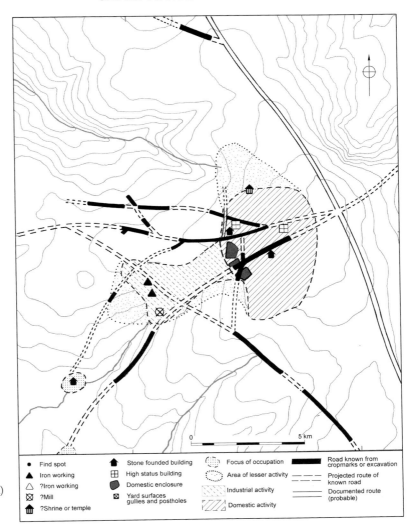

59 Weston-under-Penyard (Ariconium) AD 250–400. (*Robin Jackson*)

Bourton-on-the-Water

Situated on a crossing point of the River Windrush, with the presence of a late Iron Age trading settlement at Salmonsbury and the Fosse Way passing close by, Bourton-on the-Water was an ideal site for a small town. Just north of the Windrush crossing two likely Roman roads head north-westwards: Ryknield Street to Alcester (Aluana) and the junction with the Salt Way from Droitwich; and Buckle Street in the same direction, though this might be following an older course. Such a position seems to demand a *mansio* and stone-built structures found by excavators have been given fanciful names such as 'the transport café' or the 'stables'. A more recent reappraisal suggests a different role.

The Bourton-on-the-Water settlement would seem to have originated in the late Iron Age with two foci at Salmonsbury and Bourton Bridge, and with a likely track between them. The Salmonsbury site was an important elite centre with long distance travel routes, but not as important as the so-called *oppida* of Bagendon or the NOGD. There is sound evidence that there was continuity of occupation at the valley fort through to the early Roman period, the ramparts being slighted at that time, and a structure 4.3m wide and 11.6m long being identified within the Salmonsbury dykes. This might suggest parallels with Ditches, although the width might not be enough for an early villa building. Occupation may have occurred into the fourth century AD. Even with an important route crossing a river there is no sign of a military presence and no defences existed. Evidence of structures in and around the Bourton Bridge area suggests indigenous roundhouses were in existence until the late Roman period. Tantalising glimpses of at least three more Roman-styled private dwellings in the form of hypocausts, and at one location a column base, indicates a very high-status structure. Whether there was any continuity of an elite presence in the movement of roundhouses from inside the Salmonsbury dykes to well-appointed rectangular structures close to Fosse Way is a possibility. Also in the Bourton Bridge area there appears to have been at least three roads off Fosse Way bounded by a ditch parallel to the main route and forming rectangular plots of land. The evidence suggests a date for this area of at least the late first century through to the Saxon period, the only small town in the area to have such a continuity of sequential occupation.

The structures identified as being parts of a 'posting station' would seem to be simple functional rectangular buildings with the evidence for smithing and flour manufacture being typical, small-scale, domestic production or, at best, serving the settlement itself. The lack of tile across the areas points to the rectangular structures having thatched or turfed roofs and there are no traces of wall plaster or mosaics connected with them.

Numerous coins have been retrieved from over large areas, which indicates that the function of the settlement was as a local market serving the surrounding Cotswold area. Such a role would continue to some extent the settlement's late Iron Age trading processes, though on a much less extensive scale.

Wickwar

A Roman settlement of some form had been postulated at Hall End near Wickwar since at least the mid-1970s, with numerous small finds having been reported, including metal objects, pottery and dressed stone. The existence of a small town was confirmed through extensive geophysical surveying and a number of small trail excavations undertaken by Avon Archaeological Unit between 2001 and 2004. The remains, believed to date from between the second and fourth centuries AD, are concentrated along a length of Roman road which runs across the site on a north–south axis, through the fields of Little and Great Blacklands. Although there is no evidence of a continuation of the metalled Roman road immediately across the Ladden Brook, it is known to exist from aerial photography further to the north of the site.

Geophysical survey results clearly show that the central area of the town comprises a considerable number of stone buildings fronting the road, likely to be of both domestic and commercial function. Beyond these buildings there is evidence of a number of dispersed small enclosures, particularly in the western part of the site. Trial excavations in the north-eastern section have demonstrated the presence of shallow and well-preserved archaeological deposits, including the remains of timber structures, a series of small lanes and ditches running at right angles to the central road and evidence of industrial activity. Substantial amounts of ironworking debris were also recovered, suggesting the presence of an iron furnace, and perhaps a connection with the Forest of Dean via the settlement at Oldbury on the Severn, 12km away to the west.

Geophysical surveys also revealed the presence of a curved feature in the north-eastern part of the site, which was initially thought to represent a corner of the defensive ditch of a Roman fort, as it appeared to be of the characteristic 'playing card' shape associated with such features. However, the Roman coin list from the evaluation trenches and unstratified finds begins with issues after AD 75, whilst there is an apparent absence of coinage military metalwork of a date immediately post-conquest and together these argue against an early military origin. This curved feature does, however, have parallels with other sites of a probable 'official' but primarily non-military function. It has been dated to the second century AD and would seem to be a *mansiones* of the *cursus publicus*.

Small Towns and their Functions

While there were some broad similarities between these types of settlements, there was no archetype of small town. However, there does seem to be two overlapping aspects of the history and functions of these sites, that of a pre-Roman existence and/or a relationship to a major road which was probably serviced in some way by these sites.

The small towns at Wycomb, Bourton and Western-under-Penyard have considerable evidence of late Iron Age, if not earlier, origins and Weston-under-Penyard may have been important enough to have had a Roman road surveyed to pass close to it. At none of these sites is there any evidence for a military occupation at an early date and this is probably a reflection of the attitude of the indigenous elites to the Roman occupation. It is possible that we are seeing the sites of pre-Roman 'canton' centres at Wycomb, Bourton and Weston-under-Penyard, which continued, in some form or other, into the Roman period and developed as the focus of *pagi*, the administrative divisions of the *civitas*. Weston-under-Penyard specifically has a number of seemingly well-appointed structures and this might be the influence of being at a distance from Cirencester and therefore developing its own political and economic profile. At each of the settlements there are materials or building plans that suggest high-status housing, often seemingly on the outskirts of the settlement, and these might indicate the continuation of political or economic power from the late Iron Age into the Roman period. Another important indicator of late Iron Age centres is the presence of a temple. At Weston-under-Penyard and Wycomb the evidence for religious buildings is sound, though at Bourton there is as yet no convincing evidence of a temple or shrine. There are indications of ritual activity at Upper Slaughter, close to Bourton, but these appear to be unconnected with the small town.

The provision of the roadside *mansiones* no doubt attracted activities which remained even after the provision became redundant. This is suggested at Dymock, which appears to have its origins in the first century as a result of administrative action, and this might also be the origin of the small town at Wickwar. It is possible that the 'fort' at Cirencester also had a *mansio* type of role. In each case, the settlement would attract other functions once a Roman market economy was set up, but it is unlikely that these facilities would have had any substantial local cultural influence. The lack of a developed street grid, even though these settlements do have rudimentary layouts, and the dearth of organised community facilities demonstrates a low measure of Roman influence. However, the rectilinear plans of the plots along the roads do indicate an acquaintance with larger settlements.

In the Gloucestershire region there is little evidence of the role of processing and redistribution of local agricultural surplus, although they could have acted as a reservoir of seasonal labour. Unfortunately, the lack of modern excavation, including the retrieval of assemblages of bones with evidence of butchery, limits what can be said about livestock markets. Whether the surplus from the villa estates was sold in the small towns or sent to the larger markets in Corinium or Glevum is hard to know, but an examination of the known facilities of the *civitas* capital were limited in this respect and it may be that the small towns did act as significant places of exchange. It is noticeable that the known small towns are distributed within a day's return journey 'circle' and there is little overlap between these areas.

The incidence of market times and the religious calendar of saints' days and feasts are well known from medieval times. In the Middle Ages transport played an important role in that fairs at locations of river and roads were favoured and while foodstuffs were important, it was the work of craftsmen that was an essential element. Foreign merchants were usually allowed to trade only at a specific period after the market had opened to enable local people to sell their wares first. Both the villa estates and the smaller agricultural settlements would have needed items that could not have been manufactured in their own communities, such as quern stones or pottery, and it is the small-town market that might have been the origin of such goods. On many rural non-villa sites the only evidence of Roman influence is often pottery and trinkets in the form of jewellery and these may have been bought at the small towns on market days.

Market days also had other functions, and in the Middle Ages Lady Day was a traditional day on which year-long contracts between landowners and tenant farmers in England would begin and end. For the local villa owner or the *civitas* administration such markets could also have ensured that all commercial activity took place in one locality and therefore could be supervised to provide taxes on trading. The small towns may also have had a role in tax collection, but the traditions of this happening on specific days would not have provided a permanent enough economic base for the existence of the town. Indeed this may have hindered the development of these small centres as money and goods were being taken from the area and not being reinvested through local trade.

For the rural population the small town could have provided a market for the exchange and redistribution of local, regional, inter-regional and even inter-provincial products, and it might be expected that these would influence the settlements through a wide range of meetings with others. That does not appear to have been the case, and this can be seen in the very diverse and complex settlements with a more 'quirky' pattern of organic growth than that of the planned and regulated larger towns.

NINE

STATUS IN STONE: THE VILLAS

Archaeologists differentiate 'villas' from farmsteads as being stone-built rectangular structures with more than two rooms (although in Gloucestershire rarely fewer than six are found) and usually associated with a rural estate. On a continuum from small house to palatial complex, the defining features are the presence, number and quality of hypocausts, mosaics and architectural ornamentation such as painted plaster which would suggest a growing depth of Roman influence. Gloucestershire is renowned for its villas, especially in the Cotswolds, and 140 potential sites have been discovered, but only 36 have been confirmed through excavation. The problem lies in the ambiguity of definition, particularly as scatters of pottery and clay roofing tile might also indicate a large nucleated non-villa settlement. The distribution of villas in the region is rather clouded by the presence of the Oxfordshire-Gloucestershire county boundary and the overall geographical spread not always being appreciated. The majority of the suspected villas in Gloucestershire lie in the Cotswolds, as do many of the 68 proposed villas in Oxfordshire. However, what has been surprising is the high incidence of villa structures discovered in the Upper Thames Valley and, increasingly, in the Lower Severn Valley.

Villas were individual private expressions of wealth and taste, unlike the communal projects in the towns. Villas were built to impress rich neighbours and the poor living locally, the motivations being very much the same as in pre-Roman times. The *civitas* capital's social and administrative status might have been expressed through the location and wealth of the rural homes around it, as well as its monumental buildings. It is becoming increasingly clear that the growing taste for Roman styles and building techniques reflect the attitudes of the builders of the villas and the status of the owner to provide an ostentatious home, whether for an individual or an extended family. Even so, we must be aware that just because there was a predilection for Roman ways of life, this did not necessarily mean adoption of any of the political, social or economic aspects of *romanitas*. Certainly villa forms are an indigenous response to Roman culture in that, not only did the conquest provide a situation in which villa construction became possible, but it also recreated late Iron Age patterns of structures accommodating kinship groups and there are numerous examples of villas being built alongside roundhouses. The buildings were not like the archetypal structures in the Italian countryside, but a reinvention demonstrating a unique display of a Romano-British civilisation. We should not presume that wealth was primarily concerned with agriculture, as those villas below the Forest of Dean on the Severn Estuary had part industrial economies. Similarly, we should not consider that a 'country house' had to be rural, as villa structures are known just outside the walls of Corinium, and indeed structures of similar design have been found within the town at the Beeches site, which may suggest that a landowner had a local estate and there was land inside Corinium for his villa.

Country homes were owned not only by members of the British *civitates*, as Continental literary evidence indicates that there were other proprietors including Roman emperors and the state, absentee owners, the army, settler groups such as discharged soldiers with capital to invest, private individuals from both Britain and overseas, religious or entrepreneurial bodies also. Although the great majority of villas in the Gloucestershire region would have been 'producing villas' and part, if not the centre, of an estate, some of the interests listed above might be responsible for the larger complexes, such as Chedworth, Turkdean and Woodchester. These might be described as 'consumer villas', with possibly little or no connection with the area around them. With the almost complete lack of inscriptions found in association with villas in Gloucestershire, it is not possible to identify the owner of even the highly luxurious structures or their origin and status, and the archaeology has to be used to identify individual ambitions and culture.

The Archaeology of the Villa

Up until recently most of the Roman villas in the area were thought of as being a mid-third to early fourth century phenomenon, yet a growing proportion have produced evidence for a second-century foundation, and a limited number of late first century date, such as Ditches, Withington and possibly Great Witcombe, indicating a marked continuity of high-status occupation. The trajectory of the construction of villa-type houses is spread over the whole Roman period, but with some peaks probably related to political and economic factors that maintain or increase wealth. In villa studies generally there has been an emphasis on plans and the relative development from a simple 'row' or 'cottage' structure, later fronted by a corridor. The next stage might be the addition of wings to this simple rectangular building and then the development into a courtyard villa through the closing up of the space between the wings. Particularly in the Cotswolds, sites have been chosen so that a number of courtyards could be built down a slope (Turkdean and Great Witcombe are examples) and this ensured that they were very public and could be seen from long distances. From the evidence of villas across the country, it does appear that these stages do not form a strict relative chronology, nor do they relate to fashions at particular dates. There would also appear to be no need for a villa to go through all the stages as at a specific site the structure may remain a simple one with just a corridor. An important way of dating a villa is the use of mosaics, as not only does this indicate wealth, but their design and content is a valuable indicator of period.

The Coln Villas

Claydon Pike, Barnsley Park and Chedworth villas are all situated along the River Coln, which rises around Andoversford and flows in a south-easterly direction to cross under the

Fosse Way, eventually joining the Thames. They are relatively close but indicate differences in size, dates of development and wealth. The three villa structures are perhaps only half of the possible number in the Coln Valley, as there are sites producing Roman materials which have not been excavated.

Claydon Pike

There is growing evidence for villas in the Upper Thames Valley and at Claydon Pike, near the confluence of the River Coln with the Thames. The remains of two consecutive structures have been excavated that are very regional adaptations of the villa structure. During the first century AD a farmstead was established on a gravel island on the Thames floodplain and operated a largely subsistence economy associated with cattle ranching and providing for the needs of growing local population centres such as Corinum. The early second century saw dramatic changes, including the imposition of large rectangular compound enclosures and, within one of them, a substantial aisled barn and house. The aisled house has, arguably, some of the characteristics of a villa. The structure had mortared masonry lower wall courses, probably supporting a timber frame, and possibly mud and stud walls. Fired clay fragments were recovered from many of the postholes and may have been part of the structure, while the reasonable amount of iron nails suggests external wooden planking, perhaps to aid waterproofing. The roof of the building was clearly constructed in ceramic roofing tile and it is likely that there were some glazed windows in the building and the presence of fine-painted wall plaster suggests a structure of comfort for the owner or at least the custodian of the complex. The use of painted plaster does suggest the presence of one or more rooms and finds indicate different zones of function or status. In the northern half of the building animal bones implied that a major part of the diet was pig and chicken, which were rare on other parts of the site, and the pottery assemblage, which consisted of flagons, jars, cups and bowls, hints that this area was used for food consumption. Outside the building, in an extension, the range of pottery and animal bone was more related to food preparation, including the use of olive oil and fish sauce. At some point during the early fourth century there was a widespread and deliberate clearing of the site, undoubtedly connected with the establishment of a modest masonry villa. It contained six rooms with timber-plastered superstructure and plastered walls. These walls were whitewashed and contrasted with the brightly coloured walls of the earlier aisled hall. The roof was most likely made up of a combination of reused roofing tiles and limestone slate. However, a hypocausted room within the building, which might have acted as a winter dining area, a large bedroom or a small dining room, would suggest a modest 'cottage'-style villa, the home of a family group of five to eight persons of relatively high social pretensions and aspirations.

Barnsley Park

Excavated between 1961 and 1979, Barnsley Park Villa is very different from Claydon Pike and also Chedworth, further up the Coln Valley. There are two interpretations of the site

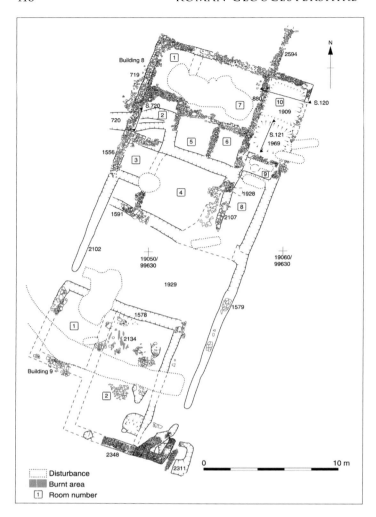

60 Plan of the Claydon
Pike Villa. (*Oxfordshire
Archaeology*)

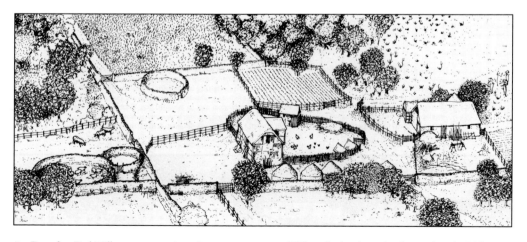

61 Barnsley Park Villa reconstruction phase 2, AD 275–315; Webster's circular animal pens, but Smith's
roundhouses. (TBGAS, *Vol. 100, p. 82*)

based on the same dating. Graham Webster, the excavator, preferred an approach in which the late Iron Age living styles of the inhabitants became romanised. Smith, the re-interpreter, while accepting Webster's structural evidence and dating, was more comfortable with the idea that the individual families farming the land decided how they would adapt the 'villa' idea to their own circumstances.

Webster suggested a date of *c.* AD 140 for the earliest structures on the site, in spite of the evidence for roundhouses and four-poster structures, which are usually interpreted as above ground, seasonal grain storage of late Iron Age date. However, only a few small pieces of pottery of this date were found. It was clear to the excavator that 'the occupants of the site at this period were Britons who had absorbed some "romanising" influences, especially in terms of the pottery that they were using, but also retained older traditions'. Consecutive rectangular timber houses were recognised from hard-packed clay and possible timber pads within the yard, the first dating to between AD 315 and 340 and the second, rebuilt structure, continued until AD 360, but with a bath house being attached to it some time between *c.* AD 340 and 360. Graham Webster concluded that the first recognisable house was a stone building which could be dated by coins to *c.* AD 350–60. He also detected the presence of a number of round, stone-built structures dating from *c.* AD 315–40 to *c.* 340–60, which he interpreted as animal pens. From AD 360–80 a stone-winged corridor was built and expanded with two hypocausted rooms until being abandoned about AD 380–400 and the main building being converted entirely to agricultural use. After AD 400 the villa building was reduced to a stone platform. There was at least one stone circular structure surviving until *c.* AD 375–80.

Smith has taken issue with the interpretation given by Webster, although accepting the relative development of the structure if not the tightness of his dating. He considers the site to have originated with a family/kinship group from a late Iron Age way of life, albeit in the second century, whose relationships are represented by the reinterpretation of Webster's cattle pens as stone-walled roundhouses. A timber hall was built in the yard with the round-houses still in existence, and then a stone bath house was attached to it. Smith considers the

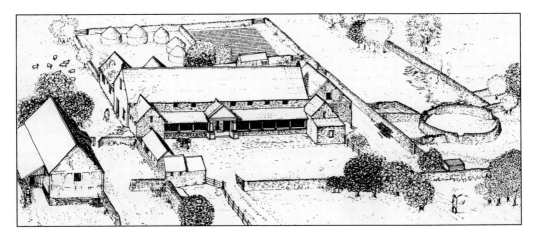

62 Barnsley Park Villa reconstruction phase 7, AD 375–380. (TBGAS, *Vol. 100, p. 86*)

early fourth-century timber hall to be a communal feature and a sign of Roman influenced use of surplus wealth.

This developed into a stone structure, a 'winged-corridor' villa, with the hall being shared by two families whose rooms were either side of it. The relative size of the rooms at each end and the provision of heated rooms in the southern part all pointed to the different statuses of the kinship groups at specific periods. This concept of more than one family in a villa has been suggested for a large number of sites which have distinct, and what might be independent, structures. At Barnsley Park there certainly appears to be some direct relationship between the spatial layout of the roundhouses and their development into a stone villa.

Chedworth

Chedworth Roman Villa lies at the western end of a small Cotswold valley which is also a tributary stream of River Coln and in a very private location. The villa was largely excavated between its discovery in 1864 and 1866, and whereas excavations have been undertaken since that time, none has been completely published. The results from the programme of recent work managed by the site archaeologist, Phil Bethell, indicates that there was Roman occupation at Chedworth from the second half of the second or early third century in the form of a substantial wooden structure in what is now the lower garden area. In the late third to early fourth century, the first clearly identifiable rectangular stone villa was on the top of the combe rather than at the bottom. The archaeology suggests that the modest, row-type, stone-built villa dated from the late third and early fourth centuries and had a series

63 Reconstruction of the late fourth-century Chedworth Villa. (*After Eds J. Burrow and B. Byron*)

of separate buildings. This first stone-built phase had mosaic pavements and painted wall plaster in the west range and its corridor, and so was luxurious, even if not to the extent of what followed. There was a south range at some distance from the west range and at a lower level, and perhaps a further separate structure to the east.

In the mid-fourth-century phase there was a complete remodelling of what now appears to be a relatively modest villa into one of the largest in Roman Britain. There was an ambition of scale not seen before at the site, achieved in a relatively short time, and representing a transformation rather than gradual development. The earlier structures were incorporated into the vast edifice which must have taken decades to build and have required huge wealth and status. The finished building, with its dozens of mosaics, architectural embellishments, two bath houses and integral shrine, must have cost very large sums of money and added to this would have been the expenditure for the huge amounts of earth being moved about the site, major terracing works on the north and south sides, and the levelling of the garden court. This all suggests an investment of wealth on a very grand scale in a short space of time by an individual or family of some significance in the province, and probably not a member of the Dubonnic elite using 'old family money' extending a villa incrementally over several generations.

Great Witcombe

Great Witcombe Villa was placed to get wide views towards Crickley Hill and the Lower Severn Valley and to be glimpsed at from those localities. At the present time, only the hut covering the mosaics of the 'lower baths' can be seen from Crickley Hill, with the main site being obscured by a wood. However, Cooper's Hill Farm is visible immediately adjacent to the villa and as a three-storeyed structure gives some indication of the effect that a Roman building of greater dimensions would have on a less full landscape.

There have been a number of excavations at Great Witcombe, begun by the inimitable Reverend Mr Samuel Lysons in 1818, after the finding of the villa by workmen removing an ash tree. Each of those excavations has left a legacy of poor preservation of the walls and foundations and unsympathetic reconstruction, therefore little of the present display represents the original positions of many aspects of the building. Phase 1 of the villa was a late Iron Age settlement close by and there is the possibility that the rectangular suite of seven rooms by the stream, some with plastered walls and floors, might have been a very early villa similar to Ditches. This supports the suggestion that the area inside the Cooper's Hill earthworks overlooking the Great Witcombe site might have played the same role as Bagendon. While Ditches remained in the same exposed position in order to be seen from Roman Ermine Street, the early Great Witcombe Villa was more sheltered, but could still be seen from the same Roman road as it descended the Cotswold scarp. The possibility of an earlier set of buildings on the main villa site was raised when it was discovered that the lower baths were at right angles to the proposed earlier structure by the stream. Clifford, in her excavations of the north-west wing, which contains the lower baths, suggested a date before the end of the first century for its construction. However, Leach concluded that there was little evidence for a structure on the site before the early

Cleeve Crickley & Birdlip
Camps from Witcomb Roman Villa.

Ed J Burrow 1918

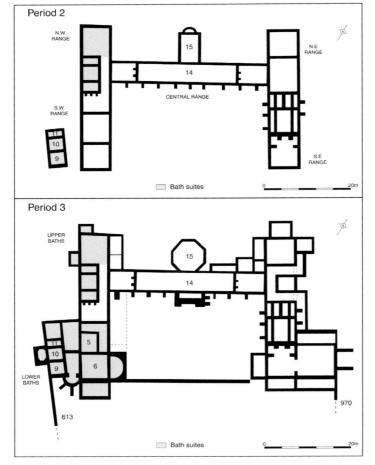

64 The view from the Great
Witcombe Villa in 1918
with the course of Ermine
Street marked by the row of
trees in the middle distance
descending the hill.
(*Ed. J. Burrow*)

65 Great Witcombe Villa:
the development of the villa,
after Leach. (TBGAS, *Vol.
121, p. 184*)

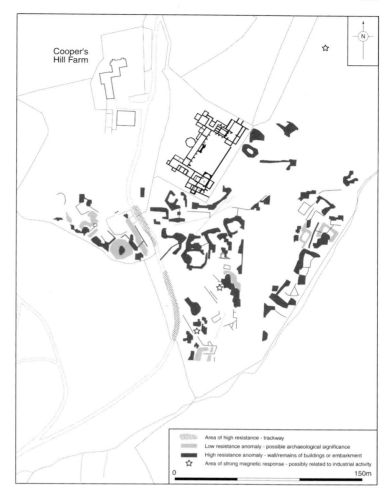

Cooper's
Hill Farm

Area of high resistance - trackway
Low resistance anomaly - possible archaeological significance
High resistance anomaly - wall/remains of buildings or embankment
☆ Area of strong magnetic response - possibly related to industrial activity

0   150m

66 Great Witcombe
Villa geophysical survey.
(TBGAS, Vol. 121, p. 193)

third century, although since then it has been proposed that the mosaics in this phase should not be dated later than AD 200.

The layout of the later building was ambitious, unified and planned to impress especially in its use of the hillside slope. A gallery formed the 'crossbar' that linked the east and west wings of the H-shape which framed it, giving a satisfying perspective both from and to the villa. The gallery had a mosaic pavement flooring it and halfway along was an apsidal space later converted into an octagonal structure which may have served as a dining room. Reconstructions of the villa suggest that the gallery and both wings could have had an upper storey due to the angle of the hill-side slope. However, the presence of the springs necessitated the buttressing of the gallery and the west wall of the east wing, and perhaps argues against a higher structure with more weight. The detached bath house mentioned above was close to the south-west range.

The final phase, in the late third or fourth century, saw the structure become a court-yard-type villa with the addition of a southern boundary wall. It would seem that the additions and modifications to the villa structure were piecemeal, with two major episodes

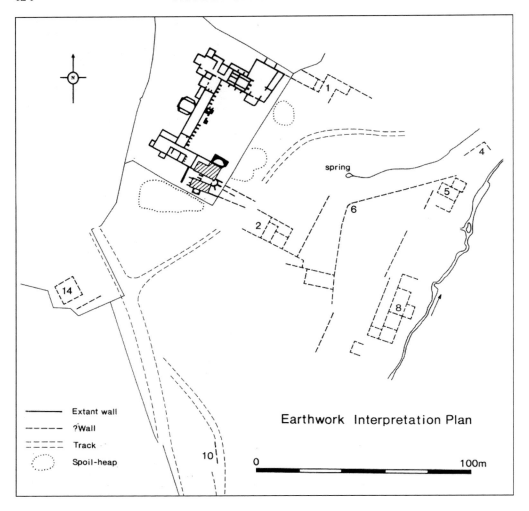

Extant wall
?Wall
Track
Spoil-heap

Earthwork Interpretation Plan

0   100m

67 Great Witcombe Villa. Interpretive plan of the field survey: Platforms 1 and 2 possible further ranges of
the villa flanking an outer court; 4 the possible mill and 5 an associated structure; 8 a simple villa (like the
early phase at Ditches); tile wasters found below 8 indicate an industrial use in this lower area; 14 a possible
temple or mausoleum; 10 an area of burnt material possibly indicating industrial activity. (TBGAS, Vol. 121,
p. 196)

in the incorporating the 'lower' baths into the south-west wing and its decoration with
painted plaster and mosaics with geometrical and aquatic designs. Extensions to the south-
east wings added the kitchen and stores with possible accommodation for farm labourers.
Presumably residential accommodation was on an upper floor. Additions and modifications
to the house continued in the fourth century, but the basic footprint of the original design
did not change.

   In 2002 the Cotswold Archaeological Trust undertook a programme of field surveying,
the results of which identified platforms indicating that there were further substantial ranges
flanking an outer courtyard that may have incorporated a formal landscape garden and
which would have further emphasised the gallery as the centre of the perspective. The villa

seems to have continued into the fifth century, but in a much dilapidated state. The subsequent hill-side slumping must have been slow, but dramatic, damaging the side ranges but leaving the central gallery largely intact and burying the lower parts of the site enough to protect the stratigraphy and artefacts of the south-west lower baths.

The survey work of the CAT in 2002 identified a number of potential structures, including a possible mill. The discovery in the stream of tile wasters indicating their manufacture was also supported by the discovery of areas of strong magnetic response from possible kilns and hearths south and north-east of the villa, far enough away and downwind so as not to cause problems for the inhabitants. Evidence for the working of copper alloy and lead had also been recorded previously, as well as the possibility of pewter vessels being manufactured at the villa.

Clearly, a site in such a magnificent position for flaunting wealth and status, and planned with so much care and effort to ensure the effectiveness of such spectacle, indicates an important individual of power and wealth. The Cooper's Hill earthworks above the site, and the rich late Iron Age burials at Barrow Wake at Birdlip further along the ridge, might suggest the presence of a dynastic group perhaps represented later by the possible mausoleum platform found during the 2000 fieldwork, which could indicate continuity from the late Iron Age into the Roman period. Whether the site had a political or social relationship with either Glevum or Corinium is difficult to know in spite of the use of pottery made in the *colonia* and a ring with an eagle on it being found in the villa.

Frocester

Excavations at Frocester by Captain H.S. Gracie took place until his death in 1979 and then each summer by Eddie Price who is a farmer. It is an interesting experience to read about the workings of a Roman farm written by a present-day practitioner. The settlement at Frocester is situated above the River Severn and demonstrates unbroken continuity from the late Bronze Age, with the shape of its surrounding boundary ditches not changing from the middle Iron Age until *c.* AD 275.

Up until AD 100, the site might have been described as late Iron Age with a transition to Roman, which was exemplified by the appearance of a small quantity of first-century Samian Ware and other imported fine wares such as a *terra nigra* platter and Lyons ware, probably coming via Bagendon. An early degree of prosperity is suggested by large numbers of brooches as well as a few coins. Some time after AD 275 the traditional boundaries of the settlement were extended to the west, adding 0.7ha (1.8 acres) of undisturbed ground. Increasing Roman influence is seen in a row-type building constructed in a compound delineated by ditches. The building unusually had massive foundations of 1.5m (5ft), which may indicate a structure of two or even three storeys. The simple row house, 32m (104ft) long and 10m (33ft) wide, was divided internally into a large central hall (Room 2), either side of which were smaller rooms (1 and 4). Room 1 was designated a workroom from the evidence of iron and bronze metalworking debris, and an oval, partly stone-edged hearth. Room 2, the central room, appears to have been partitioned into three parts; each, with a floor of different material, had a kitchen in its south-west part with a gravel floor repaired

69a–e Reconstructions of the sequence of development of Frocester Villa. (*E. Price*)

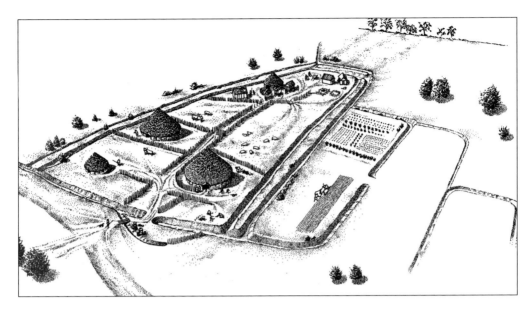

a AD 50–100

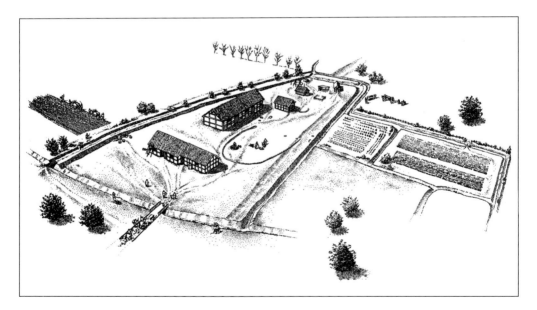

b AD 100–200

Opposite, from top
c AD 200–270
d AD 270–300
e *c.* AD 360

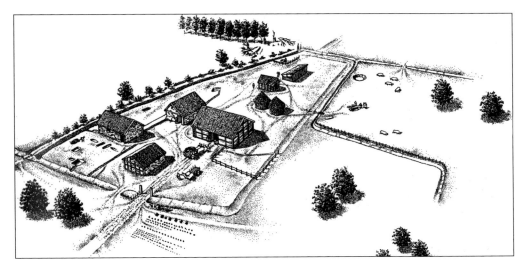

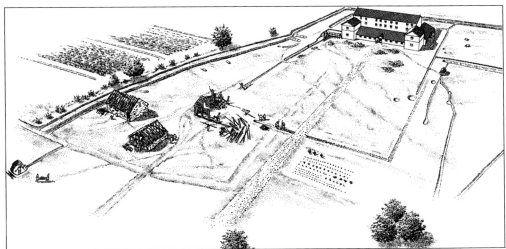

with potsherds and sand. Two ovens were apparent, a bread oven or large boiler and a typical domestic oven. The quality of the excavation and recording can be seen in the comment that the oven was not always used as 'two half egg shells, one inside the other, lay on the floor in the eastern corner of the room where they had been dropped'. Room 3 was a cross passage or accommodated a stairway and Room 4 may have been a steward's room, indicating at least one domestic storey. At some point after *c.* AD 300 a corridor was built fronting the row house, with wings added at each end. The excavator considered them to be part of a holistic plan for the villa rather than later attachments. In the fourth century a mosaic was placed in the front corridor at the entrance to the main structure and, probably at the same time, the eastern wing was provided with a hypocaust. The next stage of the villa saw the construction of a rear corridor (Rooms 8–10) with an iron-bound chest (a strong box?) being found in Room 11. About AD 360m a bath suite was added to the east side of the house. In front of the house was a courtyard, built towards the end of the third century, with formal gardens as well as a kitchen garden. It seems that the villa began to decline at some time, although there are traces of fifth-century occupation, and before the beginning of the seventh century it was abandoned.

Woodchester

The villa at Woodchester lies just below the Cotswold Edge in a valley of a tributary stream of the Severn, in a very similar position to the Great Witcombe house. Similarly, there is good access to both the river and the Cotswold plateau. While Cirencester is 18km (11 miles) to the east, Gloucester is a similar distance to the north. In terms of pottery supply, it is Glevum that would seem to be the main source, although whether this represents any other relationship is not apparent. The villa was extensively cleared by the Rev. Samuel Lysons in the 1790s and his account is still the main source of our knowledge of the villa. He located 65 rooms arranged around three rectilinear courtyards on substantially the same axis, which may reflect the formality of Great Witcombe, though Woodchester is larger. What is unique about this villa is a room (possibly domed) 15m (50ft) square, the largest known in Britain, which contains the 'Great Pavement' featuring Orpheus as the roundel in the centre. The mosaic lies under a former churchyard and has been uncovered three times since 1945; an exact scale replica has been made by local craftsmen. Part of the problem with Lysons' work is that he did not recognise the stratigraphy of the structure and so the dating of its development is obscure, but he thought it all of one build. Giles Clarke, undertaking a keyhole excavation in 1973, suggested a hypothetical scheme for the growth of the structure with a range of rooms, not dissimilar to a row villa in AD 79–117, followed by the centre and outer courts in the late second to early third centuries and finally the inner courtyard in the first half of the fourth century. Limited finds and mosaics might indicate that there was a structure on the site at the end of the first century, and Clarke has related this to the late Iron Age site at Rodborough Common.

There can be no doubt that some parts of the building were sumptuously decorated with marble sheathing, wall plaster and statues, and this has led to discussions of its function and ownership. It has been considered by some that there were no agricultural or

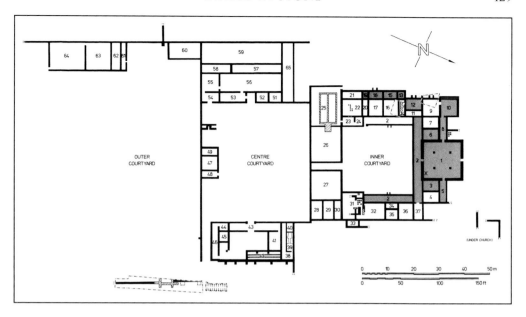

70 Plan of Woodchester Villa with Room 1 being the site of the 'Great Pavement'. (Britannia, *Vol. 116, p. 196*)

industrial components to the villa, although in the light of such limited excavation this
might be presumptuous. This has led to the assumption that Woodchester Villa might have
been the home of a high-status political figure. Giles points out that in his dating scheme
the 'Orpheus range' would have been completed before Cirencester became the important
capital of the province of Britannia Prima. Even if his dating is correct, there is still the
possibility of a relationship to Gloucester and the *colonia* which may not have come into
Cirencester's orbit (and is also a candidate for the capital of the province). Whether the villa
had gone through three structural changes or had been conceived as a single entity, there is
no reason why it might not have been the centre of a single estate, with perhaps Frocester
and other local villas in its boundaries. Kingscote may well have been part of the estate,
considering the incidence of pottery from Gloucester. This rich and exceptional residence
within the cultural influence of Glevum indicates strongly that it was owned by someone of
high standing from another part of the empire rather than a local magnate.

Kingscote

The possibility of a wider ownership of villas than just the elites of the Dobunni is presented at Kingscote, where fieldwalking, aerial photography, geophysics and excavation have
all been brought to bear on this large, enigmatic and particularly windswept site of *c.* 30ha
(75 acres) just east of the Cotswold Edge. The Kingscote settlement consisted of a possible
75 buildings, whose layout appears to have been planned on a north-east to south-west and
north-west to south-east axis, though there is no sign of a grid. Two tracks or roads have
been seen running through the settlement, one seemingly connecting to a route obliquely

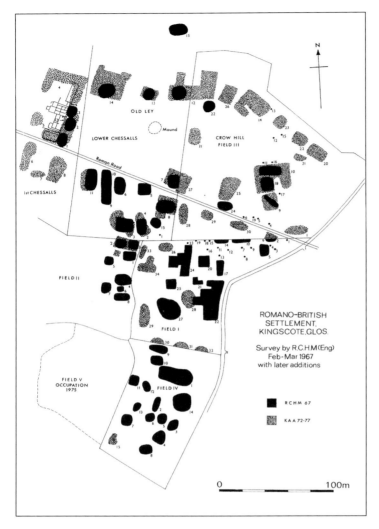

OLD LEY

LOWER CHESSALLS

Mound

CROW HILL
FIELD III

Roman Road

1st CHESSALLS

FIELD II

FIELD I

ROMANO–BRITISH
SETTLEMENT,
KINGSCOTE,GLOS.

Survey by R.C.H.M.(Eng)
Feb-Mar 1967
with later additions

FIELD V
OCCUPATION
1975

FIELD IV

RCHM 67

KAA 72-77

0   100m

71 The villa centre at
Kingscote with the
excavated building in the
Chessal's field. (*Kingscote
Archaeological Association and
RCHM*)

down the Cotswold Edge to Frocester and the Sea Mills–Gloucester road and another, or
branch from the first, heading for the Fosse Way.

There was continuous occupation between the first and fourth centuries, probably at its
most extensive in the fourth century, and at the centre of the settlement is a large central
building in Field III, with the appearance of a courtyard villa which has produced no evidence for any administrative or official role. There is also evidence of three multi-roomed
structures, possibly also villas, at the south end of Field IV. Other structures appear to have
been comfortable, if modest, and suggest accommodation for workers. The evidence col-
lected indicates the main function of Roman Kingscote to have been agricultural, with at
least two barns, a number of corn driers and querns and agricultural tools being common
finds through fieldwalking. The evidence of cattle bones and butchery give little indication
of whether the people were producers or consumers of meat. Metalworking, smithing not
smelting, appears to have been extensive but no more than to satisfy a local population for

72 The steelyard weight
from the excavated building
at Kingscote. (*Cotswold
Archaeological Trust*)

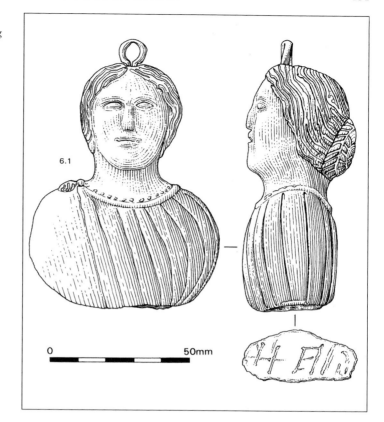

73 The cube seal from
the excavated building
at Kingscote. (*Cotswold
Archaeological Trust*)

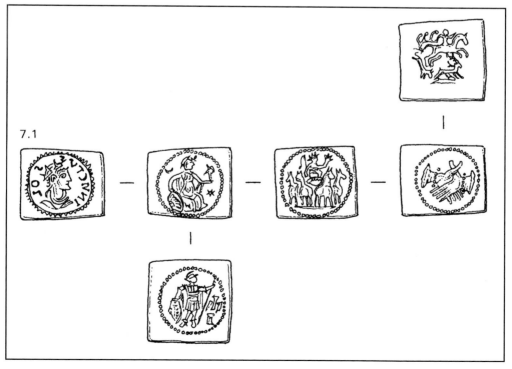

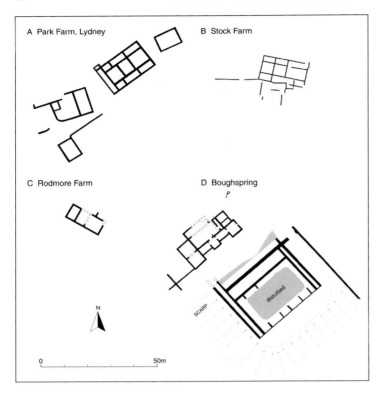

74 Villa building plans from the Forest of Dean. A: Park Farm, Lydney after M. Fitchett; B: Stock Farm, Clearwell after H.D. Atkinson and J. Blake; C: Rodmore Farm, St Briavels after J. Blake; Boughspring, Tidenham after D.S. Neal and B. Walker. (*Cotswold Archaeology*)

everyday life. The settlement itself seems to be self-sufficient with no significant evidence of imports from the local area other than corn. Kingscote might have had an official role in tax collection, and the presence of large millstones could be the result of the lack of substantial villas in the surrounding area to undertake this process. There is no evidence for a substantial temple building or any other public structures, though a stone relief of Fortuna, a head of Mercury and a representation of a mounted Mars would indicate a shrine being present somewhere in the vicinity or within it.

The single excavation produced evidence of craft specialism in the form of, what appears to have been, workshops with ovens, and perhaps some connection with furniture making. In the same building a particularly fine wall painting and a mosaic of Venus over a hypocaust were found in a small room, which appear to have been dated to the late third to fourth centuries. There were spectacular finds indicating an administrative function for the Kingscote settlement, such as the steelyard weight with what appears to be a draped bust of a young woman, possibly Emperor Constantine's wife, Faustina. The use of the portrait of a member of the emperor's family might indicate official sanction for the transactions being undertaken. Another unique object was a cube seal of copper alloy, possibly of the second half of the third century. The faces of the cube had incised portraits of Roma, Sol (the sun god), Mars, a side with two hands being clasped which may indicate an emperor in accordance with his army, and a hunting scene. It has been suggested that it acted as a seal for official letters but the reason for so many portraits is unknown. Otherwise the finds would not seem out of place in any rural or urban settlement.

There are a number of dispersed farmsteads within a radius of 6km around the Kingscote settlement, but only one villa. This could suggest that the community was the centre of an estate with a large courtyard villa and at least three well-built satellite structures within it servicing the surrounding area. The settlement was certainly well connected by road to the Fosse Way and also Gloucester, and this might indicate a wider role, possibly an administrative one. Its closeness to the magnificent villa at Woodchester and also to Frocester suggest the owner of such an estate as being of high status, possibly of provincial or even imperial standing.

Forest of Dean

The best-known sites are the villas situated on the more productive soils of the mudstone, sandstones and River Severn terrace deposits. At Boughspring, Tidenham, a potentially luxurious villa was discovered which was divided into six or seven rooms, one of which may have been a bath house. The site was interpreted as a second-century structure which was extended and eventually abandoned in the late fourth or early fifth century. Finds from the site have included pottery, tesserae, floor tiles and wall plaster. Near Park Farm, Aylburton, a possible corridor villa with a mosaic pavement was excavated in 1955. Finally, at Woolaston Grange, the site of a tripartite corridor Roman villa with wings was revealed by excavation in 1988. As far as can be ascertained, these villas were involved in seasonal ironworking, but also seemed to have mixed farming regimes. The evidence for a hypocaust and bath building at Blakeney is dated to the first and second centuries, but at this early date any structure is more likely to have been a *mansio* on the road between Gloucester and Caerleon. Other sites have been identified from scatters of pottery but cannot be given any specific function.

TEN

EARTHWORKS: AGRICULTURE AND INDUSTRY

Agriculture

The agricultural organisation of landscape at the large scale is probably now better known than the small scale of individual sites. Most villas have produced evidence of small-scale iron smithing, such as craftsmen's tools (knives, pruning hooks, chisels, spades and hoes) as well as horse snaffles, horseshoes and ox-goads and, in the case of Barnsley Roman villa, two scythes and large shears for sheep shearing. A new development in the Roman period was the use of watermills for crop processing, as well as for raising water for the land, such as at Weston-under-Penyard and Great Lemhill near Lechlade. The very basic excavation techniques of the time when most villas were explored has meant that there is little information in the form of seeds or pollen to give us indications of the farming regime in the period and how it changed. Frocester Villa is our main source of information and, having been excavated by a farmer, Eddie Price, we have an incisive account of the evidence. Pollen evidence was retrieved from wells demonstrating a wide variety of native species of trees: field maple, birch, box, hazel, hawthorn, ash, ivy, poplar/willow, blackthorn, apple/pear, oak, bramble, elder and elm. Curiously, there was little trace of beech, which is the most common tree on the slopes of the Cotswold escarpment. The cereal evidence shows a change from the emmer and spelt wheats grown at the end of the first century AD to the introduction of bread wheats and rye and oats between then and the end of the Roman period. Besides the chaff from the plants, the change in cultivation practices is also indicated by the weeds such as corncockle, stinking mayweed and cornflower that were not present when the traditional late Iron Age crops were being grown. The only plants of undoubted economic value were coriander, walnut and plum (all Roman introductions) and hazel. The bone assemblage indicates the change of species through the period. The Roman period appears to have little effect on the relative numbers of cattle and sheep, the latter rising sharply at first, but declining again in the fourth century. Pig numbers remained fairly constant, and there were always a small number of goats present, but many might have been taken on the hoof to Uley Temple, which was close by for sacrificial uses. Horse numbers dropped with the Roman arrival but then recovered and increased steadily. Unsurprisingly, dogs were always present, but very few cats. Wild animals formed little of the diet at Frocester, although both deer and wild boar were present in small numbers.

A similar picture comes from the Thames Valley where at Claydon Pike there may have been a small horticultural plot and garden area with evidence for trees and shrubs, including pear, damson, blackberry, rose and hazel. Celery and coriander were also grown in this area.

The Industrial Landscape around Corinium

Corinium is often seen as a 'consumer city', its development not based on economic factors but on social and political power, which was apparent from the outset and reflected in its fine buildings. The difference between the two settlements was that Corinium was certainly a consumer city, but not a functional centre for commercial exchange or redistribution of goods, whereas Glevum had a more pragmatic industrial base, the differences probably stemming from the communications advantage of a navigable river. It should not forgotten that Corinium was blessed with being at the node of an important road system, especially with its connections with the south-east and London. Perhaps the most important influence on both towns was the availability of raw materials. Storage facilities at Roman Claydon Pike and a series of villas at that point indicate that the Thames could have been used by medium-sized vessels as far up as Lechlade. Transport of corn downstream and the moving of pottery up from the Oxford area also supports this limited navigability. The tributaries, such as the Leach, could easily have been used for transporting stone to build the floodplain villas and possibly also be part of the transport system for the limestone to build the *civitas* capital. Where the timber came from to construct the early buildings of Corinium is difficult to know as the aerial photographic cover of the Upper Thames Valley does not indicate a great deal of woodland and the Cotswolds must be the firm candidate for the supply of wood for building.

Building Materials

Aerial photographs do indicate quarries for construction uses (the Corinium amphitheatre was placed in one) and there are extractive pits, probably for lime for burning and using on the land. The Upper Thames (and indeed Lower Severn) floodplains would also have supplied the gravels for building many types of structure. A major extractive industry was brick making at Minety in Wiltshire, where extensive clay deposits occur near the surface of the flat farmland. There was probably total of up to 10 kilns and associated buildings producing roofing tile, pilae for supporting floors above hypocaust systems, sub-floor and flue tiles. Today large mounds are covered with Roman brick and tile fragments, some wasters, and fieldwalking has identified probable ancillary buildings for the preparation of the clay products. What is unusual about the products from the Minety establishment is that the tiles are stamped with a selection of letters of unknown origin: TPFA, TPF, TPFL, LLH, ARVERI, and this practice is unique in Britain. It may well be that the stamping of tiles was copied from Gloucester, but since it was a common practice abroad it may reflect a group of immigrant workers bringing with them their traditional methods. Of the whole process, from the clay being dug and allowed to weather and prepared until the storing, it is only the making and firing that might need expert skill and it is most likely that these two processes took place in the summer. We might well be seeing tile-making as part of the agricultural year. This raises a further question of whether tile makers were itinerant throughout the region or based at specific spots and whether the tiles were transported by road or river even over 40km (25 miles) or 50km (31 miles), much as stone was from the Forest of Dean

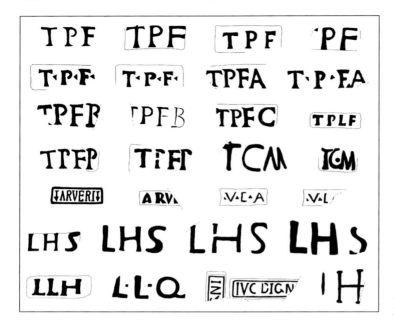

75 Tile stamps from Minety. (*Britannia, Vol. 9, p. 357*)

to Corinium. No doubt much of the Minety output ended up on the roofs of Corinium, *c.*10km (6 miles) distant. TPF tiles seemed to have used Ermine Street as a route for transport, with examples found at Wanborough, Cirencester and Hucclecote, as well as the Fosse Way to Easton Grey and Rodmarton. LHS tiles have been found as far away as Silchester and Old Sarum near Salisbury. VLA tiles appear to be centred on the Cotswolds and may indicate a small villa estate exploiting clay from its Thames Valley lands.

Mosaics, Sculpture and Furniture Making

Mosaics are a very powerful way of demonstrating status through conspicuous consumption. The theme of a mosaic gives sometimes subtle, sometimes blatant, insights into the tastes and aspirations of the commissioning owner of the property. The less subtle equation of time to constructing mosaics = cost = status, indicates that the larger the pavement, the more construction time, the richer or more important the patron. The Cotswolds especially are renowned for the number and range of mosaics to be found in the countryside villas and the *civitas* capital; Corinium may have had 88 in McWhirr's count and many isolated fragments have been seen since then. Considering how little of the area of Corinium has been excavated this must be only a small proportion of the total. Similarly, the villas have an astonishing array of mosaic pavements and those on view Chedworth, with its fragments of 12 individual floors, is especially sumptuous. At Woodchester, at least 20 rooms in the palatial establishment had mosaics, even if some were plain, but the magnificent Orpheus pavement needed 1.6 million tesserae (small tiles).

Mosiacs have long been attributed as being made by various 'schools' which are assumed to have been urban-based *officinae* (workshops), even though no workshop ever belonging to a school has been discovered archaeologically (whereas evidence of the preparation of tesserae on site sometimes has). So, all locations are speculative as there is no evidence of permanent *officinae* in any British town, including Corinium, which is often seen as the base of two schools – the Corinium Orpheus and Corinium Saltire – with names based on the recurring motifs in mosaics designs. There are remarkable similarities in motifs, composition, style and themes, in the huge numbers of mosaics found in Britannia, but there is also much overlapping. It would appear that interchange took place between individual mosaicists and this casts doubt on the existence of a close-knit association of craftsmen. It is likely that some links in design and subject matter suggest at least the movement of pattern books, if not actual craftsmen as well. The organisation of mosaicists in Britain is very uncertain – they may have been totally itinerant, having temporary rather than permanent bases depending on the circumstances, perhaps spending a season at one villa before moving on to work at another, presumably through patrons' recommendation. There may have been a complex linkage of workshops with branch workshops, independent imitators and jobbing craftsmen. Specialists from elsewhere may have been brought in to do a figured mosaic, lesser specialists to complete plain pavements or even simple geometric ones with symmetry, mechanical repeated patterns and simple proportions. These lesser specialists may well have used the knowledge gained while watching more complex pavements being laid to become masters somewhere else.

Even if mosaics were prefabricated, there is no reason why this should not have happened away from the site. A table alongside the pavement being constructed would have been adequate, and often loose tesserae found at sites might indicate this part of the process. Even at sites such as Chedworth Roman Villa, with the remarkable range of design and size, the use of local materials usually gave a range of colours: blue/black, red, white and yellow. The palette of four or five colours were from natural stones found in the vicinity, apart from terracotta red, where ceramic tiles had been cut up and reused.

The oolitic limestone of the Cotswolds is soft and allows deep grooves to be cut with relative ease, enabling detail of hair and clothes to be shown in luxurious detail. Other more expensive materials, such as marble, as well as completed statuary, would have been imported, but there can be no doubt that a thriving local industry, with sculptors of varying abilities, provided the towns and villas with decorative, religious and civic carvings. There must be a variety of industries and crafts that were important to furnishing houses in Corinium (and Glevum) that we can get sight of through surviving artefacts, but which we are unable to place in the landscape. Presumably there were craftsmen's shops producing materials in wood, and perhaps furniture in stone of which there is evidence from Kingscote. It is likely that the monumental buildings of the forum and basilicas were constructed by itinerant masons and sculptors, and perhaps this explains the lateness of the Corinium's civic buildings in that the craftsmen were in great demand elsewhere. Where were the soft furnishings made or the clothes? Each of these activities would have been vital to developing a sense of *romanitas*, would leave little evidence behind and often that is so small a part of the decayed whole that it can't be identified.

The Severn Estuary, Trade and Industry

Today the River Severn has an extreme tidal range – the second highest rise and fall in the world, with rocks just below the surface at high tide as well as unstable, moving sand shoals. Small craft with oars and sails have particular difficulties with the channel becoming deep and stable only after the great bends at Arlingham, 10km below Gloucestershire, where there was probably a ferry in Roman times. There may have been no change in the river's configurations since the Roman period; however, the channel may have been deeper and more stable further down river than is the case today and the estuary may have migrated upstream. Near Oldbury and Hills Flats settlement was clearly some distance in front of the modern seawalls and this is can be seen in the reworked and worn pottery deposits found on the rocky ledges.

Such a major tidal estuary made a prime location for transhipment ports and the unloading of larger sea-worthy vessels, while some materials would have been transferred to smaller craft. At Gloucester, two periods of river frontage 100m apart have been found with evidence for a possible major bridge across the Severn. The quay in the second/third century was in the form of a wall *c*. 1.4m (4.5ft) wide retaining redeposited soil to its east, with water-laid silts to the west. The evidence of clays beneath the redeposited soil showed that this land had been reclaimed and that the previous river front had been further east, near the fortress defences. A timber-planked landing area about 100m to the east was thought to have been the first-century quay. Small ports were specialised sites with trade as a major function, which would have formed a distinctive element in the settlement pattern – dominated by the infrastructure of moving and storing goods such as quays and warehouses with relatively little domestic occupation or other activities. The position of Oldbury beside a major tidal channel of the River Severn gave it access to both estuary traffic and small boat movements inland. A great range of metal waste and scrap seems to be in situ metalworking with lead, tin, bronze and brass demonstrating imported ores and likely cross-river trade. That it was only a transhipment port is evidenced by the poor status of the settlement with a very small number of non-ceramic artefacts and a dearth of fine wares. Also of importance may have been the transport of agricultural produce down the river to places like Oldbury from the villas at Deerhurst or from the postulated small town of Tewkesbury. Moving pottery by land is a difficult process, being heavy and fragile, as well as being shaped in curves that do not fit together easily, resulting in many breakages; however, transport by water is much easier for bulk quantities and results in fewer damages. It is worth noting that in the second and third centuries, Severn Valley Ware pottery was used on the west end of the Antonine Wall in Scotland, the pottery being transported by sea through army contracts. It is not just the River Severn that would have been an important route, as the Wye was important locally. Villas at Hadrock and Huntsham and a settlement at Clearwell were close to the Wye and evidence of iron making has been found at each. Larger settlements including Monmouth (Blestium), Whitchurch and Weston-under-Penyard were only 2–3km from the river and 4–5km from the source of the iron ores.

Iron Mining

The Forest of Dean has been seen as the pre-eminent producer of iron in Roman Britain. Accessing and extracting the ores was done either from cutting down through the ground surface or mining into the underground cave-like features in which the ore had been deposited. Unfortunately, there is little secure dating for these extraction sites, locally known as 'scowles', simply because any site of Roman date might have been subsequently used or even filled with modern rubbish. Except for iron mines at the Lydney Roman temple sites, which were capped by third-century floors, no dateable structures sealing these types of features have been found. One of the problems of not being able to date iron extraction or iron-processing sites accurately is that it becomes difficult to see whether there was any pattern behind the growth or shrinkage of the industry and then to attempt to relate this to either its organisation or the demands for the product or both as they would be likely to be inter-dependent.

There are also the questions of the organisation of mining in Dean – were mineral-rich areas the property of the state, as iron was not only an important strategic commodity but also economically valuable in itself, or was mining undertaken by groups who were 'licensed' or given concessions and in turn taxed by the state? What evidence there is does not suggest a centralisation of the industry under military control in the first century, although the growth in the number of smelting sites at particular times might have been related to the need for iron by the army in its campaigns in Wales and further afield on Hadrian's Wall. There must also have been a rising demand from the *colonia*, as seen in the tip lines of charcoal-saturated loam layers with lenses of iron hammer scale and iron slag used to level up areas for new buildings. The *civitas* capital at Corinium and the need for agricultural equipment in the developing Severn and Thames valleys must also have been important. Two sites demonstrate both small- and large-scale iron processing at Chesters Villa and Weston-under-Penyard.

The Chesters Villa, Woolaston

It is important to remember that the definition of a villa as a rural building does not necessarily mean that it was solely concerned with agriculture and that its wealth may have come either partially or wholly from other sources. Chesters was the middle villa of those close to the right bank of the estuary; 3.5km (2 miles) to the north was the Park Farm Villa at Lydney, while 4km (2.4 miles) south was Boughspring Villa, Tidenham. All three had evidence associated with iron making. The three estates divided the landscape westwards from the Severn and to the high ground of the Forest and the Wye. A series of excavations at Chesters were sparked by iron-making residues in plough soil and increased magnetic susceptibility which resulted in the recovery of two furnace sites associated with numerous types of slag. The site revealed evidence for each of the stages of the process of producing iron. The primary smithing was when ore was smelted into blooms, a porous mixture of slag and iron, and then shaped into billets, usually rectangular bars of iron for ease of transport. The secondary smithing into tools and other finished items would take place elsewhere.

The excavation revealed a large mid-third-century area of industrial activity covering *c.* 7250 sq. metres (8671 sq. yards). A timber-framed building consisted of two parallel rows of padstones with two large mounds of red clay which were the remnants of successive pairs of iron-making furnaces. Associated with the furnaces were pits for water as well as ore-crushing units. The excavators suggested that the iron making was 'seasonally inter-leaved' with elements of the agricultural cycle. Wood, mainly from hazel and oak, coppiced small bore up to 30mm (0.9 feet); roundwood, on a five- to seven-year rotation, was cut in the autumn or winter before being dried and burned for charcoal. If the same workforce was engaged in farming, woodland management and iron making, the most likely time for smelting would be between spring sowing and the late summer harvest. While charcoal and clay for the furnaces could be accessed from the villa's own estate, iron ore and coppiced timber might also be brought from other riverside and wetland locations along the estuary or needed to be brought in from elsewhere, and the river was paramount in transporting the ore in and the billets out. It is reasonably certain that iron making formed only part of the villa's economy and that it was not founded nor did it prosper simply because of iron. Forestry was also probably important, as was the quarrying of stone above the villa and the provision of clay for the construction of the furnaces. The presence of a leat to power a watermill at Chesters indicates that more corn than the villa estate needed for subsistence was being produced and exported.

Both Weston-under-Penyard and Monmouth have produced considerable evidence for Roman ironworking. At the former slag has been recovered from a wide area of the first to early second-century settlement. This appears to have been focused around the settlement core and to its immediate west. Some activity may have continued at the Great Woulding site to the north, but this seems to have been abandoned by the early part of the second century, perhaps reflecting nucleation of settlement and industrial activity at the main site. During the early part of the second century, a new ironworking area was established to the north of the domestic core, possibly reflecting a reorganisation which saw production concentrated in a defined zone of the settlement. This industrial area zone remained in use until about the middle of the third century AD, when the area appears to have been given over to the disposal of domestic rubbish. Abandonment might reflect further reorganisa-tion or result from some other factor affecting production, such as the drying up of a water supply, competition from elsewhere or simply that the area had become too unpleasant and cluttered with slag waste for the industry to continue effectively. However, ironworking remained an important activity, with a new industrial area created to the south-west towards the end of the second century, which continued in use through the third and into the fourth century. There have been indications of smelting at Rodmore Farm near St Briavels, where excavations by the Dean Archaeological Group since 1993 have revealed a rectangu-lar stone-built structure of 17m (55ft) long by 6.4m (21ft) wide with flagged and cobbled floors. Nearby was an enclosure with at least one iron-smelting shaft furnace and associated waste pits and dumps of charcoal.

Sites outside the Forest of Dean

One of the characteristics of the Forest of Dean ore production is that the smelting of the ore to make blooms often took place at a distance rather than locally. Cross-river trade is indicated by smelting residues found along the east bank of the Severn at Oldbury and Hills Flats, as well as Elmore, and there would also appear to have been iron making up to the Cotswold scarp, as evidence from Quedgeley, Alvestone, Falfield, Frocester and Cromhall villas suggests. There is further evidence for iron production along at least 100km (62 miles) of the Severn Estuary, with a widespread dispersal of sites from Hills Flats to Worcester where considerable evidence has been retrieved for smelting in terms of huge quantities of slag; this may demonstrate the importance of the river and the richness of the Forest of Dean iron outcrops. While it is abundantly clear that the rivers Severn and Wye could have played a significant role in the locality, the excavators pointed out that the manufacture of iron is a 'resource-oriented' industry which involves a considerable weight loss as opposed to a 'market-oriented' industry where processing produces a weight gain. To have trans-ported iron ore, and possibly charcoal, 40km upstream from the Forest of Dean to Worcester, in order to redistribute it as blooms, would have been entirely uneconomic. A much more plausible solution would have been to smelt ore at its source and then to transport the lighter, but more valuable, finished blooms to their particular markets. Even if the richness of the forest ores might have balanced the distance disadvantage, there is still the problem of transporting charcoal, which would have rapidly disintegrated when conveyed over any great distance, hence it would be easier to bring the ore to the charcoal source. If we are considering a local industry smelting ore as part of a repertoire of activities, then perhaps this problem is less of an impediment. However, it would still imply the presence of consid-erable woodland in the landscape.

Bricks, Tiles and Pottery

Making tiles and bricks by exploiting river clays appears to be the only industry found around both Corinium and Glevum, although both had very different distributions. Excavations at St Oswald's Priory in 1975–76 identified a municipal tilery, probably the principal, if not the sole manufacturing site, exploiting the river clays of the Severn. Bricks, *tegulae* (flat roofing tiles), *imbrex* (half round tiles for fitting over the gap between the *tegulae*) and box tiles for hypocaust systems were produced somewhere in this area evidenced by the kiln wastes found and may have been situated between the first-century quay and the third-century river frontage. The tilery's production was stamped by the letters RPG (*res Publica Glevensis/ium*), presumably 'the Commonwealth of the Glevensians'. The tiles were produced to supply the developing *colonia*, beginning in the late first century and continu-ing through the second, with production ceasing in the third century, and the magistrates' names of the specific period of manufacture are also included but are usually undecipher-able. The distribution of tiles from Glevum was very local and largely confined to the urban area, though some appear at Frocester, 15km (9.3 miles) away, as well as at Kenchester, in Herefordshire and 60km (37.5 miles) distant. It is unlikely that these isolated cases are telling

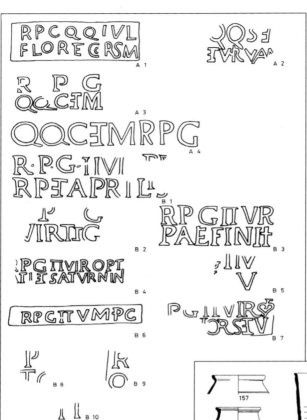

76 Tile stamps from Gloucester. (Britannia, *Vol. 13, p. 66*)

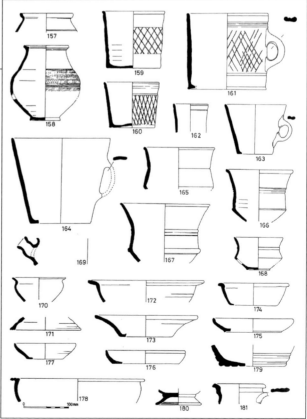

77 Severn Valley Ware from Frocester Villa. (*E. Price*)

us anything political about the *territorium*, but just reflecting the sale of the products of the municipal tile manufacturer.

In the Kingsholm or Gloucester fortresses, pottery kilns had been set up to serve the needs of the military presence in the area. The styles of the vessels produced indicate Continental origins, suggesting that the potters were military personnel, either itinerant or immigrant. The Gloucester kilns found in Brunswick Road, Berkeley Street and near Kingsholm continued in production after the establishment of the *colonia* in *c.* AD 80 to serve the civilian market inside the fortress. The range of fabrics from these kilns was indistinguishable from each other, but distinctly different from the Severn Valley Ware discussed next in terms of forms and fabrics. The forms at Kingsholm were open lamps, face urns, collared flagons, jars and bowls. In the *colonia* the repertoire was similar, producing a very specific vessel related to Roman culinary habits – storage, preparation, cooking, serving, eating and drinking and showing distinctive cultural differences, with individual military units controlling supplies, vessel shape and assemblage.

The major pottery industry in the Gloucestershire region was that producing Severn Valley Ware. This wheel-turned style of pottery appears to originate in the late Iron Age and used traditional profiles of vessels from elsewhere, particularly the Malverns and the Savernake area of Wiltshire. Severn Valley Ware had a distinctive orange fabric, although there are also less common, light grey-coloured vessels and it was used to make its typical range of forms such as jars, tankards and bowls. The earliest kilns were probably located in the Lower Severn Valley, but from late in the first century AD the small, relatively dispersed, localised industry expanded into the Middle Severn Valley to become the major provider in the West of England. The industry flourished between the second and third centuries and continued into the fourth century.

Although the 'industry' stretched from the mid-Severn Shropshire area to Somerset on the estuary, only two kilns have been recognised in the Gloucestershire area, those at Alkington and Malvern. The high incidence of up to 70 per cent of this type of pottery on sites in the central Gloucestershire area indicates that many more kilns existed but their sites are masked by the alluvium they used. During work on the M5 motorway a kiln was discovered at Alkington. It was much damaged by later ridge and furrow but survived to four courses deep of limestone and sandstone. Its furnace chamber was small, *c.* 120cm (3.9ft) long and cut 20cm (0.7ft) into the surface of Keuper Marl, and had a roughly circular stoke pit which indicated a typical up-draft walled kiln rather than domed. It was active in late first century to early second and packed with wasters after the end of use and then abandoned. Two whetstones and a sandstone 'rubbing or hammer' stone might have been connected with shaping the kiln products. There was a pond nearby and some possible postholes, perhaps of a structure associated with the pottery manufacturing process.

Outside the county, but probably supplying the northern parts of it, was the kiln at Malvern Link which gives insights into what was necessary on a production site dated from the first to early second century until the mid-late third and into fourth centuries. Similar to the Alkington kiln, it was sited on soils which were always marginal and unsuitable for cereals or arable farming, and so could be used for smoky pottery manufacture away from agricultural settlements. Potters may have used a number of different nearby sources of clay and this may be reflected in their individual preferred fabric types. Water was available from

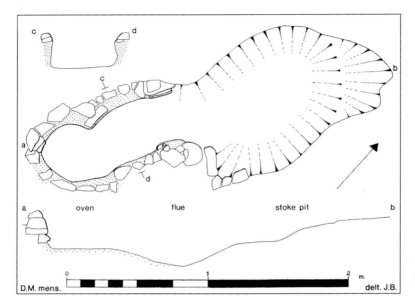

oven   flue   stoke pit

D.M. mens.   delt. J.B.

78 The Alkington pottery kiln. (BGAS, *Vol. 92, p. 21*)

a well and two streams, and wood or coal may have come from a variety of sources. The stone surfaces were possibly areas for preparing the clay – drying it out and mixing – and a series of ditches might have been used for mixing the clay with water and allowing coarser material to settle out. A piece of local stone may possibly have been used for polishing or burnishing the drying vessels. There would also have needed to be buildings close by for throwing, drying and storing the pots. It is likely that these were seasonal potteries as water-logged soils would have restricted the period of production. The single-chambered updraft kiln found produced an everyday range of forms, 60 per cent of which were jars, followed by tankards and bowls – most probably containers for food or liquids – and open-mouthed flagons more suitable for milk than wine. The output, therefore, represented food prepara-tion (medium to large bowls), serving vessels (tankards) and a small number of table-wares. Such a utilitarian assemblage indicates a relatively stable market with established forms. At both of these kiln sites there is an absence Severn Valley Ware *mortaria*, the heavy, grit-lined mixing bowl, but this need not indicate that they weren't being used in the region. There may well have been two sets of producers, those making very basic everyday wares for a market that was not adopting Roman styles of eating and drinking, and those who concentrated on items such as *mortaria* and other forms that would have been imported from the Continent and represent a Roman lifestyle in terms of the preparation of food. What the excavations at Malvern do demonstrate is that handmade Malverian pottery was being fired in kilns nearby, contemporaneously with wheel-thrown Severn Valley Ware, and indeed some forms of Malverian Ware were copied in the Severn Valley tradition. This indi-cates that an indigenous tradition was still in place throughout the whole Roman period in the region.

ELEVEN

SACRED SPACES:
SHRINES, TEMPLES AND GRAVES

Rituals and Landscape

'Sacred space' usually comprises an area which is a boundary between this world and the supernatural. Sacred spaces have psychological barriers of borders and a range of regulations for movement around and within, often including some kind of approach performance and a set of ritual practices where music, sound and smell were important. Discovering the location of cult practices in natural settings, such as rivers and bogs, is difficult as they leave no physical trace. Even when structures are present it is often difficult to differentiate them from domestic buildings, particularly as in the late Iron Age lines between the secular and spiritual were often very blurred. However, archaeological evidence in the form visual architecture, the shape of the structure, symbols like statues or painting on the walls and artefacts can help to identify specific activities related to a supernatural power. Roman documentary sources can be also be used and some 'traveller's tales' are informative, such as Julius Caesar's comments that the Gauls worshipped Mercury 'above all' as well as Apollo, Mars, Jupiter and Minerva. Caesar sees these deities through Roman preconceptions, but the similarities of the nature and function of gods and goddesses demonstrates similar needs to make sense of the world, which is a major characteristic of all religions

The Late Iron Age

Shrines are often associated with water being positioned near springs, lying at the confluence of streams and/or overlooking rivers. Within the NOGD were many late Iron Age ritual or religious enclosures known as *Viereckschanzen*, which were characterised by a generally square or sub-square outline, with a single entrance usually facing south or southeast. Most examples cover areas of less than 1ha (2.5 acres) and were constructed and used between the later first century BC and the first century AD (though some were remodelled in the Roman period), and were primarily for funerary and ritual purposes. The late Iron Age structure at Uley also demonstrates these characteristic features. The shrine was situated on a high plateau overlooking the River Severn and facing east in dense woodland which was cleared away in the first centuries AD. The shrine itself consisted of postholes and beam slots of timber buildings in association with a large, square, ditched enclosure, and a smaller trapezoidal timber structure. Votive pits were found with human and infant burials, iron

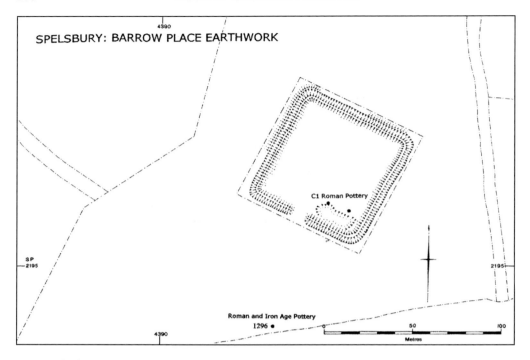

79 Viereckschanzen Barrow Piece within the NOGD. (*Richard Massey*)

projectile heads, coins and partly complete 'Dobunnic' fine-ware vessels. Miniature martial objects such as bronze shields or weapons form significant parts of the assemblage and many of these appear to have been deliberately broken prior to deposition in pits or dumps. The ritual use of animals is well attested at nearly all the sites, implying that this was a regular method of religious appropriation. The high number of bones related to goats in the Roman period, and which would not be found in a domestic context, leads to the proposition that the late Iron Age temple may have been dedicated to a horned god, which then led to the later interpretation of the deity as a native equivalent to Mercury. What was unusual about the Uley square enclosure was that it seemed to have been constructed around a pit which may have contained a standing stone, timber post or living tree and therefore the structure might have been open rather than roofed. A Neolithic/Bronze Age long barrow at Hetty Pegler's Tump is close by and the presence of a standing stone in the shrine might indicate a considerable depth of continuity of ritual. This central feature was to remain important throughout the life of the Roman temple. There was also some evidence that the ditches of the substantial palisade of the late Iron Age shrine were aligned with those of a previous prehistoric structure.

The Late Iron Age/Roman Transition

Ann Woodward, the excavator of Uley, sees continuity from the late Iron Age to Roman period at a sacred space as an attempt by the 'conqueror' to absorb and adapt the religious beliefs and practices of totally defeated tribes, and through this policy of wholesale adoption of Celtic sanctuaries an eradication of their practices was attempted. However, the Romans were perfectly prepared to accept different paths to the sacred, except where deities were threatening to the state and considered seditious because monotheistic religions such as Christianity or Judaism denied the 'living god' status of the emperor. If the empire did not expect the Britons to abandon their gods why were Roman deities adopted by the leaders of the indigenous populations? Was it because the Roman gods made more sense of both the 'old' world as well as the 'new' world of the empire, or did the indigenous elites think that because southern Britain had been occupied so successfully the Roman gods were more powerful than their own? Rather than there being just a veneer of Roman deities over the 'Celtic', the quality of the statues and the incidence of Roman dedications at the *civitas* capital of Corinium suggests the opposite. The earliness of stone statuary and bronze representations of gods became increasingly common in the early Roman period, with deities being represented visually, especially on altars. This indicates that the people of the late Iron Age did see their deities in human form and had no difficulty in accepting Roman stone representations.

One of the ways that *romanitas* might have been demonstrated was through a change in religious expression rather than in a substantial change in religious belief. This modification in religious manifestation resulted in the construction of temples with Roman architectural styles, though echoing late Iron Age floorplans. By building these Romano-Celtic temples, such as at Uley, the British peoples could be seen as expressing themselves in Roman form, but without imitating Greco-Roman styles. Romano-Celtic types of temple have a number of differentiated zones all contained in a *temelos* enclosure which often had a palisade or wall. At the centre of worship was the inner *cella* which formed the most sacred point in the complex and usually contained the cult statue of a god or goddess. There was usually a clearly defined sequence, a 'sacred ballet' of entry points from an ambulatory forming a covered walk around the sacred structure.

Roman Urban Temples

The elite, who were adopting Roman manners, importing Roman goods to underline their wealth and who were constructing grid-squared towns such as Corinium, no doubt also contributed to the expensively decorated temples with a well-carved cult statue required by *civitas* capital's charter. Members of the native aristocracy who took local office in Corinium would have had to oversee the annual religious calendar and might also have been required to appoint suitably dedicated priests of a specific cult, and overall there must have been spiritual advantages in adopting the imported deities. We know very little about the religious aspects of the *civitas* capital as no certain temple structures have been found, but ritual behaviours are known to exist from sculpture and inscriptions. Evidence of the deities worshipped at Corinium often comes in the form of incomplete figures, but the attributes of the individual god/goddess (such as appears in Christian statues of saints – St Peter and his keys, the Archangel Gabriel with his foot on the serpent) indicate the worship of Jupiter, Mercury and Rosmerta, Minerva, Ceres Fortuna

Above left: 80 Mercury & Rosmerta. (*Gloucester City Museum*)

Above right: 81 Lower Slaughter Cucullati with a possible protective Cotswold warrior god. (*Gloucester City Museum*)

Above left: 82 Matres from Cirencester Museum. (*Corinium Museum*)

Above right: 83 A bust of Attis from Gloucester. (*Gloucester City Museum*)

and Bacchus. At Silchester there is a temple *insula* and the religious structures in it are overwhelmingly of the Romano-Celtic type, but if Corinium was much bigger and with a more ambitious population it should be expected that a large temple with classical architecture would have been built.

In Cirencester, votive statues (perhaps for street shrines) comprising a *genius loci* dedicated to the spirit of the place and indigenous deities are represented by a number of examples of the hooded and mysterious threesome of the *Genii Cucallati*. The threeness, triplism or triadism had an exceptional symbolic significance in Celtic culture. Often a triplicate representation of a deity might refer to the three realms of his or her power and *Genii Cucallati* are often linked with healing and well-being functions, and appear in association with a mother goddess, a matre or a local warrior god. The Cotswold region is well known for these sculptures, the only other concentration being in the military Hadrian's Wall area. Domestic houses would have had daily worship of *die familiars*, the household deities. *Penates* were associated with protecting the food supply of family, embodying the means of subsistence for the household, and *Lares* were responsible for the safety of the family and respect for the ancestors of its inhabitants. Such daily rituals were associated with family meals in dining rooms, reception rooms or a room located at the centre of the building usually as permanent shrines, such as recesses in the wall.

The *colonia* at Glevum could have had a substantial religious influence on Corinium, being a settlement of ex-soldiers who brought Roman deities with them. We are not aware of specific religious structures at Glevum, although the presence of a huge temple complex has been proposed, which might be expected to have been dedicated to the living deity of the emperor. Few altars have been found but there are five to Mercury and Rosmerta and two representations of Attis, an eastern god, which should not be surprising considering the cosmopolitan make-up of the Roman army.

Villas and Ritual

By being patrons of both town and rural construction of temples the wealthy landowners were demonstrating that they were social, economic and political leaders of contrasting communities. This emphasis also underlined dominance over a clear hierarchical class structure, the building of rural temples using aspects of Roman architecture to highlight the pro-Roman aspirations and acquiescent attitudes to the Roman administration. The presence of shrines in a prominent position around villas gave an indication of the *romanitas* of the owners. At Spoonley Wood Villa there appears to have been a shrine centred on a large masonry foundation just north of the central entrance to the villa and was probably for both public and private rituals. Another likely shrine 800m to south was dedicated to Jupiter, represented by an eagle with folded wings in local stone. The eagle was connected with rituals of imperial cult and clearly the owner had cultural and social aspirations or was already part of the hierarchy. This might also be seen in the circa third- or fourth-century statue in Italian marble of Bacchus representing the guardian and guide for the deceased to the afterlife which was in a burial near villa. At Great Witcombe there is a doubtful temple in an octagonal room, but a possible *nymphaeum* might be located across the main corridor as three drains, carrying water from the springs in the hillside above, run from the building at this point. In Room 1, in the western wing of the complex, there may have been a sacred space in a cellar with stuccoed walls painted with different coloured panels and this might be an echo of an indigenous religion in Roman form. At Turkdean a cellar with painted wall plaster was also found in a building erected in a detached position from the main structure. The best-known private shrine is at Chedworth, where an apsidal building with 2m-high stone columns was erected to the north-west, over the spring that gathers near the villa, and was probably a *nymphaeum* dedicated to a water goddess. The residential buildings in the courtyard were skewed in the direction of the shrine, showing its possible earlier origin.

Temples and Shrines in the Countryside

Major Rural Temples
Lydney
The Lydney religious complex, possibly built in the late third century AD, was situated on the spur of a promontory hillfort overlooking the River Severn and the southern Cotswolds. The location of the Roman name 'NEMETOBALA'(?) in the Ravenna Cosmography might possibly be Lydney as the Latin term NEMETON often indicates a religious site. The layout of the temple compound was largely controlled by its location on the narrow promontory spur which was used as the *temenos* boundary. However, the existence of an iron mine, the date of which can't be easily ascertained, and a sinkhole into which part of the initial stone building collapsed, might well be important elements in the positioning of the temple. The temple seems to have thrived for at least 60 years or so, until the superstructure collapsed and much of it was rebuilt, probably around AD 370, this date being based on the evidence of a large number of coins.

The main external entrance to the site appears to have been the metalled rock-cut gully in the south-eastern corner, which led up into the precinct from the more gently sloping escarpment. Over 90 per cent of religious structures of this date in Britain face an easterly direction. The temple building seems to have been sited so as to give the maximum court-yard space in front, as this must have been where most of the public ritual would have taken place. The structure was placed on a raised podium with a flight of steps, which would have highlighted its crucial nature. The main cult statue was probably to be found in the central *cella*, as over 530 coins were found clustered in the area and so can be interpreted as the main focus for display and votive deposition. Another specific zone of deposition was the funnel built into the rear *cella* floor, which contained 21 coins and the famous bronze dog statuette. The fissured limestone underneath the temple would have allowed this funnel to have been used as a pipe for libations, liquid offerings, into the rock. Wheeler, the excavator in the late 1920s, suggested that sides were screened as special places for sacred sleep, but they well might have been subsidiary shrines designed to be viewed externally through openings in the wall.

To the north of the temple complex was a large long structure with a range of rooms, some of which had mosaics and were clearly accommodation for pilgrims, and they opened on to a veranda or corridor. There was also a bath house for public use and possibly for

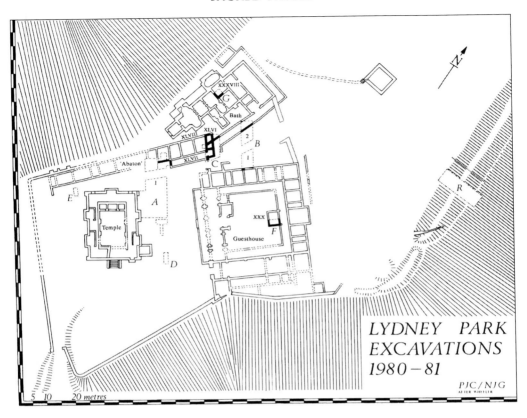

84 Lydney Park Temple. (Antiquaries Journal, *Vol. 79, p. 83*)

ritual cleansing before entry to the temple area or possibly for healing purposes. To the east
of the baths was a large aligned structure consisting of three wings around a central courtyard and a large hall on the fourth side. It is possible that this structure represents differential
wealth or the importance of pilgrims.

The type and quantity of the finds indicate some aspects of the ritual carried out on the
temple site. Coins formed the major part of the assemblage with hoards being found under
the ambulatory pavement and under the cement re-flooring of the bath house which may
indicate a ritual act. Hundreds of jewellery items were also recovered, with a particular
prominence of bracelets and pins – the latter often being associated in the Roman world
with childbirth. Further evidence for a healing aspect for the temple is the prevalence of
nine bronze and stone dog figurines whose saliva was thought to have anaesthetic qualities. Perhaps the iron-rich water of the area was an attraction because of the importance
of the mineral to a healthy body. A bronze model votive arm found on the site has fingers
showing signs of spoon-shaped nails – a condition associated with extreme iron deficiency.
Epigraphic evidence, in the form of inscribed plaques, lead curse tables known as *defixiones*
(to be discussed below) and mosaic pavement indicate that the temple was dedicated to
a conflation of the Roman god Mars and the native god Nodens – Mars Nodens. The
inscription on the *cella* floor confirms the dedication: 'For the god Mars Nodens Titus

Flavius Senilis, superintendent of the cult, from the offerings had this laid; Victorinus, the interpreter [of dreams?] gave his assistance'. Finally, confirmation of the wider role of holistic medicine is provided by the discovery of an oculists' stamp indicating the presence of a professional physician on site.

Uley

Across the River Severn and inter-visible with Lydney was a temple of very different purpose which grew out of the late Iron Age structure. The profile of coinage deposited at both sites is remarkably similar and this might indicate more than just a visual connection. Probably in the early second century AD the timber shrine was replaced, on exactly the same alignment, by a stone square structure similar to other known Romano-Celtic temples in Britain and in Continental Europe. The foundations were fragmentary, because they had been disturbed by modifications in later periods, then raised to ground level and subsequently damaged by several centuries of ploughing. However, it is possible that there were two major building phases, the first involving a slightly rectangular *cella* surrounded on three sides only by an ambulatory of even width. The main entrance was probably located on the north-east side. No original floor levels survived and the only internal features that could have been related to the temple, as it was primarily conceived, were the central pit, which may have contained a lead tank or other water container, and a mortar base centrally positioned in the south-west ambulatory. This base may have been the remnant of a foundation for a plinth intended to support the major cult statue. The finding of the head of Mercury, which appears to have been carefully buried after the collapse of the temple, may indicate a ritual that reflects the traditional respect for the head in Celtic religion and demonstrates continuity of worship from at least the late Iron Age if not much earlier.

The temple lay at the centre of a large settlement with evidence of stone buildings and industrial activity. These temple precinct buildings have parallels at a number of similar sites and presumably there would have been temporary booths or stalls set up for the selling of votive offerings which were manufactured on site to the pilgrims. There was a large structure close to the temple which may have acted as a guesthouse, but since Mercury had no healing attribution, pilgrim accommodation with ritual baths was probably not needed. The numbers of finds suggests that this was a rich rural temple in a wealthy hinterland of Woodchester and Kingscote.

As at Lydney, but in far greater numbers, *defixiones* were recovered. The small inscribed sheets of lead were an indication of 'technological magic' intended to influence the deity in order to ensure the bad luck of someone else or to correct one's own misfortune.

Wycombe

The temple lies in the Roman 'small town' of Wycombe (Syreford) on flat ground east of the River Coln and also near the springs that form its headwaters (see Fig. 56). The original excavator, Lawrence, in 1863–64, commented that in the valley 'there is a sheet of water of some 2 to 3 acres (1.2ha) and probably of much larger extent in ancient times'. The clay that seals the limestone gravel at this point made the surface of the valley impermeable; however, today this feature is represented only by a dry valley which floods periodically, largely due to later quarrying of limestone gravel causing the water table to fall. The temple appears

85 The head of Mercury from Uley Temple.

to have been the latest phase of a site of considerable antiquity and religious significance; there is evidence for Neolithic and possibly Mesolithic occupation, and the remains of a Bronze Age burial mound, which suggest a pre-conquest ritual site. As well as several pieces of sculpture from near the temple area, there are also five carved stones indicating the veneration of the *Genii Cucullati*, with some other figure on two of the locally carved crude stone panels. A well-executed bronze statuette of Mars in martial attire may have been imported from the Continent and may indicate the main dedicatory of the temple. Coins found include some 500 mostly from the temple area, indicating veneration throughout the Roman period.

The plan of the temple can be interpreted in two ways. Firstly, as a simple rectangular building with a dividing wall forming two cells which was later replaced by a square building. However, Jane Timby, in her comparisons of the site to Uley Temple, suggests that if the two structures were contemporary and the rectangular space formed a porch, then it would give either physical or visual access to the central *cella*. The entrance was on the east, similar to other early temples. There are indications of a three-sided *temenos* around the complex. The lack of comprehensive plans makes identifying ritual functions difficult, but in the centre of the main structure was a hewn stone, raised in the middle, that might have formed the base of a plinth for a statue. South of the enclosure there was a possible small detached shrine, and to the north and east there were other buildings, including a likely set of baths and accommodation or services for pilgrims.

86 Mars Romulus from Custom Scrubbs. (*Gloucester City Museum*)

87 Marti Ollvdio from Custom Scrubs. (*Gloucester City Museum*)

Of especial interest is the possibility of semi-circular foundations being part of a theatre or even amphitheatre which is common on temple sites throughout the Roman and Greek world and which would indicate a site of more than local importance. However, the curving walls identified might be part of another shrine or a roadside wall. The position of the temple and its *temenos* in the centre of the main route through the settlement and its relationship by road to the possible theatre or amphitheatre offers the possibility of a ceremonial or processional route.

Local Rural Shrines

Roman shrines in the countryside are more easily identified from the air because of their masonry footprints producing pronounced crop-marking. A square crop mark at Sapperton, a hexagonal soil mark at Pitchcombe or the circular crop mark at Cherington each indicate an area of sacred space. In the Forest of Dean there is a possible temple site at High Nash, Coleford, where the apse of a Roman building was uncovered during excavations for a bypass. At Coles Hill, Sudeley, again in the Forest, a stone eagle was recovered along with coins, rings and twisted bracelets. However, every settlement is likely to have had its own shrine, with even lower-status areas having wooden ones.

Potential temple sites have been recognised by the discovery of altars, in some cases very weathered indicating that there was no shelter of a roof of any sort. At Custom Scrubbs, north of Bisley, an inscription on a cornice of an altar reads DEO ROM[V] LO GVLIOEPIVS DONAVIT IVVENTINVS FECIT 'Gulioepius gave this to the God Romulus and Iuventinus made it'. The name Gulioepius is of Celtic origin and Iuventinus is a local sculptor. At least four altars have been found dedicated to Mars, probably in his guise as a god of agriculture, such as Marti Ollvdio. At Kingscote representations of both Minerva and Fortuna have been found, but as yet there is no evidence of the location of a temple.

Claydon Pike

The shrine was sited on an island of silts and clays, its masonry comprising three wall arcs surviving as foundations and robber-trenches, and was probably a circular building 6m (19ft) in internal diameter. Considering the thickness of the foundations, it was considered to be a one-storeyed structure, most likely roofed with thatch. A pathway curved from south-west to north-east across a marshy area, with the cobbles being packed onto the top of a foundation of gravelly clay, creating the appearance of a raised causeway. No positive evidence for an entrance was preserved, but a possible gravel pathway was identified and this may have led around the building to an entrance on the south-east side. The interior of the shrine was floored with an eroded cobbled surface which was increasingly worn towards the south-east, indicating the position of the possible doorway. An isolated layer of burnt material was located over the internal cobbled surface which may represent a hearth. There was no evidence for any cult focus, and since the causeway path led to the nearby Roman road rather than the villa, it was proposed that it was a 'semi-public' shrine. However, there was no reason to suppose that the villa's occupants were not its patron or were not responsible for its construction and maintenance.

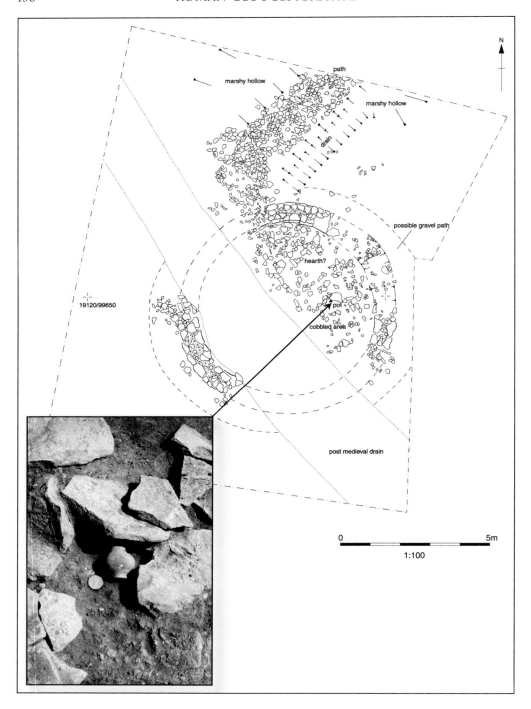

88 The central deposit at the Claydon Pike circular temple. (*Oxford Archaeology*)

The main indicator of a ritual function was the general character and context of the artefact and faunal assemblages. Two hundred and forty-eight coins were associated with the internal floor levels and, along with the 170 sherds of pottery, gave a date of the main period of activity as the later fourth century, with the use of the structure possibly ending in the early fifth. Such a large number of coins and potsherds, many of which were located within and beneath the cobbled floor surface, were seen as being unusual for a structure of this size and function. A complete small pot was deliberately buried within the cobbles, indicating, with the other finds, deliberate depositional 'zoning'. An iron chisel and a joiner's 'dog' also came from the internal cobbled layer and a miniature axe was recovered in the vicinity of the shrine. A number of animal bone fragments (417) were recovered, but only 10 per cent could be classified and their spatial pattern was unknown.

Lower Slaughter
The Chessals at Lower Slaughter was a small agricultural settlement established in the second century AD and was located immediately north of the Roman small town of Bourton-on the-Water, but seemingly completely unconnected with it. In the late Iron Age and early Roman periods there was a cult of depositing metalwork, especially iron objects, as votive offerings, either in pits or water. These votive objects also suggest a rural shrine or temple close by, and although there was no recognisable stone structure there may have been a timber building. The pottery from the site is more indicative of drinking (tankards and jugs) and serving vessels rather than a domestic assemblage, perhaps indicating feasting. The 11 wells excavated at Lower Slaughter were stone-lined and reached a depth of about 4m (13ft). Wells 1 and 3 had evidence of cattle and dog bones which are often associated with these possible ritual shafts. It was Well 5 that contained seven sculptures in the fill and a large altar lying in the water at the bottom. Damaged and weathered votive objects were in the form of two uninscribed portable altars, a similar altar with a very crude sculpture, three votive plaques of Mars and two very crude small statuettes of seated headless *Genii Cucullati*. The stone ritual objects were dated to the second and third centuries AD but were deposited in the fourth century. The carving of the figures was very much in Celtic style even though they were of Roman deities and it is likely that they represent continuation of late Iron Age practices and beliefs alongside the later Roman deities of Mars and Minerva. Among finds from the gravel working were two coin hoards, the largest of which contained 1170 coins from the mid-fourth century to Arcadius (AD 395–408), including 482 minimi (less that 10mm in diameter). Coins previously found at the Chessals include a hoard of about 1500 minimi discovered before 1881, possibly late fourth century in date.

Christianity

Before the Emperor Constantine adopted the religion in the early fourth century, mon-otheistic Christianity was condemned as a seditious threat to the polytheistic range of Roman deities, which included the emperor himself. If there were practising Christians in the region before that time the cult practices would have taken place in private and their paraphernalia hidden. As soon as Christianity became the official religion it gained ground throughout much of the empire, although there is little evidence of the depth of its establishment in Britain. It has been suggested that it was a strong lower-class religion and continued on to the sixth century, but conversely it was a set of beliefs that were favoured by the upper classes, which collapsed very quickly with other aspects of Romano-British society at the end of the fourth century.

Christianity did need sacred spaces because of the ritual of the Mass, but they did not have to be tied to a specific location. Churches probably did exist in most urban centres and, if Corinium was the capital of Britannia Prima, a large church with a bishop should be expected. However, if there were churches they need have no constituent architectural styles and were probably simple buildings. House churches may have been the norm in urban centres or in villas in the countryside, but as such would be indistinguishable in the archaeological record.

The evidence for Christian symbolism is ambiguous; partly because many of the motifs connected with Jesus were also shared by other gods, for example possible representation of the 'Good Shepherd' in a cast gemstone from Barnsley is more likely to be that of Orpheus. Several small chi-rho figures (the first two letters of Jesus' name in Greek) have been found at Chedworth Roman Villa and have been considered as evidence for the Christianity of the owners. The suggestion that the small chi-rho symbols were intended to sanctify the water shrine is unlikely as the stones on which they were carved may have been from the *nymphaeum* but were used elsewhere in random positions and not prominently displayed. There can be no doubt that the symbols were chi-rho, but their context remains a mystery.

The best evidence for the existence of Christianity comes from the Uley Temple in the form of a rectangular fragment of a copper alloy sheet found in a pit-like feature as a votive object. It would appear to be sheeting from a casket and may have belonged to people who felt the new faith was under imperial patronage and therefore very powerful. The four fig-ured scenes on the embossed sheet could be interpreted as being two settings from the New Testament above two from the Old Testament. Those on the top might represent Christ and

89a-e Burials at the London Road cemetery:
Above Gloucester: a crouched male skeleton. (*Oxford Archaeology*)

Right A prone burial. (*Oxford Archaeology*)

Below A decapitated head burial. (*Oxford Archaeology*)

Above Grave goods including a vial for perfume and pottery vessels for food and drink. (*Oxford Archaeology*)

Left The 'plague' burial. (*Oxford Archaeology*)

the Centurion and Christ healing the blind man. The lower scenes could be deciphered as Jonah and the sea monster and the sacrifice of Isaac. However, since many Roman religions share the same iconography and motifs, even in this case the interpretation is difficult. The folding and burial of this object might have been to 'kill' its significance since it was probably a part of a casket that was no longer in use.

Belief and the Afterlife

Of all the rites of passage connected with any religion (such as birth, coming of age and marriage) it is only death that is archaeologically visible in the form of human remains and the objects accompanying them as well as, rarely, a stone marker. Even the evidence for the ritual accompanying the funerary rites is limited, as there is none for the lying in state of the deceased or the procession to the cemetery and no burial in the area has evidence of a cremation pyre. In the late Iron Age there is a lack of evidence for burial, probably because of the continued use of excarnation (the exposure of the body to be skeletonised by nature) or deposition in rivers. There is also the possibility that shallow burial has meant destruction through later ploughing. Burial ritual was most likely a very conservative aspect of society, especially in rural locations where pre-Roman traditions are likely to have continued throughout the first to third centuries AD. The general trend seems to have been cremation in the early Roman period and inhumation in the third and fourth centuries, although both would be seen as the freeing of the soul. However, in the early Roman period a new and distinct funerary monument appears, probably derived from the St Albans area, where a square enclosure, from 6 sq. metres (64 sq. feet) at Roughground Farm to 16 sq. metres (172 sq. feet) at Field Farm, north of Cirencester, was surrounded by postholes within which was a central adult cremation. No cremation cemeteries are known from this period, so such burials were probably those of high-status individuals.

In the late Roman period evidence for human burial increases dramatically, with three inhumation cemeteries around Cirencester and four aligned on roads leaving Gloucester. Roman law dictated that cemeteries should be placed outside city limits and it was customary to place them along the main roads approaching the settlement. The bounding of cemeteries by walls and ditches could have ensured that the dead were kept separate from the living. In each case these cemeteries probably provide only a very small sample of the population. In all cemeteries the ratio of men to women was about 2:1, which might reflect female infanticide after birth. The Gloucester Wotton cemetery had evidence of crouched burials, usually indicating indigenous populations and suggesting that local people were connected with the *colonia*. The provision of shrouds and coffins, especially of stone, might indicate status. In the Upper Thames Valley there is evidence of small rural cemeteries probably representing a single extended family or estate group. At Horncott Quarry, near Fairford, 78 individuals were found in 73 graves. At the Cotswold Community site a cemetery for 12 individuals was focused on a late Neolithic or early Bronze Age ring ditch, which must have been visible and might have had a role in maintaining identity.

Trying to relate specific beliefs to forms of burial practices is very difficult, but it would appear that generally a belief in an afterlife was prevalent and that individual identities would survive. The journey is represented by the large number of inhumation graves with food and drink held in pots placed in the grave, and individual survival is evidenced by cases of jewellery being present. Two burials in Cirencester had coins in their mouths and one had coins covering each eye. At the Wotton cemetery in Gloucester an individual had a coin in a hand – all of the examples possibly indicating the payment for Charon, the ferryman who conveyed the dead to the underworld across the River Styx. There was a range of burial types which might suggest local superstitions or cult beliefs. The majority of individuals were buried in a supine position, lying on their backs with their face upwards. A small minority of individuals were buried with their faces down in a prone position, possibly because they were feared for some reason and might threaten the living. One of the great puzzles associated with Roman burial practice is the decapitation of the corpse after death, with the head being placed between the legs. There appears to have been no consistency of gender, status or age in this action. Explanations for this phenomenon have included preventing the dead from walking, as in prone burials, or intending to release the soul to pass into the afterlife.

Excavations by Oxford Archaeology between August 2004 and January 2006 at the Roman cemetery on the London Road, just outside the north gate of Gloucester, retrieved unique insights into burial practices and the health and longevity of the population. The excavation also demonstrated that in extreme circumstances bodies were disposed of rather than buried. This was demonstrated by a mass grave of a least 91 individuals thrown in haphazardly in a single episode during the second half of the second century. The skeletal remains are believed to have been the victims of an epidemic, perhaps smallpox, which had no respect for class, wealth or country of origin, and so gave a cross-section of the population. The Antonine Plague, an outbreak of smallpox that swept the Roman Empire between AD 165 and 189, has been identified as a possible cause of the deaths of so many individuals and the necessity to have disposed of their bodies quickly and probably by orders of the 'corporation' of Glevum.

Although the occurrence of burials aligned east–west has been thought to suggest Christianity, this position was common throughout the Roman world.

TWELVE

'HAVE YOU FOUND ANYONE YET?'

In Memoriam

While it might seem obvious that the graves of people of the period should give some clues as to their identities, human skeletons can tell us what happened to a person during life and death, but tells us little about the life choices of the individual.

While epigraphic sources can include writing on a variety of materials, such as lead and wooden tablets, we largely have only inscriptions on stone in Gloucestershire. Sadly, the 'epigraphic habit' also has limitations in that it is largely confined to the military and urban areas rather than in the countryside. The fact that the military were largely literate to some extent is obviously a factor in the creation of inscriptions, but also, being so far away from their country of origin, soldiers wanted to leave some statement of their lives. Rural dwellers would have been remembered in an oral tradition in their local communities. At their best, tombstones can give us a great deal of information about individuals. We might expect some indications of status, wealth, employment, origins/family group/clan, legal status, age and sex, slave or free, citizen or non-citizen. Surprisingly, legionary tombstones often have a minimal amount of information, a name and, if we are lucky, the title and number of the legion with which he served. It could be argued that although we can identify a person, the tombstones tell us a limited amount about that person's identity.

A good example of this is from Gloucester:

D M L VAL AVRELIVS VET LEG XX
'To the spirits of the departed and Lucius Valerius Aurelius, a veteran of the Twentieth Legion'

This suggests that being a legionary would bring with it a set of assumptions that need not be detailed. His military role would have determined his institutionalised status, wealth, location, employment. His major relationship was with the legion, so much so that his place of birth is not mentioned.

Again from Gloucester we have the tombstone of:

L(UCI) OCTAVI / L(UCI FILI) POL(LIA) / MARTIALIS / EPOREDIA /
M(ILITIS) LEG(IONIS) XX
'Lucius Octavius Martialis, son of Lucius, of the Pollian
voting tribe, from Eporedia, soldier of the Twentieth legion'

Eporedia, modern-day Ivrea, north of Turin, was in the Roman province of Italia Transpadana. It had been founded in 100 BC and set to guard one of the traditional invasion routes into northern Italy over the Alps, and as such was of strategic importance that Lucius might have wanted to draw attention to his pedigree of military prowess. Eporedia had contributed four men to other legions.

It is with the gravestones of auxiliary troopers that we can demonstrate how complex identity was as a non-legionary. As with all Roman gravestones, the date of death is not recorded. From Gloucester we have:

RVFVS SITA EQVES CHO VI TRACVM ANN XL STIP XXII HEREDES EXS TEST F CVRAVE
H S E
'Rufus Sita, a horse-trooper of the Sixth Cohort of Thracians, forty years old, served for twenty-two. His heirs, as stipulated in his will, attended to the making [of this memorial]. He lies here'

Rufus Sita's tombstone is quite plain, with the body appearing to be totally bare, but like other military tombstones his dress and armour would most likely have been detailed in paint, as would the saddle cloth. The three figures upon the gable are two lions, devourers of death, and a poorly carved sphinx.

From Cirencester we have a number of auxiliary troopers' tombstones:

SEXTVS VALERIVS GENIALIS EQES ALAE TRHAEC CIVIS FRISIAVS TVR GENIALIS AN XXXX ST XX H S E E F C
'Sextus Valerius Genialis, a cavalryman of the Thracian Wing, a citizen of the Frisiavones, from the Turma of Genialis. Forty years old with twenty years' service. He lies here. The cavalry were responsible for the making [of this memorial]'

Genialis was from a tribe in Germania Inferior; their capital was at Rijsbergen in the Baronie van Breda district of Zeeland in the southern Netherlands, close to the border with Belgium. He was a citizen, as can be seen by his three names, and his presence in an auxiliary troop is unusual. He may have been an officer as he is dressed in parade armour, and the standard that he is carrying is not typical of those used in combat. It is more likely to be more applicable to the parade ground rather than the battlefield, giving a signal for a manoeuvre for part of a ceremony. The fact that 'the cavalry' erected the memorial and it was not part of his will, or an heir doesn't seem to have been involved, may demonstrate status.

DANNICVS EQES ALAE INDIAN TVR ALBANI STIP XVI CIVES RAVR CVR FVLVIVS NATALIS IT FLIVS BITVCVS EX TESTAME H S E
'Dannicus, trooper of the Indian Wing in the turma of Albanus, with sixteen years' service, a citizen of the Raurici. Fulvius Natalis and Flavius Bitucus organised [this memorial] as stipulated in his will. He lies here'

Dannicus' origins lay in a tribe from the Upper Rhine Valley in Germania Superior. Their capital city was Augusta Raurica, now known as Augst on the Rhine in northern Switzerland. Dannicus appears to be in battlefield dress, but with the stylised sculpture for a cavalry auxiliary, and the tombstone was most likely cheaper to produce than that of an officer, perhaps indicting a local sculptor.

Each of these tombstones demonstrates ostentatious behaviour, with the cavalryman on horseback and his spear driving down the defeated enemy – something that must have happened to his own tribe and therefore portraying a shift in sides from defeated enemy to powerful conqueror. These memorials also ascertain membership of, and positioning in, the wider and strictly hierarchical community of soldiers in which social identity was expressed in inscriptions and sculptures in terms of rank. Cavalry troopers were paid more than auxiliary foot soldiers, which resulted in higher status and allowed for the expense of long inscriptions and a rather stereotyped sculpture which again demonstrated membership of a specific military community of the regiment.

Language and literacy were an essential element of a Roman soldier's identity. All the orders and regulations were in Latin, and it was essential in a polyglot and ethnically diverse unit. Rufus Sita and probably Dannicus are romanised versions of names given on enlistment, and each would be able to read each other's tombstones (whichever died first) even though they were from different parts of the empire. However, the local people could not read the language and as such they are excluded from the military community and this made an important difference between two sets of non-citizens. We don't know whether these troopers retained any element of the ethnic identities of which they were so clearly proud. That would be a question for archaeology, at least in terms of food, and perhaps specific artefacts related to the region of origin. However, we have no way of connecting the tombstones with contemporary archaeological deposits connected to these men.

We don't know the status of civilians who were represented on other tombstones found near Cirencester, but we can get insights about the development of a Roman town:

D M P VICANAE P VITALIS CONIVX
'To the shades of the departed Vicana, her husband Publius Vitalis placed this [memorial]'

Vicana is a Latin version of a British name, but her husband has a purely Latin name. Whether this was adopted to demonstrate a *romanitas* or he was from another part of the empire is unknown.

D M NEMONNI VERECVNDI VIX AN LXXV H P
'To the spirits of the departed and Nemonnus Verecundus, who lived for seventy-five years, placed here'

Again we see Latinised British names, but on a particularly Roman method of memorialisation. We also have evidence that Corinium was a particularly cosmopolitan town:

AURELIUS IGENNUS VIXFIT ANNIS VI \ EX MESE X. \ AURELIUS. \. EUTICIANUS.
\ PARENS POSSVIT

'Aurelius Igennus aged six years and ten months, whose father's name, Aurelius Euticianus, suggests a Greek background'

PHILVS CASSAVI FILI CIVIS SEQV ANN XXXXV H S E

'Philus the son of Cassavus, a citizen of the Sequani, forty-five years old, he lies here'

The Sequani tribe lived in the Jura foothills of Germania Superior, now the Upper Burgundy region of eastern France.

Just as we can empathise with Aurelius Igennus' parents at the sad and early death of their child, so there is also pathos in the relationship between a young slave and his owner, perhaps a boy of his own age.

M [...] RTIALIS C [...] SERV [...] [...] XIII [...]E

'Martialis, the slave of Corius (?) aged 14 lies here'

Unfortunately we know very little more about these people, the unique lives they led, how they dressed and other aspects of their identities, and for this we must turn to archaeology.

The Curse of *Defixiones*

Defixio is the Latin word for a binding spell for controlling, coercing, compelling or constraining a cursed person. The word could also refer to the fact that the curses were written on lead tablets which were rolled, bent or had nails put through them. Lead is easy to write on and may have been prepared on and sold at the site. When folded they were usually buried or thrown into water, their power being dependent on the curse not being discovered in case the cursed wrote to the god annulling it. *Defixiones* are very personal and direct, and reveal the hopes and fears, ambitions and failures of people and are examples of private magic that were used to vent petty frustrations.

The examples that come from the Gloucestershire region have been found at Lydney, in the temple of Nodens and at the Uley shrine to Mercury. Typically they are about largely about stolen property, which is the most common theme in Britain. There seems to be a formula, possibly copied by a scribe or an individual, who invokes the god, sets out the complaint and then lists the consequences of not complying. At times the meaning is so tortuous that it seems the writer is copying from a board of some sort and mis-scribing the words and their order. No doubt some individuals had enough Latin to undertake writing their own curse, keeping it very private, though others might have needed the resident scribe(s).

Here are some from Uley, the words in brackets being added did not exist in the original: 'Biccus gives Mercury whatever he has lost [that the thief] whether man or male may not urinate nor defecate, nor speak, nor sleep, nor stay awake, nor [have] well-being, unless he bring [it] in the temple of Mercury, nor gain consciousness of [it] unless with my intervention.'

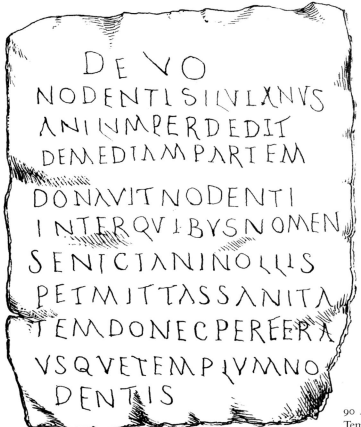

DE VO
NODENTI SILVLANVS
ANILVMPERDEDIT
DEMEDIAMPARTEM

DONAVITNODENTI
INTERQVIBVSNOMEN
SENICIANINOLLIS
PETMITTASSANITA
TEMDONECPEREERA
VSQVETEMPLVMNO
DENTIS

90 A *defixionio* from Lydney
Temple. (*After M. Wheeler*)

Cenacus complains to the god Mercury about 'Vitalinus and his son Natalinus concerning the draught animals they have stolen from him that they have neither health before or unless they return at once to me the draught animals'.

An anonymous curser writes that 'This sheet [of lead] which is given to Mercury that he exact vengeance for the gloves that have been lost that he take the blood and health from the person who has stolen them'.

It was not just men who felt abused by others:

A memorandum to the god … Mercury from Saturnina a woman, concerning the linen cloth which she has lost. [She asks] that he who has stolen it should not have rest before or unless or until he brings the aforesaid property to the aforesaid temple, whether man or woman, whether slave or free.

Perhaps one can feel sorry for the anonymous person who complained to Mercury about 'those who are badly disposed towards me and who are acting badly [??]. whether slave or free, whether male or female. Do not allow them to sit or stand to drink or eat or to buy off the provocation unless with their own blood.'

At Lydney a *defixio* was found in the temple precinct in a room attached to the temple which was used by the priest for storing such things: 'To the god Nodens. Silvanus has lost a ring; he hereby gives half of it [half of its value] to Nodens. Among those who are called SENICIANUS do not allow health, until he brings it to the temple of Nodens.'

We can deduce that the two men, who were probably visiting Lydney for health reasons, had been staying in the guesthouse from which the one stole the other's ring. From the later addition of the word *redivivia*, renewing the curse, it is clear that Silvanus did not immediately recover his ring. However, the story does not stop there. At Silchester, a polygonal gold ring has been found, inscribed on the interior with the legend 'May thou live in God, Senicianus'. It has been suggested that this was the missing ring, and John Wacher tentatively postulated that Senicianus had converted to Christianity after his healing pilgrimage to Lydney failed to yield the results he wanted, little knowing that he had been cursed.

Archaeology and Identity

Because the 'epigraphic habit' appears largely confined to minorities in urban areas, the vast majority of the people in the towns and the countryside remain anonymous. While archaeology may not be able to identify individuals it can give us information about identities, not who they were but what they were. While the whole question of identity in the archaeological record can seem very abstract, it is largely about the sorts of things that people choose to consume. We need specific types of evidence in order to understand the complex needs and aspirations of small groups and individuals in the past, particularly at a time when there were the opportunities for large social change. The body is a major aspect of portraying identity through the way we dress, manage our physical appearance, ensure our personal hygiene, seek medical treatment and, lastly, how we treat the body in death. Similarly, 'foodways' define groups through what they eat, how it is prepared and by whom, how and on what it is eaten. Behaviour as consumers using a wide range of goods and services is a vital part of how individuals present themselves. Finally, the way physical space is organised inside and around the homes is a very important indicator of the identities of individuals, families and communities. Each of these aspects of identity is reflected in the very stuff of archaeology: artefacts, eco-facts, such as seeds and bones, and the remains of structures.

These are a Few of my Favourite Things

There is some evidence of Roman military accoutrements being found in pre-conquest contexts in parts of southern Britain, and hints in classical written sources are suggestive of the sons of the late Iron Age elite serving in the Roman army, possibly in auxiliary regiments. It is difficult to assign specific sites to this type of occurrence, but at Greet Road, in Winchcombe, pieces of Roman military adornment were found in connection with early first-century pottery, including exotic imports, that indicate a sophisticated way of life. Fragments of amphorae, used for exporting wine or olive oils from the Mediterranean area, and Gaulish Samian Ware suggest that the owner of the site wanted to impress at the dining table. The Greet evidence indicates a late Iron Age site of a high status, with continuity seen through the building of an early Roman structure, which went out of use in the early second century. The inhabitants clearly had some sort of connection with the Roman army and at such an early date this is unlikely to have been a retired legionary having settled in the *territorium* of Glevum. That Roman habits were developed among the late Iron Age elites and their descendants in Britain may be more of a reflection of their choices rather than Rome's demands.

At Claydon Pike, in the late Iron Age and early Roman period, the quantity of small finds suggests a quite conservative rural society with nothing to indicate new styles of hair or dress. There were lots of brooches, but they did not have Roman characteristics. The pottery was of the local type, although a large assemblage of amphora for transporting and storing wine or olive oil and imported *mortaria* for mixing herbs and spices demonstrates an increasing move towards a Roman style of food consumption, but it seems that this would concern only a small percentage of the total population. These patterns might suggest the increasing status of individuals and communities on the site, with imported goods being part of a chain of gift-giving, which strengthened bonds with different levels in a hierarchy, perhaps with the elites at Bagendon or those who lived at sites such as Ditches, where structures and artefacts demonstrate an early need to be seen as sophisticated.

During the second and third centuries, at Claydon Pike, there were clear distinctions between different parts of the Roman complex. The eastern zone had higher-status artefacts and a richer finds assemblage than the western zone, where the buildings were less elaborate. The patterns of food consumption also indicated a more Roman way of life with a change in butchery practices and new ways of preparing drinks also detectable through the pottery assemblage, a drop in the occurrence of jar forms and an increase in vessels associated with drinking, such as tankards, cups and beakers. As well as an increase in amphora and *mortaria* associated with storing and preparing food, bowls and platters for serving food in new ways were also more prevalent. There was an increased presence of wildfowl and domestic fowl in the diet, providing clear evidence for hunting and fishing, and with the presence of celery and coriander indicates a Roman 'foodway'. The finding of considerable amounts of oyster shells, typical of long-distance trade also reinforces this interpretation. Pins and combs hint at the adoption of different hairstyles and the wearing of Roman types of footwear implies a more luxurious consumption which is supported by the finding of an ivory die and a copper alloy lamp. However, most personal items, such as brooches and hairpins, were still of local British forms. This evidence does imply a dramatic change in the use of all aspects of material culture and occurs at the time of large-scale landscape reorganisation. Hilary Cool, who analysed the small finds on the site, asked the question: 'Would a woman who had spent her girlhood on the site have lived to see her granddaughter adopting new fashions or would she have seen an alien population?' Her answer was that the grandchild would have been part of a very deep-seated lifestyle change, as the 'Roman package' was adopted wholesale by some of the inhabitants, but there is no reason to think that the population of the earlier period had moved elsewhere or that they thought of themselves as Dobunnic or British, which were both Roman terms.

Buildings and Identity

Chedworth Roman villa was largely excavated in the mid-nineteenth century; the majority of the finds have disappeared and what we are left with is the footprint of the structure, the location in which it was built and some beautiful mosaics. We can't identify the owner, even if we do have the name 'Censorinus' on a fourth-century silver spoon (unfortunately now lost), but he was certainly showing how he wanted to be seen through the design and quality of the buildings at Chedworth. What is certain is that the aspirations and tastes were very much those of a Roman way of living that can be recognised through the earlier writings of Vitruvius (b. *c.* 80–70 BC; d. after *c.* 15 BC) on architecture and the *Letters* of the Younger Pliny (AD 61–*c.* 112), which describe life in the countryside and its elaborate houses. While these are more trustworthy sources than those describing military and political events such the conquest period, it must be remembered that they were written about structures designed for the climate of Italy, and not the much colder north-west provinces.

One of the advantages of the Chedworth site is that its location in a combe alongside the River Coln is accessible on a footpath, part of the Macmillan Way from Yanworth, which runs through woods alongside the Coln and gives a sense of a 'choreographed' approach to the villa from the Fosse Way. The route would have passed a magnificent temple/mausoleum on the left, now on private land and often infested by adders, but the site itself would not have been seen easily from anyone travelling down the valley from the rather self-advertising location of the villa at Turkdean. This suggests that the owner of Chedworth

91 The inner court at Chedworth in the fourth century. (*Ed. J. Burrow*)

had great wealth and status and did not to need to display them in a public setting. In terms of the location, it is rather curious that it is not only sheltered from winds, but also from the sun and is often very cold in winter and distinctly chilly at times in the summer, so much so that the question of whether the villa was used all year around or whether the owner went to another villa or town for the winter is a pertinent one.

One way of defining the spaces within the villa is by trying to determine which areas the owner wanted as public, which were for the entertainment of invited daily or longer-term guests and which areas were completely private. Often this can be done by examining the sizes of the rooms, the quality of the mosaics – plain, patterned or with figures – or by analysing access to rooms: if you have to go through a room to get to another, it is likely that the furthest room is the most private. Using a plan of the villa, it is not hard to appreciate the effect on the visitor in the fourth century travelling up into the combe. Once in the lower courtyard, probably used as a public space, the effect of being overhung by the roofs of the inner court and the two-storeyed west and single-storeyed east wing on either side would have been daunting, but anticipatory for those invited to visit.

The inner court was a flat space and must have been impressive when the amount of earth needed to level it was considered, and another statement of the wealth of the owner. This could be an entertainment space for playing games, as we know that it was not a formal garden. The opulence of the surrounding structures can be appreciated by looking at the west and north ranges, with the small gap between them enticing the eye to the magnificent structure of the *nymphaeum* and its natural spring, and possible monumental structures above. The privacy of the west range was clearly of importance and was empha-sised by the lack of a direct sight line between the entrance to the inner court and that of the main block, as the doorways are staggered. The corridor fronting the west range had fine mosaics and painted plaster on the inside walls and although these might have been fronted by a colonnaded wall, as in warmer climates, it is as likely that they would not have been exposed to the elements in this way. As a corridor with windows, the experi-ence of entering into the building was a more intense experience, a continuation of the processional route into the main rooms of the house. Off the corridor, the quality of the mosaic pavements gives clues to the status of each of the rooms. The deeper into the house a person got, the more private and decorative rooms would become. The dining room and baths are at two ends of the range and both have to be entered through another room. Pliny, in a letter to his friend Calvisius, describes the order of events taking place 'when he is told that the bathing hour has come ... then he plays at ball for a long spell, throwing himself heartily into the game ... after his bath he lies down and waits a little while before taking food, then dinner is served'.

Such a highly Roman building begs the question about whether the owner was a for-eigner, a member of the local elite using 'old' money accrued over 13 generations in which there was enough time to become fully Roman, or a rich administrator from Corinium. It is unlikely that we will ever know, but the aspirations of the owner, as demonstrated by the buildings, indicate that not only was he wealthy but cultured in a very Mediterranean manner and may well have been personally familiar with that part of the empire.

Vicana in the *Civitas* Capital

Evidence from Roman writers indicates that the lot of women in the late Iron Age was a good deal better than in most societies of that time. They were technically equal to men, owned property and could choose their own husbands. They could also be war leaders, as Boudicca later proved. This changed during the Roman period and, again, if we use the evidence of classical authors, the relationship between Publius Vitalis and Publica Vicana would have been expected to have been one of companionship, with the wife acting as helper. Vicana would have sat next to her husband at banquets and parties and shared his authority over the children, slaves and the household. Nobody required Roman wives to live secluded lives, mainly because the Roman attraction to family and social life led to a relaxed approach. With marriage, Roman women gained considerable autonomy and they could freely receive visitors, leave the house, visit other households or leave to go shopping in the centre of Corinium. However, there was an important aspect of town life that women probably would not have been involved with – the client system, which was considered earlier in the book.

THIRTEEN

THE END OF ROMAN GLOUCESTERSHIRE: BANGS, WHIMPERS AND ECHOES

Anyone born in Corinium in AD 365 would have access to markets, pottery from a wide range of industries throughout southern Britain and abroad, and specialist craftsmen to manufacture mosaics, furniture and other items. There was an extensive economy based on coinage that ensured the survival of towns through collecting taxes to support the administration and soldiers as well as the central Roman government. The rural villa was at its most imaginative in terms of architectural embellishment and the town was surrounded by more of them than in any other part of the province. This state of affairs was quite different from other parts of the province, which appear to have slowed economically, with other towns not renewing public buildings as they aged (Verulamium and Calleva each had a forum and a basilica that were in terminal decline in the early-mid fourth century) and the numbers and wealth of the urban population decreasing. However, at the age of 60 years, in AD 425 our inhabitant of Corinium would have lived in a town that was seemingly abandoned, with coinage no longer in use and barter or gift exchange supporting a different, but probably still viable, local economy. As Roger White has put it, town life may have ceased to be that of the Roman Empire as we understood it earlier in this book, but life in towns continued and perhaps people still felt 'Roman'.

Why did this change happen? A number of views have been put forward to explain the ending of Roman Britain in the fourth and fifth centuries. Some would argue that Britannia had been in decline since the early-mid third century, yet others would suggest that there was a period of great prosperity which suddenly and dramatically collapsed at the end of the fourth century, with most traces of Romano-British culture quickly disappearing. A very different scenario has also been suggested which proposes that the towns of Britannia maintained their political, economic, administrative and high-status domestic functions even at the beginning of the fifth century, and these gradually wound down over the following centuries. What happened at province or empire level that might support these scenarios? What can archaeology tell us about the effect of the events of those years on the Gloucestershire region and which model, if any, fits the evidence?

Tyrants and Empires

St Jerome (c. 347–30 September 420) called Britain 'A province fertile in tyrants'. The problem has its sources in the relationships between the north-west provinces and the emperors, especially in Britannia, where there seems to have been little imperial support but a long tradition of using the island as a source of metals and corn. The other factor was that the emperor deliberately kept the legions and their power in the provinces as far away from Rome as possible, again leaving them isolated. In AD 259–73, there was a successful secession of the north-west provinces which saw the setting up of the 'Gallic Empire' of the provinces of Britannia, Gaul, Germany and Spain. There was a 'British Empire' in AD 286–96 which forced Emperor Constantius Chlorus to take Britannia back into the Roman Empire through invasion. The evidence in Gloucestershire for these events is limited to a fourth-century defended settlement at Dorn, 1.5km (1 mile) north of Moreton-in-the-Marsh, where a walled circuit with a broad ditch surrounding it was created to one side of Fosse Way. The function of this settlement could have been administrative and may have been established by Constantius Chlorus as part of his campaign to recover the province in the years following AD 296.

Britannia Prima

At the end of the third century Diocletian divided the two provinces of Britannia Superior in the south and Britannia Inferior in the north (the result of administrative changes under the emperor Severus in the early third century) into four provinces. He hoped that by separating the military command from the administrative branch of each province the revolts that were happening throughout the empire might be stopped. The new province of Britannia Prima probably consisted of the whole of Wales, Cheshire, Shropshire, Herefordshire, Gloucestershire, Somerset, Dorset, Devon and parts of Worcestershire. The capital of Britannia Prima has been the subject of some debate. At Cirencester the base of a Jupiter column carries the inscription of dedication: 'To Jupiter, Greatest and Best, His Perfection Lucius Septimus, Governor, of Britannia Prima, restored this.' The inscription is dated to AD 296–313 and illustrates some of Diocletian's reforms, in that this person is probably from Rheims in France, a non-local official immune to corruption. However, this evidence need not indicate that the governor was resident in Corinium, just that at one point in time he was in the city or even that he authorised the column to be dedicated in his name. Glevum, having the status of a *colonia*, was higher up the hierarchy of towns and therefore a had a better claim to be the capital of the new province, but we know so little about this period there that it is perhaps best to keep an open mind until further evidence surfaces.

The case for Corinium is supported by the growth within the urban area at that time, certainly going against the trend of the shrinkage of other towns. New building may have taken place because of the need for a *praetorium*, where the provincial governor would have been and civic and financial activities would have taken place. No doubt there would have been a need for buildings for meetings with those who wanted to climb the political and social ladder. This is a very different situation from Corinium as a *civitas* capital where the local elites lived and paraded their position and wealth. This increasing provincial importance of Corinium may be evidenced by the first programme of public building work since the late second century. The basilica remained in use throughout the fourth century and in mid-century the rooms in the back range were remodelled, their entrances being walled up and internal partitions reorganised or demolished. At about the same time the portico was demolished and a wall constructed across the street between the forum and *Insula VI*, to the south, and is dated by a coin to AD 367. At the end of the third century or beginning of the fourth, a time roughly coincidental with the foundation of Britannia Prima, an internal portico was walled in and rendered externally with red-painted plaster in the forum. In the fourth century the forum was re-floored with a fine mosaic of geometric patterns. In AD 360 at the earliest, the forum piazza itself was resurfaced using slabs of fine pennant sandstone from the Forest of Dean or South Wales – it being highly worn and fragmented indicated heavy use. The central courtyard may have remained an open space for longer period. The possible temple/*macellum* in *Insula VI* was occupied and the amphitheatre was radically changed in *c*. AD 350/60.

There is more evidence of pressure for increased accommodation within the town. Houses for officials would have been needed and the presence of a large number of mosaics of this date indicates people of some status and wealth. The amount of military equipment found suggests large groups of soldiers whose duties may have been to protect state officials and respond to threats from outside and within the area. The amphitheatre appears to have fallen out of use in the late third to fourth century and modifications, like a widening of the entrance to allow vehicles to enter, might indicate a change of function, such as an external market.

The evidence for Glevum is thinner, but there appears to have been some form of military presence in the *colonia* and the city wall was strengthened in the later third to early fourth century. Mosaic floors were still being laid in the last quarter of the fourth century. There is also evidence for timber buildings being constructed in the later fourth century and into the fifth century. The building or improving of the walls around Corinium and Glevum, especially by adding external towers, may have been a response to unrest in the empire as a whole and not in response to any particular local threat. With such a long perimeter of walled circuits, the idea that small bands of attackers would only approach one side of the towns and therefore the defences would hold them is rather naïve. However, the walls and external towers may well be the result of the prestige reflected by the siting of the capital of Britannia Prima at Corinium. There are no signs of stress in the countryside of the Gloucestershire region, as seen in the undefended and lavish villa estates of the period. There were threats from without though, such as the 'Barbarian Conspiracy' of AD 367, when Picts, Irish and Saxons overran and plundered large parts of Britain. The Gloucestershire region was protected by the 'Saxon Shore Fort' at Cardiff and the fleet, and no doubt the port of Gloucester, would have had some place in this defensive scheme.

The Beginning of the End of Roman Gloucestershire

Many of the threats to the province in this period came from inside it rather than out, as Britannia had acted as a springboard for wider challenges to the imperial centre, resulting in men and materials being drained from the province. On each of the previous occasions of revolt, the legions were to return, but things began to change; the failed revolts of Magnus Maximus in AD 380 and Constantine III were to have catastrophic effects on the people of Britannia and in these attempts to satisfy the British elites' demands for proper attention, the island had been denuded of any first-line military protection. The British usurpers had led to the ruin of Britannia and the entire province had alienated itself from an increasingly fragile empire. Possibly in AD 407 there appears to have been a revolt in Britannia when Zosimus tells us that 'the inhabitants of Britain and some of the Celtic tribes ... were obliged to throw off Roman rule and live independently, no longer subject to Roman laws'.

In the popular imagination, the end of Roman Britain has been seen as a sad event as the Roman ships leave and the Celts and the soldiers' girlfriends wave goodbye from the Cliffs of Dover. Rosemary Sutcliffe in *The Lantern Bearers* (the last of her 'Eagle of the Ninth' trilogy) sums up the emotions perfectly: 'Aquila's gaze lengthened out across the marshes in the wake of the galleys, and far out to sea he thought that he could make out a spark of light. The stern lantern of a transport; the last of Rome in Britain.'

This book has been focused on 'Britain in Rome' and the end of Roman Gloucestershire was set in a wider process that was as complex, regional and piecemeal affair as the conquest of AD 43. While AD 410 is a convenient date for those who study Roman Britain, it was not an end to *romanitas* in Britannia Prima. Even the destination of the letter of Emperor Horarius, telling Britons to look to themselves for defence, may have actually been scribal error for Brettannia or Brettia Brittia in Bruttium, now Calabria, in southern Italy.

It is clear that the end of the province was a process rather than an event, and this impacts on the type of evidence available to us. Throughout the Roman period both coins and pottery were the mainstay of the dating process, with coins being seen as more accurate than ceramics. Although there had been variations in supply of coinage in the previous decades, after AD 402 no coinage enters the province. One of the results of the lack of coinage in late Roman Britain was that the pottery industries, such as that in Oxfordshire, collapsed and our other main dating source of evidence goes with it. However, the Oxfordshire industry and those from the Nene Valley did not change the style of their wares, making it difficult to distinguish between early and late fourth century, and this compounds the problem. A further complication is that of 'curation' of pottery perhaps for at least 20 years, in a society that was much less prepared to discard materials because of fashion or even if the artefacts were broken. There is plenty of evidence that pots were repaired by riveting or used for other jobs, such as cutting down for spindle whorls. If biodegradable materials like wood, also in the form of basketry, and leather were used, there would be no trace in the archaeological record. Pottery and human bone are frequently found in the 'dark earth' that covers both Glevum and Corinium, the result of rotting vegetation and the collapse of structures. Datable organic matter is lacking because to survive it needs either a watery context, therefore lacking the oxygen responsible for decay, or to have an impervious material, such as a road, seal it. However, just because these materials do not exist does not necessary imply abandonment.

Alternative sources of supply were bound to move into a region to fill the vacuum created. Grass-tempered ware from the Midlands was crude and handmade, and strongly reminiscent of later Iron Age pottery. Produced at the end of the Roman phase, grass-tempered ware is often used as an indicator of some sort of continuity. It has been found at Frocester, in the Victorian backfill at Chedworth, at Barnsley Park (but not in the structure that may have survived) and outside Cirencester, but not within the walls. This suggests that farmland was still being used if not the villa structures themselves.

The Post-Roman Period in the Gloucestershire Region

In the cases of both Cirencester and Gloucester there are indications of towns operating in some sort of administrative capacity, as both were captured by Anglo-Saxon forces in AD 557. In the light of this, perhaps we should not look for either continuity or change in the continued existence of Cirencester and Gloucester, but reinvention of ways of living. In the case of Cirencester there is evidence of occupation right up to the end of the fifth century, but it is poorly understood or dated. However, what traces there are point to occupation, even if it was not extensive. Coins of Theodosius (AD 388–402) were found on the latest floor surfaces of the basilica, suggesting occupation into the fifth century. There is also evidence for timber buildings being erected in the fifth century. At the amphitheatre there may also have been a substantial post-built structure within the arena, along with the continuing market. The arena might also have been defended and used as a refuge, maybe from plague, as two unburied human bodies found in a street's side ditch may point to that of AD 443 or of a century later.

At Gloucester, town centre buildings were already in decay but sub-divided for domestic and industrial use, including metalworking. A building in front of the forum was burned down, levelled over and rebuilt in timber with large sleeper beams set on the ground. The radiocarbon dating of the timber suggested a date of *c.* AD 430 and associated coins suggested a construction date of AD 370. The forum seems to have been dismantled in the later fourth century and became an extensive well-metalled area which was extended at the end of the fourth or early fifth century. The large open space was bounded on one side by still standing columns and may have had a market function which continued well into the post-Roman period. The well-made metalling might be construed as being undertaken by a capable civic organisation that initiated a fifth-century re-planning and may have been living in stone buildings, possibly constructed in parts of the town after AD 370. Some sort of military presence may have continued into the post-Roman period. The walled area may have been largely deserted by sixth or seventh centuries except for some agricultural use – the Roman west gate may have been a farmstead.

The Countryside

Evidence of late villa structures is rare due to imprecision of early excavations, but relatively plentiful late Roman artefacts were often found. Although the fourth century saw the further growth of villas and their estates, they appear to have shrunken in the mid to late century, with Chedworth, for example, being used as an agricultural site. There seems to be some measure of continuity at Whittington Villa, and at Turkdean the building continued in use until the late fourth century, but there was an accumulation of rubbish within the outer courtyard in the period AD 364–88 which may mark the beginning of the decline of cleanliness and ordered rubbish disposal. It is likely that some form of activity did survive until the last decade of the fourth century and almost certainly into the fifth. Other villas across the region, but especially around Corinium, demonstrate a similar pattern where they have been excavated carefully.

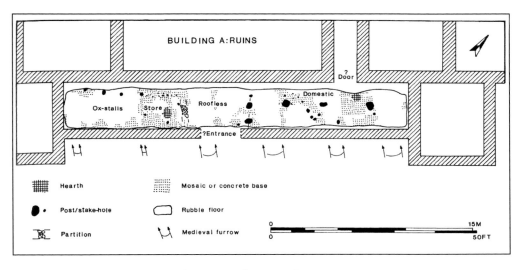

92 Evidence for post-Roman use of Frocester Villa. (*E. Price*)

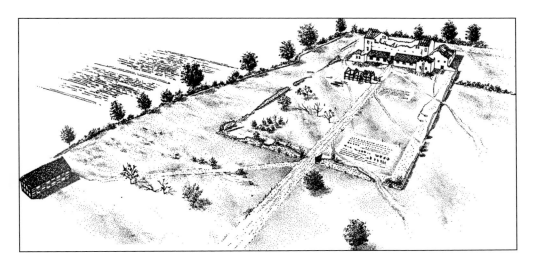

93 A reconstruction of the post-Roman Frocester Villa. (*E. Price*)

Some villas may have been partially demolished in order to maintain a part of the build-ing as a dwelling and walls knocked down for safety reasons, with waste being dumped everywhere. Evidence suggests that while there may be a reduction in circumstances of some of the larger villas, rural life in general continued without significant archaeological destruction up until the end of the fourth century, as far as dating evidence can take us. Claydon Pike, in the Upper Thames Valley, was abandoned at the end of the fourth century, but there is little evidence for Anglo-Saxon occupation until at least the later fifth century. At Barnsley Park evidence suggests that people were adapting to a new environment; they were not 'squatters' but could not keep up standards as skills were lost – such as those of the mosaicist and mason. A possible timber building on a platform erected after the villa building became ruinous indicates the skills of the carpenter and joiner were more prized than previously. The inability to maintain stone structures does not necessarily mean degradation and timber buildings could be as grand as those that went before.

Farming probably continued, particularly in lower-status areas, which were less affected by economic or political instability. There does not seem to have been a reversion to forest or scrub, and the main routes remained open until the Saxons gave them their own names. At Frocester there was occupation into the fifth century, when the villa house was destroyed by fire. Subsequent occupation within the former courtyard and the shell of the ruined house was associated with grass-tempered pottery, though these structures may not demonstrate continuity. The corridor at the front of the house was adapted as a long-house type dwelling, with habitation at one end and animals at the other, while structures were placed within and around a courtyard, one being dated to AD 540–656. At the other end of the spectrum, there is evidence at Crickley Hill for a refortification of the hillfort, comprising a timber-palisaded enclosure containing rectilinear houses located towards the centre of the hillfort, with a small cluster of rectilinear sunken-floor buildings associated with grass-tempered pottery and located adjacent to the hillfort gateway. Was this associated with Great Witcombe Villa?

The Destruction of Roman Gloucestershire?

Just as this book began with Dio Cassius' tantalising account of the AD 43 invasion, so we will end with another equally frustrating piece of documentary evidence. The closest historical source to AD 410 is that of Gildas, a cleric born (probably) in the late fifth century (c.490–570?), at a time when contemporaries of his grandparents might actually have experienced the end of Britain in Rome. Gildas' principal work, *De Excidio et Conquestu Britanniae* (*On the Destruction of Britain*), is full of historical errors; however, as a near-contemporary source to the events of the early and mid-fifth century, we cannot ignore it. It is a sermon in three parts condemning the acts of his contemporaries, both secular and religious (and more the British than Romans). The first part comprises Gildas' explanation for his work and a brief narrative of Roman Britain from its conquest to Gildas' time. The account itself, and its implications, will be discussed below, but recent research throws an unexpected light on the author and his possible relationship to Cirencester. An account of Gildas' life by an eleventh-century monk from south Brittany comments that he was with St Illtyd in Llantwit Major, Wales, and then he 'bade farewell to his pious master and his venerable fellow-disciples, and proceeded to *Iren* that, as a diligent enquirer, he might also ascertain the views of other teachers both in philosophy and divinity'. As early as AD 315, the bishops of the capitals of three of the four provinces, York, London and Lincoln, attended the Council of Arles, and it is inconceivable that there was no bishop or his representative from Britannia Prima. Andrew Breeze, using linguistic analysis, has argued that the *Iren* is not Ireland, as has been previously suggested, but Cirencester, which would have been a suitable place for a classical education considering its size and the richness of its buildings and countryside. This throws a new light on Corinium at the end of the fifth century, in that it was surviving not only as a settlement, but as an important centre of Roman culture, which is reflected in the type of flowery, often bureaucratic Latin used in the *De Excidio et Conquestu Britanniae*. It also suggests that some remnants of a governmental organisation of Britain, closely based on a Roman heritage with Christian influences, must have survived into the sixth century. Richard Sharpe, in his study of local saints of the period, has further proposed that Gildas was not a town dweller and suggests that he wrote in the villas around Cirencester, Gloucester and Bath.

Gildas' view of the Britons was basically that the land was a long way from Rome, divided and full of rebels. He believed that although Britain acquired a veneer of Mediterranean culture because the army had given it no choice, the province never actually became Roman, When Roman power had gone, the British were exactly the same as they had always been. If he was writing in the countryside around Cirencester, Gloucester or Bath, he might have seen those urban places as remaining 'Roman' and it was those rural dwellers who he referred to as the 'Britons'.

That some people during the Roman period willingly adopted Mediterranean ways of life is beyond doubt, though in a province on the edge of the empire it is questionable how committed they were to the culture. The Roman client system may not have been that different from late Iron Age practices, and some noble families could have counted on the support of many people, in the cities as well as in the countryside towns, and the unwavering loyalty of clients could keep families in power for centuries. The client system might explain the continuities between the pre-Roman and Roman periods, as well as the endurance of power, the growth of family wealth and the relationships with the countryside, especially through villa life in the late Roman period. While the indigenous pre-Roman relationships, with groups being led by elites, may have survived through the Roman interlude, there is every reason why keeping Roman lifestyles should have continued after the 'convenient' date of AD 410. After all, what others identities would they choose having been brought up in such a culture, with pre-Roman ways of life being 13 generations before? A Roman way of administration and governance may have survived in Corinium and Glevum, but there was no need for collection of taxes and the countryside might well have reverted to elites leading followers in a social structure that had been in the foreground for hundreds of years.

BIBLIOGRAPHY

I have tried to select the most recently published books which are accessible to the general reader, and I have chosen the latest archaeological report for a site in that will contain the necessary references to earlier ones if needed. All of the translations from Roman documentary evidence are taken from Ireland, S., *Roman Britain: a source book* (London: Routledge, 1996). Jones, B. & D. Mattingly, *An Atlas of Roman Britain* (Blackwell: Oxford, 1990) is still a valuable source for locating sites mentioned which are outside the region. I have tried to avoid using abbreviations for journal articles except *TBGAS*: Transactions of the Bristol and Gloucestershire Archaeological Society. Where a source is used in a number of chapters, it is cited in full at first; thereafter a shorter reference is made to it. Most of the published material on Roman Gloucestershire and the national journals referred to are available for study in the BGAS library collection, held at present in the Archive Room of the University of Gloucestershire.

Preface: Justifying the Text
Archaeologies of Gloucestershire have been written before: Sir Atkyns, R., *The Ancient and present state of Glostershire* (first published 1860, E.P Publishing Ltd in collaboration with Gloucestershire County Library, 1974); Lysons, S., *The Romans in Gloucestershire, and the results of their residence in this county considered in an historical, social and religious point of view* (London: Hamilton, 1860); Witts, G.B., *Archaeological handbook of the County of Gloucestershire* (Cheltenham: 1883). Each reflects changing approaches to the Roman past and also the audience for whom it was written. Some of the prints I have used are from Burrow, Ed. J., *The Ancient Entrenchments and Camps of Gloucestershire* (Cheltenham: Burrow & Co. Ltd, 1919), which, although only partially concerned with Roman monuments, is nevertheless valuable in that he gives a view before modern methods of agriculture and transport.

The most recent account is by McWhirr, A., *Roman Gloucestershire* (Stroud: Alan Sutton & Gloucestershire County Library, 1981) and remains an incisive view of the archaeology of the county, especially concerning Cirencester, where he excavated extensively. Saville, A. (ed.), *The Archaeology of Gloucestershire* (Cheltenham: Cheltenham Art Gallery & Museums & BGAS, 1984) is a review of all periods with a substantial section on the Roman era which has been substantially updated by Holbrook, N. & J. Jurica (eds), *Twenty five Years of Archaeology in Gloucestershire. A review of New Discoveries and New Thinking in Gloucestershire, South Gloucestershire and Bristol 1979–2004: Bristol and Gloucestershire Archaeological Report No 3* (Cirencester: Cotswold Archaeology, 2006). The most recent book on the countryside of the county is Pilbeam, L.S., *The Gloucestershire Landscape* (Stroud: The History Press, 2006); however, Finberg, H.P.R., *The Gloucestershire Landscape* (London: Hodder & Stoughton, 1975) still remains the most valuable account. For similar publications about the regions adjacent to Gloucestershire, Henig, M. & P. Booth, *Roman Oxfordshire* (Stroud: Alan Sutton, 2000) is a detailed account of a highly populated area of the Cotswolds and Thames Valley, and Howell, R., Searching *for the Silures: An Iron Age Tribe in South-East Wales* (Stroud: Tempus, 2006) describes a completely contrasting, yet equally fascinating, landscape.

1 Lost and Found: Defining Roman Gloucestershire

The definition of 'Roman' is adapted from Faulkner, N., 'The Debate about the End: A review of Evidence and Methods', *Archaeological Journal* 159 (2002), pp. 59–76. The post-colonial approaches of Mattingly, D., *An Imperial Possession: Britain in the Roman Empire* (London: Allen Lane, 2006) and Creighton, J., *Britannia: the Creation of a Roman Province* (London: Routledge, 2006) have influenced my thinking, but a more Roman-centred and classical view is provided by De la Bédoyère, G., *Roman Britain: A New History* (London: Thames & Hudson, 2010). Although now not easily available, Reece, R., 'My Roman Britain', *Cotswold Studies Volume 3* (Cirencester: Cotswold Studies, 1988) in many ways foreshadowed post-colonial ways of thinking and demonstrates how he has always had a great capacity for new insights and his work will be met often through this book. General and approachable texts on archaeological methods include White, N.M., *Archaeology for Dummies* (London Wiley & Sons, 2008), and Greene, K. & T. Moore, *Archaeology: An Introduction* (London: Routledge, 2010). The examples of the use of fieldwalking, geophysical techniques and metal detector use can be found in Roberts, A.J., 'Fieldwork at Willington Court Roman Villa, Sandhurst, Gloucestershire', *Glevensis* 42 (2009), pp. 17–28. Charlesworth, D. (ed.), *Seeing Through the Trees: The Cotswold Edge LIDAR Project* (Gloucester: Gloucester & District Archaeological Research Group, 2010) demonstrates how effective the technique is in finding low visibility monuments.

2 The Late Iron Age Foreground

The *oppida* in the area are reported in Dunning, G.C., 'Salmonsbury, Bourton-on-the-Water, Gloucestershire', in *Hillforts: Later Prehistoric Earthworks in Britain and Ireland*, ed. D.W. Harding (London: Academic Press, 1976), pp. 75–118; Copeland, T., 'The North Oxfordshire Grim's Ditch: a fieldwork survey', *Oxoniensia* 53 (1988), pp. 277–92; and Clifford, E., *Bagendon: a Belgic Oppidum: A Record of the Excavations 1954–56* (Cambridge: Heffer, 1961), which was augmented Trow, S.D., 'The Bagendon Project 1981–1982: A brief interim report', *Glevensis* 16 (1982), pp. 26–8 and Jackson, R., *Ariconium, Herefordshire: An Iron Age Settlement And Romano-British 'Small Town'* (Oxford: Oxbow Books, forthcoming). The comparisons with the St Albans area are dealt with in the very readable Niblett, R., *Verulamium* (Stroud: Tempus, 2001).

For the problem of the Dobunni, Ecclestone, M., S. Gardner, N. Holbrook & A. Smith, *The Land of the Dobunni: A series of papers relating to the Transformation of the Pagan, Pre-Roman Tribal Lands into Christian, Anglo-Saxon Gloucestershire and Somerset* (King's Lynn: Heritage Marketing and Publications Ltd, 2003) is a valuable survey in continuity, but Moore, T., & R. Reece., 'The Dobunni', *Glevensis* 34 (2001), pp. 17–26 is more thought provoking and is the stance adopted here. A recent survey of approaches to the late Iron Age is given in Moore,

T., 'The Iron Age', in *Twenty five years of Archaeology in Gloucestershire* (cited above). A more detailed account is in Moore, T., 'Life on the Edge? Exchange, Community and Identity in the Later Iron Age of the Severn-Cotswolds', in *The Later Iron Age in Britain and Beyond*, ed. C. Haselgrove & T. Moore (Oxford: Oxbow Books, 2007), pp. 41–61. The Western Series of coins is the focus of Van Arsdell, R.D., *The Coinage of the Dobunni: Money supply and coin Circulation in Dobunnic Territory, Oxford University Committee for Archaeology, Monograph 18* (Oxford: Oxford University Committee for Archaeology, 1994), and has extensive photographs of the coins. The Ditches site is reported in Trow, S., S. James & T. Moore, *Becoming Roman, Being Gallic, Staying British: Research and Excavations at Ditches 'Hillfort' and villa 1984–2006* (Oxford: Oxbow Books, 2009).

3 Securing the Surrender: Forts, Boundaries and a 'Lost' Garrison

De la Bédoyère, G., *Eagles Over Britannia: The Roman Army in Britain* (Stroud: The History Press, 2001) is a good general account of the military. The strategies for the invasion are presented by Frere, S. & M. Fulford, 'The Roman Invasion of AD 43', *Britannia* 32 (2001), pp. 45–55, who favour the Kent landing site, Sauer, E., 'The Roman Invasion of Britain (AD 43) in Imperial Perspective: a response to Frere and Fulford', *Oxford Journal of Archaeology* 21:4 (2002), pp. 333–63, and Manley, J., *AD 43: The Roman Invasion of Britain* (Stroud: Tempus, 2002) argue for a site near Chichester for at least part of the invasion force.

More site specific papers can be found in Sauer, W.E., 'Alchester, a Claudian "Vexillation Fortress" near the Western Boundary of the Catuvellauni: New Light on the Roman Invasion of Britain', *Archaeological Journal* 157 (2000), pp. 1–78; McWhirr, A. & J. Wacher, *Early Roman Occupation at Cirencester: Cirencester Excavations I* (Cirencester: Cirencester Excavations Committee, 1982) gives the evidence for a fort, as does Hurst. H.R., *Kingsholm Gloucester Archaeology. Rep 1* (Gloucester: Gloucester Archaeological Publications, 1985). Atkin, M., 'Excavations in Gloucester 1985; an interim report', *Glevensis* 20 (1985), pp. 3–12 suggests a more detailed chronology for the Kingsholm base.

4 Roman Roads: a Straightjacket for the Region

The classic, and still relevant, account is Margary, I.D., *Roman Roads in Britain: I. South of the Foss Way–Bristol Channel* (London: Phoenix House, 1955). Davies, H., *Roads in Roman Britain* (Stroud: The History Press, 2008) has considered the surveying and engineering factors in great detail. Specific routes in Gloucestershire are analysed in Copeland, T., *Akeman Street: Moving through Iron Age and Roman Landscapes* (Stroud: The History Press, 2009) and Mudd, A., J.W. Williams & A. Lupton, *Excavations alongside Roman Ermine Street, Gloucestershire and Wiltshire: the archaeology of the A419/A417 Swindon to Gloucester Road Scheme, Vol. 1* (Oxford: Oxford Archaeological Unit, 2000). Hargreaves, G.H., 'The road network in the vicinity of Cirencester', in *Cirencester: The Roman Town Defences, public buildings and shops: Cirencester Excavations V*, ed. N. Holbrook (Cirencester: Cotswold Archaeological Trust, 1998), pp. 11–7, has solved the problem of the routes around the *civitas* capital very elegantly.

5 Displaying Compliance AD 43–100

The importance of the Tar Barrows was first proposed in Reece, R., 'The Siting of Roman Corinium', *Britannia* 36 (2003), pp. 276–80 and a report on fieldwalking and geophysical survey was published as Guest, P., 'Tar Barrows', *Britannia* 40 (2009), pp. 206–8. Holbrook, N., 'Cirencester and the Cotswolds: the early Roman evolution of a town and rural land-scape', *Journal of Roman Archaeology* 21 (2008), pp. 200–19, discusses the wider landscape in the Cotswolds and Thames Valley in relation to Cirencester. McWhirr, A. & J. Wacher (1982 – cited above) is important in understanding the development of the early Roman occupation at Cirencester. The early villa at the Ditches site is reported in Trow, S., S. James & T. Moore (2009 – cited above). The development of both Glevum and Corinium from military roles into towns can be found in Webster, G. (ed.), *Fortress into City: The Consolidation of Roman Britain, First century AD* (London: Batsford, 1988).

6 Romans and Countrymen: Glevum and Corinium

The sources for the *colonia* are not as full as those for the *civitas*, largely owing to the built-up town centre at Gloucester and its status as a conservation area resulting in few opportunities for excavation. The papers of the conference held in Gloucester on 5–6 July 1997 were published as Hurst, H.R. (ed.), 'The Coloniae of Roman Britain: New Studies and a Review', in *Journal of Roman Studies Supplementary Series* No 36 (Portsmouth, Rhode Island: 1999) contains the most up-to-date summaries of the archaeology of Glevum, particularly in Hurst's 'Topography and Identity in *Glevum colonia*', pp. 113–35, and 'Civic Space in *Glevum*', pp. 152–60. Michael Fulford's 'Veteran settlement in 1stc. Britain and the foundations of Gloucester and Lincoln' is a valuable account of the role of *coloniae* pp. 117–80. The debate about the foundation date of Glevum *colonia* between Henry Hurst and Mark Hassall is presented as 'Soldier and civilian: a debate on the bank of the Severn', pp. 181–90. Heighway, C., 'The East and North Gates of Gloucester', *Bristol Western Archaeological Trust Monograph 4* (Bristol: Western Archaeological Trust, 1983) was an important foundation for Hurst, H.R., 'Gloucester: The Roman and Later Defences', *Gloucester Archaeological Reports*, Vol. 2 (Gloucester: Gloucester Archaeological Publications, 1986). One of the most informative volumes on towns, though in some cases a little out of date, is Wacher, J., *Towns in Roman Britain* (London: Routledge, 1997). More recent and useful for the general audience is, de la Bédoyère, G., *Roman Towns in Britain* (Stroud: The History Press, 2003). We are particularly fortunate in having the excavations of the last 30 years in Cirencester published in full: Wacher, J.S. & A.D. McWhirr, *Early Roman Occupation at Cirencester: Cirencester Excavations I* (Cirencester: Excavation Committee, 1982); McWhirr, A., L. Viner & C. Wells, *Romano-British Cemeteries at Cirencester: Cirencester Excavations II* (Cirencester: Cirencester Excavation Committee, 1982); McWhirr, A. (ed.), *Houses in Roman Cirencester: Cirencester Excavations III* (Cirencester: Cirencester Excavation Committee, 1986); Holbrook, N. (ed.), *Cirencester: the Roman Town Defences, Public Buildings and Shops: Cirencester Excavations V* (Cirencester: Cotswold Archaeological Trust, 1998); and Holbrook, N. (ed.), *Excavations and Observations in Roman Cirencester 1998–2007: Cirencester Excavations VI* (Cirencester: Cotswold Archaeological Trust, 2008), which demonstrates the frustrations of contract archaeology in urban contexts. Smaller excavations are reported in Reece, R., *Cotswold Studies Vol. II: Excavations, Survey and Records around Cirencester* (Oxford: Oxbow Books, 1990).

The contrast between the towns is considered in the 1999 *coloniae* volume cited as Richard Reece's 'Colonia in context: *Glevum* and the *civitas Dobunnorum*', pp. 73–85, which explores the relationship between the two urban areas and their areas of influence. Hurst, H.R.

'Roman Cirencester and Gloucester Compared', *Oxford Journal of Archaeology* 24: 3 (2005), pp. 293–305 considers some of the artistic differences in terms of buildings and sculpture. A statistical approach is taken by Clarke, S., 'Acculturation and continuity-re-assessing the significance of Romanization in the hinterlands of Gloucester and Cirencester', in *Imperialism: Post Colonial Perspectives Leicester Archaeology Monograph, 3*, ed. Webster. J. & N. Cooper (Leicester: University of Leicester School of Archaeological Studies, 1996), pp. 71–84. Buckman, F.L.S. & C.H. Newmarch, *Illustrations of the Remains of Roman Art in Cirencester the site of Antient Corinium* (Cirencester: George Bell, 1860) has some magnificent hand-coloured drawings of the town's mosaic pavements.

7 Contrasting Landscapes, Contrasting Archaeologies

There are two valuable summaries of the extensive excavations in the Upper Thames Valley: Booth P., A. Dodd, M. Robinson & A. Smith, *The Thames through Time: the Early Historical Period AD 1–1000 The Archaeology of the gravel terraces of the Upper and Middle Thames Valley Landscapes Monograph No 27* (Oxford: Oxford Archaeology, 2007); and Lambrick, G., *The Thames Through Time: the First Foundations of Modern Society in the Thames Valley 1500 BC–AD 50. The Archaeology of the Upper Thames Valley: Thames Valley Landscapes Monograph No 29* (Oxford: Oxford Archaeology, 2009). A more specific site account is Miles, D., S. Palmer, A. Smith & G.P. Jones, *Iron Age and Roman Settlement in the Upper Thames Valley: Excavations at Claydon Pike and other sites within the Cotswold Water Park Valley Thames Monographs* (Oxford: Oxford Archaeology, 2007). For the origins of the development of archaeology in the Thames Valley Leech, R., *The Upper Thames Valley in Gloucestershire and Wiltshire: Archaeological Survey of the River Gravels* (Bristol: Western Archaeological Trust, 1977) is valuable.

A major contribution to our understanding of the Cotswolds was Royal Commission on Historic Monuments (England), *An Inventory of Historical Monuments in the County of Gloucestershire. Volume I, Iron Age and Romano-British Monuments in the Gloucestershire Cotswolds* (London: HMSO, 1976), and this work continues through the National Mapping Project working with Gloucestershire County Council Archaeological Service. Individual and contrasting sites are in Ayers, K. & K.M. Clarke, *Birdlip Quarry* in the Ermine Street excavations volume cited above, Marshall, A.J., *Farmstead and stronghold: development of an Iron Age and Roman settlement complex at The Park-Bowsings, near Guiting Power, Glos. (UK)* (Guiting Power: Cotswold Archaeological Research Group, 2004); and Parry, C., 'Excavations near Birdlip, Cowley, Gloucestershire 1987–88', *TBGAS* 116 (1998), pp. 25–92.

The increase in our understanding of the countryside in the Severn Valley is summarised in the Holbrook, N. & J. Jurica (eds), *Twenty-Five Years of Archaeology in Gloucestershire* (cited above) particularly pp. 108–14. Cotswold Archaeology has an excellent record in making the results of their work available quickly and thoroughly, and Holbrook, N., *Iron Age and Romano-British Agriculture in the North Gloucestershire Severn Vale Bristol and Gloucester Archaeological Report No 6* (Cirencester: Cotswold Archaeology, 2008) has a particularly well-written synthesis of recent work. The problems and gains of contract archaeology in a rural setting in Coleman, L., A. Hancocks & M. Watts, *Excavations on the Wormington to Tirley Pipeline, 2000 Cotswold Archaeology Monograph 3* (Cirencester: Cotswold Archaeology, 2006). Allen, J.R.L. & M. Fulford, 'Romano-British wetland reclamations at Longley, Gloucestershire, and the evidence for the early settlement of the inner Severn Estuary', *Antiquaries Journal* 70 (1990), pp. 288–326, explores the changes in land use during Roman times.

8 Small Towns: Unique, Complex and Very Un-Roman

The problems of defining these types of settlements and an exhaustive, thorough and analytical account of the, often sparse, evidence for each of them is contained in Timby, J., *Excavations at Kingscote and Wycomb, Gloucestershire* (Cirencester: Cotswold Archaeological Trust, 1998). 'Roman Dymock: Archaeological Investigations', *TBGAS* 125 (2007), pp. 131–246, reports a recent research on the settlement. Jackson, R., *Ariconium, Herefordshire: An Iron Age Settlement and Romano-British 'Small Town* (Oxford, Oxbow Books, forthcoming).

9 Status in Stone: the Villas

The most recent book of Roman villas is Smith, J.T., *Roman Villas a study in social structure* (London: 1997 Routledge). Excavations at Barnsley Park Villa are reported in a 'The Excavation of a Romano-British Rural Settlement at Barnsley Park' was published by Graham Webster and others in Part 1, *TBGAS* 99 (1981), pp. 21–78, Part 2, *TBGAS* 100 (1982), pp. 65–189 and Part 3, *TBGAS* 103 (1985), pp. 73–100 – this final part focuses on the Roman field system still surviving. The findings of Webster were challenged by Smith, J.T., 'Barnsley Park Villa: its interpretation and implications', *Oxford Journal of Archaeology* 4:3 (1985), pp. 341–51 and responded to by the excavators in Webster, G & Smith, L., 'Reply to J.T Smith's suggested re-interpretation of Barnsley Park Villa', in *Oxford Journal of Archaeology* 6:1 (1987), pp. 69–89. The exemplary excavations at Frocester Villa are reported in Price, E., *A Romano-British Settlement, its Antecedents and Successors Vol. 1: The sites and Vol. 2: The finds* (Stonehouse: Gloucester and District Archaeological Research, 2000). The development of the structures from the prehistory through to the late Roman period is fully illustrated. Turkdean Roman Villa was the subject of a Time Team excavation and the findings were published by Holbrook, N., 'Turkdean Roman Villa, Gloucestershire: archaeological investigations, 1997–1998', *Britannia* 35 (2004), pp. 39–76. The Claydon Pike Villa in the Thames Valley was described in the specific excavation report cited above. At present the most extensive account of Chedworth remains Goodburn, R., *Chedworth Roman Villa* (London: National Trust, 1970); however, recent work has demonstrated a completely different interpretation, especially for the chronology, and this will be reported in a new guidebook and academic volume in future. The Great Witcombe Villa is represented by Leach, P., 'A report on excavations by Ernest Greenfield 1960–73', *BAR British Series*, 260 (Oxford: British Archaeological Reports, 1998) and the geophysical and total station surveying techniques used to evaluate the immediate area around it is in Holbrook, N., 'Great Witcombe Roman villa, Gloucestershire: Field Surveys of its fabric and environs 1999–2000', *TBGAS* 121 (2003), pp. 179–200. The large but enigmatic villa at Woodchester is discussed in Clarke, G., 'The Roman Villa at Woodchester', *Britannia* 13 (1982), pp. 197–228.

10 Earthworks: Agriculture and Industry

Greene, K., *The Archaeology of the Roman Economy* (London: Batsford, 1992) remains a good overall empire-wide view. Sim, D., & I. Ridge, *Iron for the Eagles: The Iron Industry in Roman Britain* (Stroud: The History Press, 2002) is a good background reader. Of more local significance are Barber, A. & N. Holbrook, 'A Roman Smelting Site at Blakeney Gloucestershire: excavations at Millend Lane', *TBGAS* 118 (1997, 2000), pp. 33–60; Hoyle, J., L. Butler, G. Tait & D. Wooton, 'The Scowles and Associated Iron Industry Survey: project No 334,, a Gloucestershire County Council Report Archaeology Services Report', available at http:// ads.ahds.ac.uk/ [accessed 29 November 2010]; Fulford, M.G. & J.R.L. Allen, 'Iron making at the Chesters Villa, Woolaston, Gloucestershire: survey and excavation. 1987-1991', *Britannia* 23 (1992), pp. 159–215. Witts, P., *Mosaics in Roman Britain: Stories in Stone* (Stroud: The History Press, 2005) provides a helpful context, but the definitive account of the individual mosaics in the region is Cosh, S.R. & D.S. Neal, *Roman Mosaics of Britain, Vol. IV: Western Britain* (London: Society of Antiquaries, 2010). Ceramic roofing materials are discussed in McWhirr, A. & D. Viner, 'The Production and Distribution of Tiles in Roman Britain with particular reference to the Cirencester region', *Britannia* 9 (1978), pp. 357–77; Heighway, C.M. & A. J. Parker, 'The Roman Tilery at St. Oswald's Priory, Gloucester' XIII 1982', *Britannia* 13 (1982), pp. 25–77. Pottery production in the region is described in Timby, J., 'Severn Valley Wares; a re-assessment', *Britannia* 11 (1990), pp. 243–51. A view of the pottery industry from another angle is Cooper, N.J., 'Searching for the blank generation: consumer choice in Roman and post-Roman Britain', in *Roman Imperialism: Post-Colonial Perspectives Leicester Archaeology Monographs 3*, ed. J. Webster & N.J. Cooper (Leicester: University of Leicester, 1996), pp. 85–98.

11   Sacred Spaces: Shrines, Temples and Graves

There is no recent popular account of religion and ritual in the period, but Woodward, A., *Shrines and Sacrifice* (London: English Heritage, 1992) is highly readable, particularly for the late Iron Age period. De la Bédoyère, G., *Gods with Thunderbolts: Religion in Roman Britain* (Stroud: The History Press, 2002) is strong on the Roman gods and styles of worship. Petts, D., *Christianity in Roman Britain* (Stroud: Tempus, 2003) has few references to Gloucestershire, but is a thoughtful overview of a contentious subject. Adams, G.W., *Power and Religious Acculturation in Romano-Celtic Society: An Examination of Archaeological Sites in Gloucestershire BAR British Series, 477* (Oxford: Archaeopress, 2009) explores links between religion, towns and especially villa owners. A highly imaginative account of continuity of worship is given in Yeates, S.J., *The Tribe of Witches: The Religion of the Dobunni and Hwicce* (Oxford: Oxbow, 2008).

Besides the Cirencester Excavation Committee Volume II on cemeteries, Bateman, C.M. & N. Holbrook, 'The South Gate Cemetery of Roman Gloucester excavations at Parliament Street, 2001', *TBGAS*, 126 (2008), pp. 91–106; and Simmonds, A., N. Márquez-Grant & L. Loe, *Excavation of a Roman cemetery with a mass grave at 120–122 London Road, Gloucester* (Oxford: Oxford Archaeology, 2008).

Lydney Temple has the classic Wheeler, R.E.M., 'T.V. Report on the excavation of the prehistoric, Roman and post-Roman site in Lydney Park, Gloucestershire' (London: Reports of the Research Committee of the Society of Antiquaries, 1932) and the site was which was re-examined by Casey, J.P., F. & B., 'Hoffman Excavations at the Roman Temple in Lydney Park, Gloucestershire in 1980 and 1981', *Antiquaries Journal* (1999), pp. 59–79. Woodward, A. & P. Leach, *The Uley Shrines. Excavation of a ritual complex on West Hill, Uley, Gloucestershire 1977–9* (London: English Heritage, 1993) is particularly well illustrated and accessible to the non-archaeologist. Both the shrines at Wycomb and Lower Slaughter are discussed in Jane Timby's volume on small towns. The Claydon Pike site is discussed in the Thames Valley excavation report in the landscape section.

12 *'Have you found anyone yet?'*
Specialist texts are Mattingly, D., 'Being Roman: expressing identity in a provincial setting', *Journal of Roman Archaeology* 17 (2004), pp. 5–12; and Jones, S. (ed.), *The Archaeology of Identity: Constructing Identities in the Past and Present* (London: Routledge, 1997). Allason-Jones, L., *Women in Roman Britain* (London: British Museum Press, 1989) remains the only thorough account, and her *Daily Life in Roman Britain* (Oxford: Greenwood World, 2008) complements Cool, H.E.M., *Eating and Drinking in Roman Britain* (Cambridge: Cambridge University Press, 2003); Croom, A.T., *Roman Clothing and Fashion* (Stroud: Tempus, 2000); and Perring, D., *The Roman House in Britain* (London: Routledge, 2002). The uses of space and decoration in historic structures is dealt with in Copeland, T., *Mathematics and the Historic Environment* (London: English Heritage, 1992). More specialist texts are Clarke, S., 'The social significance of villa architecture in Celtic north west Europe', *Oxford Journal of Archaeology* 9.3 (1990), pp. 337–53; and Witts, P., 'Mosaics and room function: the evidence from some fourth-century Romano-British villas', *Britannia* 31 (2000), 291–324.

13 *The End of Roman Gloucestershire: Bangs, Whimpers and Echoes*
The argument for the demise of the province in a 'whimper' beginning in the mid-third century is pressed by Faulkner, N., *The Decline and Fall of Roman Britain* (Stroud: The History Press, 2001); and Faulkner, N., with a contribution from Reece Richard, 'The Debate About the End: A review of Evidence and Methods', *Archaeological Journal* 159 (2002), pp. 59–76. This view has been emphasised more recently by Laycock, S., *Britannia: The Failed State* (Stroud: The History Press, 2008), and further questioning about just how much of an impact Rome really had on Roman Britain is the theme of Russell, M. & S. Laycock, *UnRoman Britain* (Stroud: The History Press, 2010). Esmonde-Cleary, S., *The Ending of Roman-Britain* (London: Routledge, 1991) tends to prefer the 'bang' theory, sudden and possibly brutal, while Dark, K.R., *Britain and the End of the Roman Empire* (Stroud: The History Press, 2002) suggests continuity for some decades after AD 410. White, R., *Britannia Prima* (Stroud: The History Press, 2007) adopts the same position, but considers centuries rather than decades. Breeze, A., 'Gildas and the Schools of Cirencester', *Antiquaries Journal* 90 (2001), pp. 131–8 has some completely convincing 'Celtic' linguistic arguments.

INDEX

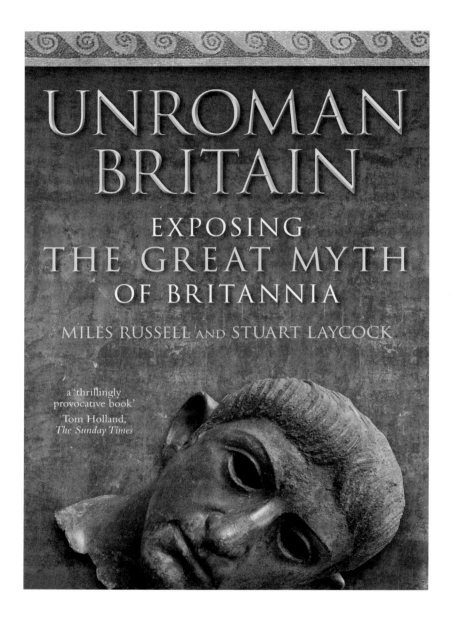